# The Royal Seal of Mahamudra

# The Royal Seal of Mahamudra

*Volume Two: The Supreme Complete Path of the Ocean of Profound Meaning*

The Third Khamtrul Rinpoche,
Ngawang Kunga Tenzin

Translated by Gerardo Abboud

Snow Lion

Snow Lion
An imprint of Shambhala Publications, Inc.
4720 Walnut Street
Boulder, Colorado 80301
www.shambhala.com



Cover art: Thangka painting of Ngawang Kunga Tenzin used courtesy of
Drugu Choegyal Rinpoche

Cover design: Gopa & Ted2, Inc.



9 8 7 6 5 4 3 2 1

First Edition
Printed in the United States of America

♾ This edition is printed on acid-free paper that meets
the American National Standards Institute z39.48 Standard.
♻ Shambhala Publications makes every efferort to print on recycled paper.
For more information please visit www.shambhala.com.

Snow Lion is distributed worldwide by Penguin Random House, Inc.,
and its subsidiaries.

Library of Congress Cataloging-in-Publication Data

Ṅag-dbaṅ-kun-dga'-bstan-'dzin, Khams-sprul III, 1680–1728, author.
[Phyag rgya chen po lhan cig skyes sbyor gyi dgnos gźi'i khrid yig zab
don rgya mtsho'i lam tshang bla na med pa. English]
The royal seal of mahamudra: a guidebook for the realization of coemergence /
The Third Khamtrul Rinpoche, Ngawang Kunga Tenzin; translated by Gerardo Abboud.
pages cm
Includes index.
ISBN 978-1-55939-437-6 (Vol. 1)
ISBN 978-1-55939-489-5 (Vol. 2)
1. Mahāmudrā (Tantric rite)—Early works to 1800.
2. Meditation—'Brug-pa (Sect)—Early works to 1800.
I. Abboud, Gerardo, translator. II. Title.
BQ8921.M35N3313 2014
294.3'4435—dc23
2014013424

# Contents

THE DALAI LAMA

# FOREWORD

MAHAMUDRA IS a set of teachings and practices that represent the essence of Highest Yoga Tantra, highest of the four classes of Buddhist tantra. It is generally associated with the Chakrasamvara cycle of tantras and is known for being a unique tradition for the practice of clear light, the nondual wisdom of bliss and emptiness. The Kagyu, Sakya, and Gelug traditions of Tibet each transmit lineages of mahamudra presented in their own distinctive manner of explanation and with their own individual style of meditation. The tradition was brought to Tibet primarily by Marpa Lotsawa, who received it from his Indian masters Naropa and Maitripa.

I welcome this English translation of the *Royal Seal of Mahamudra*, a work of practical instructions in the profound practice of mahamudra by the late seventeenth–early eighteenth-century Drukpa scholar Ngawang Kunga Tenzin. He was the Third Khamtrul Rinpoche and founder of the monastery popularly known as Khampagar. The book adds to the growing body of authentic Buddhist tantric literature available in English. I congratulate Gerardo Abboud for the evident dedication he has brought to the work of translation and offer prayers that readers who are moved to engage in the spiritual practices outlined in this book will meet with success.

Tenzin Gyatso, the Fourteenth Dalai Lama
April 5, 2014

# Foreword

## BY THE NINTH KHAMTRUL RINPOCHE, SHEDRUP NYIMA

This exceptional text containing a complete and vast series of
instructions
On mahamudra, the heart of the profound true meaning,
Was composed by Kunga Tenzin, an emanation of Guru Rinpoche.
The devoted and learned translator Gerardo,
With no regard to hardships, for a long time
Took on himself this good deed with a pure motivation,
Through the power of which he translated this book into English—
A medicine for the Dharma and sentient beings.
I dedicate this merit toward great enlightenment.
May it be the cause for establishing all beings in everlasting
happiness.

—by the Tulku bearing the name Dokhampa

# Foreword

## BY DRUGU CHOEGYAL RINPOCHE

THIS GUIDEBOOK to the main practice of mahamudra by the great Third Khamtrul Rinpoche, Ngawang Kunga Tenzin, is for me a deep wisdom melody resounding in the heart and awakening innate enlightenment. For anyone who reads this mahamudra text translated by my Dharma friend Gerardo Abboud, I am sure it will be the same. This book can help us to achieve the most precious glory of our wonderful human life, the realization of mahamudra—a goal far superior to material success or freedom from mental stress. How wonderful it is to awaken to the innate infinite wisdom, filled with the true wealth of genuine love and selfless compassion toward all beings in the whole of space! This book is a living book: every word speaks with the profound, boundless, warm, loving breath of the author up to the present lineage masters.

# Translator's Preface

One of the meanings of the term *mahamudra* is "great seal," the analogy being that just as the subjects of a kingdom do not go beyond the command-seal of the king, all phenomena of samsara and nirvana without exception are not beyond mahamudra, or suchness.

For a practitioner of mahamudra, or any of the contemplative traditions of Tibetan Buddhism, instruction guidebooks are a source of advice on how to enhance inspiration and tune our practice so that mistakes can be avoided. Such manuals have been written by truly realized beings who express their immense experience of practice and realization in the written word. Whether in an isolated retreat hermitage or at home, practitioners often do not have ready access to a teacher the very moment that advice is needed; however, a manual—though in no way equal to the direct instruction from a qualified teacher—remains always at hand to help clarify doubts and suggest techniques for removing obstacles.

This guidebook for the main body of the practice of mahamudra is one of the most complete and detailed commentaries on the four yogas: one-pointedness, simplicity, one taste, and nonmeditation. I started reading it many years ago while in India, and decided to translate it in 1983, while I was in retreat at Ven. Sengdra Rinpoche's retreat center in Nepal, near the border with Tibet. Although the first draft was completed there, I was only able to resume work on it in 2010.

The Tibetan text has two main sections: the first covering the introduction and main body of the practice and the second including an introduction to mind essence from various approaches as well as detailed instructions for removing obstacles, enhancing the experience, distinguishing between experiences and realization, and elaborating on other aspects that complete the mahamudra path.

In the Drukpa Kagyu lineage this manual is highly regarded as perhaps the most comprehensive commentary on mahamudra practice. Whether referring to the physical posture required for meditation or the various points to be examined in the process of vipashyana, it covers a great number of possible mistakes and misconceptions that might arise and, in each case, offers specific and practical advice on what remedies to apply. It is therefore used primarily by the yogis and yoginis in all Drukpa Kagyu retreat centers.

The unique feature of this presentation is how, right from the beginning, the author gives instructions on the main aspect of vajrayana practice: how to use thoughts and emotions, experiences of happiness and sadness, and so on, as the path. This is a characteristic of the Drukpa Kagyu system that has as its special teaching the conduct of equal taste, which deals with how to utilize all experiences, thoughts, and perceptions as the path to enlightenment. Although many mahamudra texts deal with instructions on shamatha and vipashyana, we rarely find such clear advice on how to carry out these practices suffused with insight into the nature of mind.

As with any translation from the Tibetan, in this text too one encounters the basic difficulty of rendering in a structured Western language a text that was originally written in a language that has fewer elements to freeze a concept. We should consider that texts like this one have been written by realized persons for whom the conventional level of reality is at all times perceived to be indivisible from the absolute level. Probably due to this there is often a certain ambiguity in the writing that leaves entire passages open to interpretation, and it frequently happens that a given quotation from a scripture is explained by scholars or lamas in different ways. Sometimes a whole line of explanation begins addressing instructions on conceptual mind, ending without warning with directions that apply to natural, nonconceptual mind. Although in Western languages we find and appreciate such ambiguity in poetry, we expect greater clarity and precision in prose and texts of a more technical nature. Another difficulty resides in a single term being used in various contexts with different meanings, and it is up to the translator to choose the right meaning according to context.

This translation has been divided into chapters for the sake of modern readers, and the titles assigned do not belong to the original text. Despite my careful efforts to render the translation as accurately as possible, errors and imprecise concepts may have unfortunately remained. These are exclusively due to my limited capacity and I rely on the reader's kind understanding and sympathy to forgive any such mistakes that I might have made.

## The Drukpa Kagyu Lineage of Tibetan Buddhism

The Drukpa Kagyu lineage shares the same origin as most of the other Kagyu lineages: from Buddha Vajradhara to Gampopa, through Tilopa, Naropa, Marpa, and Milarepa. In the *King of Samadhi Sutra,* Buddha asked who among his disciples would spread that teaching, and Bodhisattva Chandraprabhakumara, Youthful Moonlight, took upon himself that commitment. On the basis of his aspiration and Buddha's prediction, Youthful Moonlight was reborn in Tibet as the physician Sonam Rinchen, known as Gampopa.

One of Gampopa's main disciples was Phagmo Drupa (1110–1170), a very learned practitioner who had trained in the Sakya tradition before he met Gampopa. During his first meeting with Gampopa he offered his understanding and realization, upon which Gampopa, who was holding a morsel of tsampa in his hand, said that although he appreciated that realization, he still preferred the tsampa. Giving the morsel to Phagmo Drupa, he told him to go to a nearby forest and meditate. Shocked by the master's response, Phagmo Drupa did what he was told, and an overwhelming devotion to Gampopa arose in him, dissolving obscurations and leading him to the true realization of the nature of mind. From Phagmo Drupa no fewer than eight Kagyu schools arose.

One of his eight main disciples was Lingchen Repa. When approaching Phagmo Drupa's residence for the first time, Lingchen Repa started to perceive all the surrounding forest, birds, and animals as emanations of the master. He later went to a cave to start a long-term retreat, but after only three days he came back to his guru, who asked him what had happened in the retreat. At this he replied:

> Lord, you told me to meditate on the innate essence,
> And meditate is what I did.
> It so happened that both meditation and meditator simply vanished,
> And no postmeditation was there to maintain.

Seeing that he had attained instant full realization, Phagmo Drupa praised him, declaring, "On that side of the Ganges is Saraha; on this side is Lingchen Repa."

Lingchen Repa's foremost disciple was Tsangpa Gyare Yeshe Dorje (1161–1211), the founder of the Drukpa Kagyu lineage. From Lingchen Repa he received the full transmission of mahamudra and the six yogas of Naropa, mastering them to the point of becoming immune to extreme cold. In fact, he wore only a white cotton robe even in high snowy mountains. After attaining complete realization he went to Lodrak in Central Tibet. There he revealed a treasure of teachings called the six cycles of equal taste, which had been brought from India by Rechungpa but concealed in a rock for later discovery by a destined disciple.

Later, after meditating under a tree for three months without moving, Tsangpa Gyare had a vision in which seven buddhas appeared to him and revealed a teaching called the Seven Interdependencies. Following his guru's instructions, he founded the Shedrup Chokor Ling Monastery in Tsang. Then he went to Central Tibet to establish another large monastery. When he and his followers reached Namgyi Phu, nine dragons (pronounced "*druk*" in Tibetan)—said to have been manifestations of nine Indian mahasiddhas—reared up from the earth and soared into the sky, roaring with the sound of thunder, while flowers miraculously rained down. Because of this the lineage became known as the Drukpa Kagyu, which translates as Dragon Kagyu. The monastery thus founded was named Namdruk and remained the principal seat of the Drukpa Kagyu for a long time.

The Drukpa Kagyu order became famous for the purity, simplicity, and asceticism of its adherents and the profundity of its teachings. Tsangpa Gyare passed away in 1211 at the age of fifty-one, and was later known as the First Drukchen, the head of the lineage. After his cremation, his heart, eyes, and tongue remained intact. His skull bore the images of Avalokiteshvara, Manjushri, and Vajrapani, and twenty-one images of Avalokiteshvara appeared engraved in twenty-one of his vertebrae, some of which are still kept in Bhutan and in other sacred places. He predicted that he would be succeeded by nine masters with the name Senge (Lion), three of whom would be emanations of the Three Protectors (Avalokiteshvara, Manjushri, and Vajrapani), after which he would return to guide the lineage once again, as the Second Drukchen. Today the head of the lineage is the Twelfth Gyalwang Drukpa.

Three main branches followed, each deriving its name from its location: Gyalwa Gotsangpa spread the tradition in Western Tibet, and his branch was called Upper Drukpa. Choje Lorepa branched out to form the Lower Drukpa. And Onre Dharma Senge was the head of the Central Drukpa. In this way the lineage spread far and wide to China, Mongolia, Nepal, Afghanistan, Ladakh, Lahoul, India, and Bhutan. In Tibet itself, the great number of followers and influence of its practice led to the popular saying, "Half the population are Drukpas, half of the Drukpas are mendicants, and half of these mendicants are siddhas."

This lineage closely followed the example of Milarepa in terms of renunciation, simplicity, dedication to practice, and devotion to the guru. The main teachings are subsumed into what is known as the five oral instructions with the command seal: the view is mahamudra, the meditation is the six doctrines of Naropa, the conduct is the six cycles of equal taste, the fruition is the seven interdependencies, and the dearest of them all is the profound path of guru yoga.

## The Khamtrul Rinpoches

Among the most prominent masters of the Drukpa Kagyu school, the Khamtrul Rinpoches are considered the principal architects of the lineage in the Kham region of Eastern Tibet. Through their attainments and due to their work for the enlightenment of all beings, the successive incarnations were great masters, examples of perfect knowledge of the teachings and practices as well as the ideal of the bodhisattva. Their invaluable creative work in the preservation and spread of the Dharma greatly benefited the peace and harmony among Tibetans. The biographical sketches that follow are excerpted from information on the lives of the Khamtrul Rinpoches prepared by Drugu Choegyal Rinpoche, in the Khampagar Monastery archives in Tashi Jong, India.

## Ngawang Kunga Tenzin, the Third Khamtrul Rinpoche

The author of the work translated here, Kunga Tenzin, the Third Khamtrul Rinpoche, was born in the Iron Monkey year (1680) at Gongar Kyid, southwest of Lhasa. Prior to his birth many miraculous auspicious songs were heard. It is said that when his mother came to see the third Choegon Rinpoche, Choekyi Wangchuk, the protector Chagpa Melen appeared, took the baby from her lap and placed it on Choegon Rinpoche's lap while saying, "This is Karma Tenphel's [the First Khamtrul Rinpoche's] reincarnation and you should recognize him as such!" So, when he was only three months old, he was recognized as the Third Khamtrul Rinpoche.

He was ordained by Choegon Rinpoche and given the name Ngawang Kunga Tenzin (Lord of Speech, All Loving, Holder of the Doctrine). At the age of two, he had a vision of Guru Padmasambhava. When he was four he realized the nature of mind. As he himself wrote, "When I was three months old I was recognized by my root guru Khyabdak Choekyi Wangchuk, and at the age of four I realized the nature of mind, a realization that never changed even after many years of practice."

He completed his preliminary practices at the age of seven. Following that he received teachings from over a hundred great lamas from all schools of Tibetan Buddhism. In addition to Choegon Rinpoche, some of his most important teachers were Gampopa Zangpo Dorje, Khedrup Yarphel Wangpo, Minling Trichen Terdak Lingpa, and Lochen Dharma Shree. For many years thereafter he most vigorously put into practice the teachings he received from his teachers. Although he practiced both mahamudra and dzogchen equally, he mostly instructed his students on the mahamudra system.

Meanwhile his popularity spread widely and he attracted many disciples. At the age of thirty-two, he instructed his disciples to spread the message of the Buddhadharma, and then, in the Water Dragon year (1712), he retired to Rocky Mountain Vulture's Cave (Dzagyal Gowo Khyung Phuk) in Chamdo, for a meditation retreat. On the tenth day of the Monkey month, as Kunga Tenzin meditated facing east, he saw a bank of perfect white clouds amassing before him. Amidst a bright colorful rainbow Padmasambhava appeared and greeted him with radiant warmth, saying, "Chief of my devoted sons, listen to me without distraction." Then Padmasambhava predicted in verse all the sorrows that would befall the Tibetan people in the years to come. He then advised Kunga Tenzin that it was time to leave retreat and help other sentient beings, telling him, "You, who sleep in the Vulture's Cave, it is time to fly within sight of open country." By "fly within sight of open country" he meant that Kunga Tenzin should propagate the Dharma for the benefit of others impartially.

Padmasambhava advised Kunga Tenzin to perform the dance festival according to that vision, together with the sadhana of Padmasambhava for the benefit of all beings. In accordance with these instructions, Kunga Tenzin composed the Great Tsechu Lama Dance festival based on the teachings from the original tantric text on dance, as well as the additional dances that he witnessed in his visions. Then he left his retreat, traveled all over Kham, and successfully organized over seventy great rites of accomplishment (*drubchen*) of Guru Padmasambhava, performing the dances on all the occasions and dedicating the merit for the welfare of all beings, removing evil influence, and establishing peace.

Between the Water Tiger and Water Mouse years (1722–1732), he made 100,000 statues of Guru Padmasambhava, carved 100,000 vajra guru mantras in rock, built 100,000 stupas, and printed 100,000 copies of prayers to Guru Padmasambhava and 100,000 copies of Guru Padmasambhava's life story.

His fame and honor flourished extensively and he attracted wide appreciation for his invaluable work devoted to the welfare of all beings in general but especially to the Tibetan people. Among his distinguished admirers was the Mongolian king Gushri Khan of the Jungar dynasty, who paid generous tribute to Kunga Tenzin for his outstanding contribution to the preservation and spread of the Dharma. His Holiness the Sixth Dalai Lama, the spiritual and temporal head of Tibet, paid similar tribute to Kunga Tenzin and presented him with a scroll testifying to his great work in reforming and unifying the different spiritual communities in Tibet. In the latter part of his life the king of Lhathok in Kham prayed that Kunga Tenzin would build his permanent monastic seat within the king's realm. Pal Phuntsok Choekhor Ling (Glorious and Prosperous Dharma Sanctuary) was thus founded at Karmoe Rikhuk, about three kilometers from the present site of the monastery.

Kunga Tenzin was a master of painting, sculpture, astrology, physics, and medicine. In every field of the arts and sciences, his work represented a unique and outstanding achievement. It is commonly believed that such skill in just one of these arts would take a lifetime to develop. The collection of his works consists of seventeen huge volumes covering a range of subjects from mahamudra to various ritual initiations, including comprehensive teachings on basic practice and literature.

During his lifetime, he had over a thousand disciples and countless followers, among whom was the renowned Amkhar Dechen Dorje, who departed to the land of the dakinis in his own earthly body along with his entire family. The couple could often be heard arguing, but one fine morning their neighbors heard celestial music and wondered what was happening. When they went to Amkhar's house they saw mist and rainbows in the sky above the house. Amkhar himself was walking along on the clouds with his family and his dog trailing behind. This spellbinding appearance was witnessed by many of their fellow countrymen.

Dhimar Geshe Tenzin Phuntsok was another disciple considered to be the greatest master of medicine in the latter period of history, as well as being a great philosopher of all ten sciences. Another prominent student was Situ Pandit Chokyi Jungney, who received teachings on the Great Tantric Treasure of the Kagyu (Kagyu Ngag Dzod Chenpo) and other teachings from Kunga Tenzin and was a great commentator of philosophy and literature. Among other students from different traditions were Surmang Rolpei Dorje, Surmang Chetsang, Sungrab Gyamtso and Zagyud Choe Tashi, one of Tibet's greatest artists.

At the age of forty-nine, in the upper region of Zachu, Kunga Tenzin passed away. His last words were these:

> I will rest in the nature of mind, within the inner mandala of Padmasambhava. Although I will enjoy the peace of nirvana, I cannot abandon suffering beings; so, even if each sentient being takes millions of years to be freed, I will emanate in many incarnations for them and for the Dharma. I have no wish to care only for my own tradition or just for those who respect me and are attached to me—I wish to be helpful to all beings without discrimination.

## Notes on Volume 2

Volume 1 of *The Royal Seal of Mahamudra* presented the introduction to and main body of the practice. Volume 2 concludes the discussions and brings the text to completion. The mahamudra path entails discovering the true nature of our being and stabilizing that realization so that our whole experience eventually takes place from within that level of truth—in contrast to our present samsaric experience, which is sustained and underlaid by mistaken apprehensions.

For this stability to be attained there are other conditions to be observed. To begin with, there must be an introduction to the right view of mahamudra, or the nature of mind, so that all misconceptions may be eliminated. Once this view has been recognized, we must avoid deviations in our practice that would take us away from attaining the right fruition. For this process to be swift, we should also enhance our experience and realization by applying specific techniques. The progression toward the fruition is traditionally laid out in terms of what are known as the four yogas: one-pointedness, simplicity, one taste, and nonmeditation. And each of these is subdivided into different levels that indicate how our mind releases itself from subtler and subtler fixations.

Here we will find a detailed description of all these points, as well as the relationship between these levels of accomplishment based on mahamudra practice and the paths and bhumis in the general Buddhist system. In this way, together with the discussions found in Volume 1, the text covers an immense range of topics related to the practice, experience, and realization of mahamudra, rendering it as perhaps the most comprehensive work ever written on this profound teaching.

## Acknowledgments

This translation could not have been done without the assistance of the following people who patiently offered their knowledge, and to whom I am deeply grateful: Drugu Choegyal Rinpoche for his brilliant clarifications of obscure concepts and terms; Drubwang Tsoknyi Rinpoche who always supported me with explanations; Khenpo Choying Lhundrup, the head teacher of Khampagar Monastery *shedra*, who also contributed to the right understanding of difficult passages; Elizabeth Grindey who so kindly and accurately edited the text, along the way giving me priceless advice on English grammar; and the team of Shambhala copy editors led by Casey Kemp.

May this complete work on such a precious gift as the mahamudra path help many practitioners to cut through the constant deceptions of self-centered experience and realize the infinite expanse of wisdom and compassion, the true nature of our being.

Gerardo Abboud
Buenos Aires
November 2019

# The Supreme Complete Path of the Ocean of Profound Meaning

*A Guidebook to the Main Practice for Connecting with Coemergence, the Mahamudra*

༄། །ཕྱག་རྒྱ་ཆེན་པོ་ལྷན་ཅིག་སྐྱེས་སྦྱོར་གྱི་དངོས་གཞིའི་ཁྲིད་ཡིག་
ཟབ་དོན་རྒྱ་མཚོའི་ལམ་ཚང་བླ་ན་མེད་པ་ཞེས་བྱ་བ་བཞུགས་སོ།།

# 1. Defining and Pointing Out Mahamudra

III. Conclusion
- A. Defining and Pointing Out Mahamudra
  - 1. Extensive Definition
  - 2. Pointing Out the Absolute Level

## Defining and Pointing Out Mahamudra

This consists of: (1) extensive definition, and (2) pointing out the absolute level.

## Extensive Definition of the Name

Many aspects could be considered here, such as the meaning of the name, synonyms, virtues, and faults regarding knowledge or ignorance of the distinctions, and so forth. However, since at this time there is no need to deal with synonyms, distinctions, and so on, we will only discuss the definition of the name and pointing out the absolute level.

The term we are considering is *mahamudra* in Sanskrit or *chag gya chenpo* in Tibetan ("great seal"). Some people object that this is inadmissible because *maha* (great) is *chenpo* and *mudra* (seal, symbol) is *gya,* which is not the term *chag gya*. However, the term *chag* being implicit in *gya,* it must be brought out, as will be seen in the following quotations.

In general, *mudra* has three definitions: seal, significance, and precise significance.[1] *Seal* stands for "to be stamped" or "was stamped." For example, when someone seals something this would be referred to as "it was sealed or stamped" (*mudra*). Similarly, since this mahamudra seals all phenomena of samsara and nirvana without exception, it is *mudra,* a seal. Secondly, the significance of *mudra* is that it stands as a symbol. For example, in the present world the subjects never go beyond the command of the king or minister nor can they do so. Likewise, no phenomenon of samsara and nirvana, without exception, is beyond this mahamudra of true meaning, and this is what is referred to by the word *mudra.* As said in the *Discourse Requested by Arya Akashkosha*:

> What is meant by *mudra* in the phrase "sealed by the mudra of the Tathagata" is the inseparable absolute suchness: indistinguishable, inactive, free from attachment, immutable, without producing movement, that cannot be moved by the worlds of gods, humans, and asuras. Why is that? It is because the worlds of gods, humans, and asuras are sealed by that mudra. The Tathagata's mudra is the utterly unoriginated mudra, the mudra utterly free of characteristics, the utterly wishless mudra, the utterly unconditioned mudra, the passionless mudra, the suchness mudra, the ultimate perfect mudra, the space mudra, and so forth.

Regarding *maha*, this Dharma of true meaning is the meaning of all Dharmas. Since there is nothing higher than this, it is called *maha*, "great." In the *Realization of the Secret* it is said:

> There is no tantra higher than the fourth.
> It is what brings about full enlightenment.
> There is nothing higher
> Than mahamudra meditation.

Also in a text from the hearing lineage, the term *chag gya chenpo* is explained as:

> *Chag* is recognition of nondual wisdom.
> *Gya* is opening the knots of samsara.
> *Chenpo* is the birth of the torch of indivisibility.

In the *Mahamudra Bindu* it is said:

> This is *chag gya chenpo.*
> *Chag* is the wisdom of emptiness.
> *Gya* is liberation from the phenomena of samsara.
> *Chenpo* is their indivisibility.

Since these two quotations have the same connotation, this is the meaning we will discuss. *Chag* refers to the recognition of the self-knowing awareness wisdom[2] of emptiness where there is no duality in phenomena-emptiness, awareness-emptiness, and so forth. In the *Five Stages* it is said:

> Here, *chag* means to properly see
> This awareness wisdom that knows itself.

*Gya* refers to freedom from the seal of samsara: the subject-object[3] dualistic fixation of ignorance and delusion; it means that all phenomena have been or are being sealed by that freedom. In the *Assemblage of Secrets* it is said:

> [Mahamudra] is free from all things.
> It has totally abandoned subject and object duality,
> Aggregates, elements, and sense spheres,
> And arises from the equality of the two types of selflessness.[4]

*Chenpo* means that method and *prajña*, phenomena and mind, and so on, are all said to be indivisible, being united and not two. To practice in that way is considered the highest meditation. Maitripa said:

> Those who unite means and prajña
> Are yogins who practice the highest meditation:
> They are integrated with mahamudra.

The meaning of the term *mahamudra* is further found in the *Pemachen, the Elucidation of the Difficult Points of Kalachakra*:

> Regarding *mudra*, the *prajñaparamita* gives birth to all the tathagatas of the past, present, and future, so *mudra* means that bliss is sealed by the utterly nondwelling nirvana or the inexhaustible bliss. As it is superior to *karmamudra* and *jñanamudra*, and it is free from samsaric habitual patterns, it is *maha*.

In the sutras and tantras, there are exceedingly numerous references such as these, but since I fear it may be too much, I will not elaborate further.

## Pointing Out the Absolute Level

Takpo Rinpoche [Gampopa] said:

> The realization that the world and beings, samsara and nirvana, are not beyond the state of unoriginated absolute reality is *chag*. That all that appears or is possible does not transcend the genuine nature is *gya*. To realize that absolute reality is naturally free is *chenpo*.

Similarly, Lord Tsangpa Gyare, Gotsangpa, and others also said that what is called "mahamudra" is:

> All phenomena included in the world and beings, or samsara and nirvana, are in their natural condition. That all that appears from it—fresh and complete, in the three times and timelessly—is not beyond innate wisdom, is mudra. That

there is no phenomenon whatsoever that is apart from it, or
more beneficial or higher than it, is *maha*.

Also Lama Serdingpa said in the *Torch of the Vehicles*:

This is the definition of *chag gya chenpo*:
Because all obscurations of karma and afflictions
Are seen as the naturally free mind essence, the *dharmakaya*,
It is called *chag*.
Because all concepts of defining characteristics
Are unable to transcend it, it is *gya*.
Since it is greater than the vehicles
Of characteristics, *kriya*, *charya*, and the other tantras,
It is labeled with the term *chenpo*.

Other meanings of this term are similar to the ones already discussed. Let us consider the first word *chag gya*. For example, when ordinary people meet a guru or a king, they bow before them. In our case too, the obscurations of karma, afflictions, and other concepts of ignorance must all bow before the naturally free mind essence and pay respects (*chag*) to it. In other words, in actual fact the basic state of naturally free dharmakaya would be like the chief figure, and since afflictions, obscurations, thoughts, and so forth are its radiance, they would be like the subjects or retinue. Therefore, as they are not beyond the basic state, it is called *gya*. Since it is greater and more profound than all the teachings of the hinayana, mahayana, and tantras, it is called *chenpo*.

Here follow synonyms for mahamudra. In the *Realization of Wisdom* by Indrabodhi it is said:

This is the absolute, suchness.
It is unsurpassable vajra wisdom.
It is called Samantabhadra
And mahamudra.
This is called dharmakaya.
You should know that it has many such names.

In this quotation, *this* means "mind," and its synonyms are: the absolute, suchness, unsurpassable wisdom, vajra mind, Samantabhadra, mahamudra, and dharmakaya. Also, the *Seventh Unification* explains:

> Absence of true nature, suchness,
> Absolute reality, equality of phenomena, ultimate level;
> Although many such synonyms have been mentioned,
> They mean nothing other than the lack of true nature.

Further, indeed the Kagyu masters of the past also expressed many terms such as mahamudra, primordial lord, coemergent mind essence, mandala of mind essence, ground innate essence, natural luminosity, buddha nature, and dharmakaya as it is. All these are subsumed in mind, so you should know that when you say "mind," it is mahamudra, and when you say "mahamudra," it is mind essence itself.

As to the essence of mahamudra, it has been described as space: dwelling nowhere, free from all characteristics, and all-pervading. Indrabodhi referred to it in many instances, such as:

> Nondwelling like space,
> It is all-pervading and free from characteristics.
> This is the ultimate itself.

# 2. Identifying the Essence of Mind

B. Identifying and Pointing Out One's Mind Essence
- 1. The Manner of the Delusion of Samsara
  - a. Identifying the Ground
  - b. How Delusion Arises from It
- 2. The Realization of Awareness, the Undeluded Natural State
- 3. The All-Sufficient Innate Nature
- 4. The Three Coemergences
  - a. Identifying and Pointing Out Coemergent Mind Essence
  - b. Identifying and Pointing Out Coemergent Thoughts
  - c. Identifying and Pointing Out Coemergent Phenomena
- 5. The Ordinary Mind, the Unfabricated Natural State
  - a. Identifying the Distinctive Feature of Ordinary Mind
  - b. How the Natural State of the Mind Is Referred To as Ordinary Mind
  - c. Identifying Ordinary Mind Itself
  - d. Explaining How Not Wandering from It Is Mahamudra Meditation
- 6. Essence, Nature, and Characteristic
- 7. Meditation and Postmeditation
  - a. Identifying Meditation and Postmeditation
  - b. The Common Method for Sustaining Meditation and Postmeditation
  - c. The System for Sustaining Meditation and Postmeditation
  - d. How Postmeditation Arises as Illusion
  - e. The Distinction between Merged and Unmerged Meditation and Postmeditation

## Identifying and Pointing Out One's Mind Essence

In a concise way, it would be enough to consider just the three types of coemergence and the introduction through the three kayas. But there are those who know the essential meaning of Dharma and in whom experience and realization have arisen, or else those who simply know how to sustain mindfulness of self-knowing awareness and who have theoretical understanding, experience, and realization. For their sake, what is related to this introduction to mind can merge with their mind stream, and because it is necessary to arouse in them understanding, confidence, and conviction, what follows is a slightly extended and detailed explanation.

This explanation will be divided into thirteen points. These are the introduction to one's mind through:

1. The Manner of the Delusion of Samsara
2. The Realization of Awareness, the Undeluded Natural State
3. The All-Sufficient Innate Nature
4. The Three Coemergences
5. The Ordinary Mind, the Unfabricated Natural State
6. Essence, Nature, and Characteristic
7. Meditation and Postmeditation
8. Ground, Path, and Fruition
9. The Four: View, Meditation, Conduct, and Fruition
10. Mahamudra
11. Perfect Buddha
12. The Three Kayas
13. The Five Wisdoms

## Introduction to One's Mind through the Manner of the Delusion of Samsara

This includes explanations of: (1) identifying the ground, and (2) how delusion arises from the ground.

## Identifying the Ground

Regarding the natural state of the mind, Lord Gyalwang Kunga Paljor said:

> In this way, all phenomena included in the world and beings, samsara and nirvana, are none other than suchness; they are primordially perfect, created by nobody, spontaneously present, and, since they are inseparable from everything, they are not distinct. They are not contaminated by any exaggeration or denigration such as existence or nonexistence. They are free from all stains of subject, object, and so forth. They are not an object of mentally produced stopping, acquiring, and so on. Therefore, they are beyond thought, expression, and so on, as well as beyond eternalism and nihilism. They abide as their essence, the enlightened mind of the buddhas. Even if we say coemergent wisdom or dharmakaya, no phenomenon is veiled by such excellent names. Indeed, what is taught as natural mind or primordial cognizance is itself the meaning of mahamudra. Since that mind itself is nondwelling, a mere appearance, it is the basis of interdependence. It has no existence whatsoever, so it is the basis of emptiness. It does not abide as separate, so it is the basis of indivisibility. It is free from directions, so it is the basis of pervasiveness.

In a quotation from the *Vajra Peak Tantra* it is said:

> This, beginningless and endless,
> Is the mind of all beings,
> The supreme essence of the tathagatas
> And the great vajra *dharmadhatu*.

Also in the *Buddha Skull Tantra* it is said:

Mind essence is like a spotless mirror.
Whatever one thinks is like a reflection in it,
And indeed thinking is like a dream.
Yet it is caught by thought.

In the *Ocean of Dakinis* it is said:

The main point of the occurrence of the word *shri*[5]
Is to refer to the external and the internal:
The form of the conventional level
And the formlessness endowed with bliss,
As well as *evam* and other terms.
*Shri* refers to primordial wisdom.

There are many quotations such as these. Thus, the natural state of mind is by nature the dharmakaya: it is all-pervading like space, the essence of everything, indivisible from everything, and the great all-encompassing freedom from concept.

## How Delusion Arises from the Ground

In general, this nature has been primordially abiding in the mind streams of all six kinds of beings without improving or deteriorating, yet it has been veiled by ignorance. So one has neither seen one's own mind nor known one's own essence. There are five explanations as to how unknowing and ignorance have come about, as declared by Lord Yangonpa:

1. Since the natural state of mahamudra is primordial purity—emptiness beyond conceptual thought, words, knowledge, and expression—one is ignorant of the essence because the essence is free from any reference points related to something that is identified or the identifier. For example, a drawing cannot be made on empty space.

2. Since that natural state does not exist as a thing—an object perceived by a subject—one is ignorant of the essence because there is neither anything to know nor a knower. This is similar to the eye not seeing itself.

3. One is ignorant of the essence because the condition for realizing that profound truth, a qualified teacher, is missing. This is similar to a prince wandering unrecognized among his subjects.

4. Since the essence of inner space does not exist as a singular entity—indeed thoughts and so forth are the manifestation of its radiance—the essence arises as everything. However, since the radiance that arises from ignorance of the basic state is also manifold forms of ignorance, everything turns into ignorance. This is similar to medicine turning into poison.

5. Mind abides as wisdom, yet through habitual tendencies it perceives mistakenly and is deluded into ignorance. This is similar to a multicolored rope mistakenly being seen as a snake.

Also in the previously quoted *Buddha Skull Tantra* it is said:

> Yet it is veiled by thought.

In another tantra it is said:

> All beings are buddhas,
> Yet this is veiled by temporary stains.

Indeed there are many quotations such as these. In fact, the essence of one's mind has certainly been primordially pure but, at present, due to temporary defilements and various samsaric habitual patterns, it is veiled. This being so, delusion has greatly confused us and causes us to grasp at phenomena as an object, fixate on awareness as the I, hold as true what is false, cling to what is nonexistent as existent, grasp what is impure as pure, and perceive the pure dharmakaya mind essence as impure. Everything has become a perverted misunderstanding of things as they are. In terms of phenomena, which are a nonduality of oneself and others, by creating the karma of dualistic fixation of attachment, aggression, and ignorance, we are experiencing the ripening of that karma. Confused in senseless delusion, undoubtedly we are repeatedly cycling in samsara over and over again, going round and round like a waterwheel. So now we need to apply the method to counteract that extremely intense delusion: supplicating an authentic guru and sustaining mind essence without distraction. Lord Drikungpa said:

> If you master mindfulness, you master meditation.
> If you lose mindfulness, you lose meditation.

If you distractedly slip into delusion, you break away from meditation. If you have mindful knowing, you possess the practice of meditation. Therefore, for the sake of understanding it, think of it this way: instead of looking outward, turn inward; it is important that one's mind looks at itself.

Look at your mind, but since its essence is unidentifiable, rest loosely on your mind itself, simply without delusion or forgetfulness. Apart from barely remaining undistracted, don't make any corrections, not even for a moment. Rest in the continuity of undistracted nonmodification. In that state, no matter what arises or appears—stillness, movement, perceptions of the six senses—rest on whatever appears and sustain its essence. If you forget, then you need to rely constantly on undistracted mindfulness.

## Introduction to One's Mind through the Realization of Awareness, the Undeluded Natural State

One's mind rests from primordial beginning as the great self-luminosity, the dharmakaya, yet it has no doubt been obscured until now by defilements. Now, after eliminating the defilements, to realize the essence, as it is, is what is called "realization of the natural state." The essence or nature of that realization is in fact that one's mind cannot be defined as existing, it is free from all conceptual fabrications, and it is beyond being an object of thought and meditation. Furthermore, ultimately all phenomena of samsara and nirvana are free from elimination, addition, increase, decrease, bondage, liberation, action, effort, reference points, deliberate fixations, and so on. Whether you realize it as such or not, unimpeded radiance manifests in myriad forms from the state of the nonconceptual essence of your mind. Although they manifest like that, they never move from the essence when they arise. So by realizing your mind as dharmakaya, if it rests, that is the essence of dharmakaya, and if it manifests, that is the continuous display of dharmakaya. No matter how those forms arise, they are never beyond the display of dharmakaya, not even for a second. This is the knowledge that comes about. Everything is known as having the nature of dharmakaya, so there is no need to stop, acquire, accept, reject, or deem important anything whatsoever. The mind becomes spacious and open. Then phenomena are born from conditions, while emptiness is free from conditions, and these two—unoriginated and free from conceptual elaborations—arise simultaneously together. Since the variety of phenomena arises as unoriginated, phenomena are the natural expression of dharmakaya. In a nutshell, the meaning is that everything is realized as the single, vast expanse of primordial wisdom and dharmakaya.

In other words, by not leaving it as a theoretical mental image or a vague idea, you realize the natural state of your mind as it is and know the system of delusion as it is, whereby you reach a conviction about awareness and phenomena. In brief, ordinary mind[6] arises as naked dharmakaya, it is evidently seen, there are no doubts, conviction is born, certainty is found, and its potential is developed. By realizing that it is like that, you are liberated and all cognizable things are the basic state. For instance, just as when the sun rises, darkness fades away. As Toktsewa said:

> Ordinary mind is awakened in the center of the heart.
> If the six senses are purified, great bliss is continuous.

Also in a spiritual song by Chime Dorje it is said:

> *Kyemaho!*
> Unfabricated mahamudra is great bliss.
> Thoughts arise in the expanse of nonthought.
> Nonorigination embraces everything like space.
> One rests in the nonconceptual state.
> Appearance free of elaborations is great bliss.
> Free from thinking, without any conceptualization,
> The myriad thoughts are clearly seen in the mind.
> If one examines and searches, nothing is there.
> Since it is unborn, it is free of fixation.
> Everything is seen beyond conceptual mind.

It is, however, hard for our awareness and cognizance to reach such certainty. At present we may not be sure, but since we never change from that ground, when we now practice the path there is no need to have an attitude of acquiring some excellent meditation, or to think that there are other explanations elsewhere. If you think that, it would be an externally oriented cognizance. What matters is to rest in your basic nature itself, however it may be. It is sufficient to rest having determined to simply not wander from the true nature itself. In this context, if you engage in a deliberate meditation that is conceptually fabricated, fixating the mind, and so forth, that would be a stain. So do not proceed in that way but instead you should rest in the natural flow of the mind. The main point is simply not to lose the sharpness of mindfulness; nothing else is needed. Meditation is not something that can be narrowed down to "this." Since it is free from reference points, rest in the continuity of nonmeditation. If no thought arises, rest in that state of stillness. What is needed is for the mind to simply not forget itself. If a thought arises, look at its identity and rest in that state; you don't need to purposely reject it. Regarding outer phenomena, if they arise as objects of the eye and visual consciousness, recognize that and rest on it. Don't fixate deliberately. If you practice in that way, you will not waver from the goodness of the practice. Whatever arises or appears will be useful for meditation. If at all times you are constantly undeluded and not distracted, you will not be separated from meditation. To sustain in this way is what is called "thoroughly knowing the nature or perfect nature." King Indrabodhi said:

> The nature is perfect from the beginning.
> Primordial cognizance is free from conceptual elaborations,
> The essence of all tathagatas.
> I also realized it and so was liberated.

Also Lord Gotsangpa said:

> This profound, peaceful, and unconditioned space of simplicity,
> The perfect nature, great bliss,
> Abides primordially in oneself, so there is no need to look for it.
> To rest in natural lucidity is the practice.

Karma Chodrak Gyatso said:

> Following the tracks of every single one who emulated those possessing the ten powers,
> Through the kindness of the realized guru
> I realized the perfect nature, the nature of mind.
> Now I no longer think there is samsara.

## Introduction to One's Mind through the All-Sufficient Innate Nature

Although we call it "introduction," there is nothing more profound to be additionally taught, so by "introduction" we mean a reexamination of the practice instructions mentioned earlier or a more detailed exposition of the way to practice.

The great scholar Naropa himself was a *pandita* very learned in words, but he had not realized their meaning; so, based on a prediction of a wisdom dakini, he followed Lord Tilopa for twelve years, enduring twelve difficult trials. At the end, when they were in the middle of a large fearful desert plain, he was told to offer a mandala but, as he could find neither flowers nor water, he sprinkled the mandala with his own blood, cut off his ears, and offered these. At that moment, knowing that Naropa's defilements had been purified, Tilopa hit him on the forehead with his shoe, at the same time giving him the pointing out instruction through this four vajra-line verse:

> *Kyeho!* This is your own awareness, primordial wisdom.
> It transcends verbal expression and is not within the scope of
> conceptual mind.
> I, Tilopa, have nothing whatsoever to show.
> Point at yourself and know it!

In the first line, Tilopa uses *kyeho* to call Naropa's attention. In "this is your own awareness, primordial wisdom," "this" indicates that it is not some other external thing to be pointed out. So what is it that is shown inwardly? What is it that is recognized? It is what follows: one's "own awareness, primordial wisdom." Tilopa teaches that one's own awareness itself, unfabricated and fresh, pure from the beginning, has the nature of the wisdom of dharmadhatu.

The second line, "it transcends verbal expression and is not within the scope of conceptual mind," refers to the essence of the mind—the natural state, the mode of being of the dharmakaya—which is said to be inconceivable, profound, or difficult to fathom, so it transcends being an object of words, thought, cognition, or verbal expression. In other words, the nature or original face of this very mind essence is emptiness that does not exist as a form. Since it is unrestricted and does not fall into extremes, it is free of limitations. Given that it transcends being an object of mental fabrication, it has no characteristics of bondage or liberation whatsoever, so it is beyond the path of speech and is not within the scope of the intellect. This mind essence, rootless and groundless, pervades the outer and inner universes and all inhabitants, and in no circumstance does it increase or diminish. By simply looking at it, seeing ceases, so it is beyond the path of speech and transcends the scope of the intellect. Being unimpeded, the natural radiance of the basic state manifests as myriad things, yet its essence is unoriginated, unabiding, and unceasing, so it is beyond the realm of speech and is not within the scope of the intellect. In the *Cloud of Precious Jewels Sutra* it is said:

> When asked, "What is the so-called suchness?" the reply was, "What is called 'suchness' is, in a word, the 'perfect.'" This is not the self-knowing awareness,[7] and the wisdoms are unable to designate it. Why is that so? It is because it transcends being an object of all speech, expression, and thought; it is the object of the primordial wisdom of the sublime beings and abides from timeless beginning as just what it is.

This has been taught, together with the declaration, in the sutra called *Sutra Revealing the Inseparable Dharmadhatu Nature*. In the *Precious Lamp Sutra Dharani* it is said:

> You should realize the dharmadhatu as insubstantial.

In the *Great Ali Kali River Tantra* it is said:

> The perfect truth is not something that is seen.
> It is inexpressible and transcends thinking.
> One's mind is the single sphere of dharmakaya.

In the *Two Segments* it is said:

> The essence has no form and cannot be seen.
> It has no sound and there is nobody who hears.
> It has no smell and there is nobody who smells.
> It has no taste and there is nobody who tastes.
> It has no texture and there is nobody who feels the touch.
> It has no mind and there are no mental events.

Dharmakaya Samantabhadra said:

> The vast self-existing expanse is indescribable;
> It does not have the names samsara and nirvana.

The Great Brahmin [Saraha] said:

> It has neither color, nor qualities, nor can it be illustrated by words.
> How is this—which is indescribable—to be described?

Omniscient Pema Karpo said:

> To describe it in detail
> The omniscient ones are at a loss for words.
> It is not an object of conceptual mind and is not corrupted by other examples,
> So it has no frame of reference.

All these quotations refer to the key point of the meaning of non-origination and indescribability.

Let us now continue with the third line, "I, Tilopa, have nothing whatsoever to show," which refers to the inconceivable wisdom, the space beyond concepts. Why Tilopa has "nothing whatsoever to show" is because it cannot be illustrated through analogies; the absolute remains beyond description. In other words, Jetsun Milarepa said:

When confirming the view,
Not only an ignorant person like myself,
But even the perfect buddhas,
Like a dumb person or a youth describing their bliss,
Can only illustrate it by analogy;
I have seen nothing that I can actually reveal.

The fourth line reads "Point at yourself and know it!" Tilopa had not revealed the nonconceptual truth earlier, not due to lack of affection, but because it cannot be realized through someone else. Then who should realize it? Through the interdependent connection with the blessings of the guru, what is to be realized in the nonconceptual state of simplicity, indivisibility, and nonorigination is one's own mind essence. "Realize it as such!" instructs Tilopa.

Let us clarify the vastness of the understanding of this teaching. As to how to sustain the ongoing practice of awareness, one's unidentifiable mind, this cognizance of empty lucidity, free from elaborations, is not to be deliberately meditated upon with alterations. Allow the primordial lucidity itself to serenely flow of its own accord. It may be that although you rest in that way, the mind doesn't stay and various thoughts arise but, by knowing they are the absolute essence itself, at all times, whether still or moving, sustain the recognition of your own nature without forgetting. Apart from this mere not forgetting, if you search for seemingly good, elaborate virtuous practices elsewhere, you will miss the key point. Also regarding both stillness and movement, if you are overtaken by stopping and acquiring, you would be modifying and adulterating, so it would be a great fault. If the mind is still, it is the essence and nature that rest still. If it is dispersed and agitated, this would only be its natural radiance; not even for a moment would there be good or bad as two entities. Therefore, the important key point is to sustain the very nature of whatever arises: the whole variety whether good or bad, subtle or coarse. No matter what form, sound, or any of the other five outer objects arise, there is no need to accept or reject. Without engaging with the clinging of attachment or aversion regarding good and bad, look at its original face in its own place. Also, even when you forget, don't allow the unfabricated essence to slip into confusion.

## Introduction to One's Mind through the Three Coemergences

This explanation consists of three points: (1) identifying and pointing out coemergent mind essence, (2) identifying and pointing out coemergent thoughts, and (3) identifying and pointing out coemergent phenomena.

### Identifying and Pointing Out Coemergent Mind Essence

First is the introduction to the essence of mind or the basic nature. An extensive explanation would include an elucidation of the natural state of the ground, pointing this out through the designation of terms, and numerous other points. But here we will deal with this concisely. While resting on the basic nature, the very essence of your mind, without modification and distraction, when you look at its natural state or mode of being, the occurrence of thoughts—good or bad, subtle or coarse—is unimpeded. Thoughts subside by themselves and turn into their intrinsic lucidity. As a result, the mind rests unmoving within itself. Upon trying to identify the essence of that stillness, nothing is found to exist, yet there is the conviction of just awareness knowing itself. This is what is called "the mind's natural state" or "the mode of being of the basic nature." Since this is unidentifiable and insubstantial, it is emptiness. Since this empty aspect is not the nothingness of the nihilistic view, but rather this empty essence is cognizant and luminous, it is intrinsic awareness. These two are inseparable, and this is called inseparable awareness and emptiness. This inseparable awareness-emptiness itself is the nature of mind. No matter what we call it—*shamatha-vipashyana*; self-knowing awareness wisdom; coemergence; simplicity; not limited by eternalism and nihilism; unthinkable, inexpressible, and indescribable; mahamudra, and so on—there is no conflict. All are included in this mind essence itself.

When your mind rests of its own accord, thoughts subside in their original place and the mind rests free of dullness and agitation in its own basic nature. This is what is called *shamatha*, calm abiding: "calm" because thoughts are pacified, "abiding" because it rests unmoving in the essence. To clearly see by oneself the nature or essence of this shamatha is *vipashyana*, superior seeing: "superior" because the nature of mind is the supreme essence, "seeing" because its natural state is seen. In the *Ornament of Sutras* it is said:

> Because, based on perfect stillness,
> The mind settles on itself,
> And because all phenomena are fully analyzed,
> These two are "calm abiding" (shamatha) and "superior seeing" (vipashyana).

This abiding of the mind neither is dull, indifferent, distorted, nor does it remain in a neutral calm; rather it is the self-luminous essence of the mind. This luminosity is not due to light, or other such means, but it is without an object or anything to be identified. As there is nothing to be identified, there is no obstruction to its cognizance, which is vibrant, clear and open, raw, fully awake, and knows itself. Therefore, it is said to be self-knowing awareness. Because there is no knowing agent outside of it, the mind itself is the knower. As said in the *Abridgement of Words*:

> Also the mind, being a mere movement of cognizance,
> Has no true nature; it is the strength of *prana* energy.
> Its essence, empty like space,
> Abiding evenly like the sky of dharmakaya,
> Is what is called "mahamudra."

Since one recognizes what has been primordially innate to oneself, it is called "primordial wisdom": "primordial" in that it is precisely the essence of the original state, "wisdom" in that it is a cognizance that knows itself. Similarly, the supreme being Marpa said:

Self-luminous awareness is unimpeded.
Indivisible awareness is the natural flow of the innate state.
Spontaneously present primordial wisdom is seen.

Because it has never been separated from oneself even for an instant, it is called coemergent (*lhan chig kyepa*): "co" (*lhan chig*) means that from timeless beginning it has not been apart, but has been abiding jointly or together; "emergent" (*kyepa*) means that it is born and exists simultaneously from the beginning. As Gampopa said:

This coemergent consciousness,
Nakedly catch it as primordial wisdom!

Since it is free from all fixation on defining characteristics and fabricated elaborations, it is called "free from conceptual elaborations." "Elaboration" refers to the elaborations of fixation on characteristics; freedom from all such elaborations includes freedom from all defining properties. Thus, Lord Phagmo Drupa said:

The mind, pure from the beginning, is suchness.
Since it is peaceful and unoriginated from the beginning,
It is primordially free from all fabricated limitations.

The essence or nature of the mind is not something about which you can say, think, or conceptually label "it is like this." It has no identity. But even so, there is a seeing of what cannot be seen, an experience of what cannot be experienced, which you have but don't know how to put into words. While not knowing how to express it, it is known by itself, and this is what is meant by beyond speech, thinking, and description. "Speech" is to verbally express the natural condition of the absolute state. "Thinking" is to intellectually think about the nature. "Description" is to describe the mode of being of the basic state. "Beyond" means that the mind's nature transcends all speech, thinking, and description. In the *Prajñaparamita* it is said:

Prajñaparamita, beyond speech, thinking, and description,
Unoriginated and unceasing, its very nature is like space.
It lies in the domain of precisely self-knowing awareness wisdom.
I prostrate to the mother of the conquerors of the three times.

Since the mind does not exist as a thing, it does not fall into the extreme of eternalism. Since it is known and experienced by itself, it does not fall into the extreme of nihilism. So it is beyond the extremes of eternalism and nihilism. "Eternalism" stands for being a permanent concrete thing. "Nihilism" entails the view that emptiness is a void. "Extremes" stands for the limitations of eternalism and nihilism. "Beyond" is because it transcends the extremes of both eternalism and nihilism. In the *Inconceivable Secret Sutra* it is said:

Eternalism and nihilism, origination and cessation,
And all other extremes are abandoned by the mind;
It knows itself and is originally free of conceptual elaborations.
Its meaning is definitely inconceivable.

There is not a single phenomenon included in the universe and beings, in samsara and nirvana, that is beyond one's awareness. Since there is no Dharma superior to it, it is called *mahamudra*, the great seal (*chag gya chenpo*). It is a "seal" (*mudra*, *chag gya*) because all phenomena throughout the universe and beings, or samsara and nirvana, are not beyond it. It is "great" (*maha, chenpo*) because it is supreme and above all these. As is said in the *Mahamudra Bindu*:

This is *chag gya chenpo*:
*Chag* is the wisdom of emptiness;
*Gya* is liberation from the phenomena of samsara;
*Chenpo* is their indivisibility.

One's awareness is called Buddha's enlightened mind, the mind essence of sentient beings, or the natural state of things as they are. If it is recognized, it is the enlightened mind of the buddhas; if not, it is the mind of sentient beings. The mode of being of the unfabricated ground is what is called "the natural state of things." If one recognizes that, then the natural state of the absolute, the fruition, is actualized. In the *Utterly Nondwelling Mahamudra Tantra* we find:

> This is mahamudra.
> It is uncontaminated by defilements.
> In it there is nothing to stop or acquire,
> And nothing is found through paths and antidotes.
> This is the body of all the buddhas.
> This is the ground of all qualities.
> This is spontaneously present.

Siddha Virupa said:

> It is originally innate and not to be searched for elsewhere.
> Mind essence is just a name; its simplicity is mahamudra.

Krishnacharya said:

> Though buddhahood is primordial,
> Still, aspiring to buddhahood, one realizes it.

Dusum Khyenpa said:

> Buddha is found in your mind;
> It is free from the concept of accomplishment.

Lingchen Repa said:

> If you realize your own mind essence, that is buddha.
> If all misconceptions are eliminated from within, that is fulfillment.

Dharma Lord Tsangpa Gyare said:

> The mind left to settle without modifications is dharmakaya.
> Conceptual characteristics vanish into themselves.

There are innumerable vajra teachings similar to these by the Kagyu saints of the past.

## Identifying and Pointing Out Coemergent Thoughts

The essence of your mind abides as a naturally lucid, self-knowing awareness. From that state, discursive thoughts—good, bad, neutral; subtle, tangible, coarse—arise. By looking directly through the mindfulness of your awareness at the essence of whatever thoughts arise, their original identity is recognized. What is recognized is not something presenting itself dualistically as something else, so it is simply an unimpeded form arising clearly from your own mind essence; apart from it, there is no discursive thought manifesting dualistically. For example, waves are not beyond water, but rather the water itself arises as waves, the waves being nothing other than water. As to thoughts, their essence or nature has nothing substantial to be identified. When you recognize whatever thought arises without delusion—just like meeting an acquaintance—it is nothing more than a recognition because its unoriginated nature is empty. Both the empty nature of thought movement and the empty essence are naturally liberated in their original condition, and this is what is called "coemergent thoughts" or "dharmakaya thoughts." Regarding coemergent thoughts, mind essence is unoriginated and thoughts are its natural unimpeded radiance. These two being not separate, they occur simultaneously—or coemerge—at the beginning and then abide together. This is called "coemergent thoughts." As to dharmakaya thoughts, recognizing the original identity of thoughts, they are self-liberated and this itself is called "dharmakaya." If you think that the thought has turned into something "good" called dharmakaya or that there is some other dharmakaya that has pervaded the thought, you would merely be entertaining a theoretical assumption that would not serve any purpose. To say "dharmakaya thought" means that when the essence of any thought—good or bad, subtle or coarse—is seen by one's awareness looking at itself, there is no need whatsoever to reject or adopt, stop or acquire anything. The essence of whatever thought you think is a vividly clear, empty lucidity. It is the genuine state, the innate essence inseparable from you, and it is precisely that which is called "dharmakaya." To recognize that is what is called "recognizing thoughts." As Avalokiteshvara said:

> Because whatever arises is the genuine nature itself,
> When one rests on the sharp awareness of what arises,
> In that way there is no doubt that one is
> The king who masters the realization of all kinds of emptiness.

Incomparable Takpo said:

> Indeed thoughts are dharmakaya.
> Indeed they are not to be altered by antidotes.
> Indeed awareness remains in continuous lucidity.

Following the same pattern, it is only because you don't recognize thoughts of happiness, suffering, good, bad, and so forth that you cling to them as separate. Since here they are of one taste with your essence of dharmakaya wisdom, use all good and bad circumstances as the path. The root of samsara is the fixation on a self. When looking at the essence of this fixation neither the perceived nor the perceiver is found to exist, so oneself and others are not beyond being the same; they are inseparable. This being so, what is called "nonthought" is not something good to be accomplished. Further, if not recognized, this nonthought has the nature of dullness and torpor. What is called "thought" is not something to be rejected as bad. If recognized, it is not separate from the basic nature of your mind abiding as dharmakaya nature. You may think, "Well then, if it is not recognized it is not dharmakaya."

Whether recognized or not, it doesn't move from the natural state of the ground, the dharmakaya, but when not recognized, it arises as the nature of delusion. Therefore, if you stick to sustaining the natural state of awareness, in sustaining awareness on that stillness, there is no deliberate projection of thought, and if there is movement, apart from sustaining awareness on that movement, there is no deliberate concentration. Thus, by sustaining the essence of whatever arises, meditation becomes effective, your practice does not stray into partiality, and no hunger for realization occurs. That the natural state is originally pure and delusion is naturally liberated are the secret words of the precious true meaning. There are some quotations regarding this. In the *Two Segments* it is said:

> The embodiment of perfect wisdom
> And the conceptual thoughts of samsara—
> These two don't have the slightest difference.

Also, in the same text:

> This itself is called samsara.
> This itself is nirvana.
> Nirvana is not something obtained elsewhere
> After abandoning samsara.

In the *Samputa Tantra* it is said:

> Samsara and nirvana
> Are not two things.
> To know the nature of samsara
> Is what is called "nirvana."

In the *Jewel Mound Sutra* it is said:

> From nonorigination everything is born.
> Being a mere birth, it is unoriginated.

Virupa said:

> Since the myriad things are cognized as dharmakaya, the mind of acceptance and rejection does not arise.

Naropa said:

> Self-liberated thoughts are primordial wisdom.

Lord Marpa said:

> The movements of the mind, both subject and object,
> Dissolve into the simplicity of dharmakaya.

Lord Mila said:

> The inner movement of dualistic consciousness,
> When not realized, is ignorance,
> The root of all karma and afflictions.
> If realized, it is self-knowing awareness wisdom,
> And sublime qualities are perfected.
> Finally, in the absolute, there is no wisdom.
> All phenomena are brought to extinction.
> Thus it was taught.

Lord Gampopa said:

> This thought born as having characteristics,
> Nakedly catch it as dharmakaya.

Dusum Khyenpa said:

> Be free from the attitude of judging as good or bad
> Thoughts, whose nature is dharmakaya.

Jigten Gonpo said:

> The deluded thoughts of ignorance and samsara
> And self-existing wisdom,
> These two have no distinct peculiarities in the ground.

Lingchen Repa said:

> By realizing thoughts as dharmakaya
> The fixation of fault and virtue simply vanishes.

Zhang Rinpoche said:

> Don't think that suddenly arising thoughts
> Are other than dharmakaya luminosity.
> Therefore, these thoughts
> Are emptiness projecting from emptiness,
> Are dharmakaya projecting from dharmakaya,
> Are indivisibility projecting from indivisibility.

Siddha Orgyenpa said:

> In the continuous cycle of mahamudra
> There is no need for conceptual meditation sessions.

There are lots of quotations such as these.

## Identifying and Pointing Out Coemergent Phenomena

Things corresponding to the world and its inhabitants, which are mere appearances arising as outer phenomena, presently appear to those who are accustomed to the ordinary habitual patterns of delusion as existing externally and separate. In other words, indeed things seem material, but in actual fact they are projections of the mind that, based on previous habitual patterns, arise as mere forms, and since they do not exist apart from this, they are not different from coemergent thoughts. Here, forms, sounds, and so forth evidently appear as permanent, stable, and enduring to us ordinary beings, based on the common karmic perception of sentient beings.

Now we will introduce as coemergent the objects of perception that arise in the sensory consciousnesses of eye, ear, and so on. If we were to introduce the five objects one by one, it would require endless explanations, so we will briefly explain the meaning.

While resting in the basic state of knowing the nature, in the coemergent essence of your mind typical outer phenomena, such as mountains, rocks, earth, stones, or humans, animals, and so on, may arise. By looking at these things fully through mindfulness without wandering from your mind essence, any perception that appears as an object of the eye neither stops nor becomes dim. When your mind alone simply recognizes that self-appearance and sees it without distraction, the external phenomena, as well as their form and attributes, are clearly recognized. From that bare recognition no essence or identity is found, and that is emptiness. Furthermore, emptiness is inseparable from the awareness that made the recognition. In brief, neither disappearing nor becoming fuzzy, the form of outer phenomena (such as mountains, rocks, earth, stones, or humans, animals, etc.) and emptiness—their unidentifiable essence—are inseparable. They are experienced as empty appearance or appearing emptiness. Perceived and perceiver are inseparable; the empty appearance arising nakedly is seen as the coemergent essence. For example, various appearances of the universe and beings arise in dreams, yet these mere appearances do not actually exist apart from the dreaming consciousness itself. Similarly, present phenomena, no matter how they appear, are none other than the unceasing natural expression of the emptiness of your own mind, and they will continue to simply arise like this until the collective karma is purified. Merely arising, they are no other than the natural light of the emptiness of your mind. Siddha Lingchen Repa said:

> The dream you experienced last night
> Is the teacher who reveals phenomena to be mind.
> Have you understood this teacher?

Thus, apparent forms are inseparable from your mind, and following the same pattern, so are the other perceptions: hearing sounds as objects of the ears, smelling scents as objects of the nose, tasting flavors as objects of the tongue, and feeling tactile sensations as objects of the body—none are a separate duality from the mind's natural expression. Although they are not two, they arise as myriad forms; being the forms of habitual patterns, they arise as distinct. Their essence is not an identifiable object; therefore it is emptiness indivisible from your awareness. A heard sound is empty and nondual with your mind, a smelled scent is empty and inseparable from your awareness, a tasted flavor is empty and indivisible from your mind, an experienced touch and your mind are nondual. In brief, all apparent phenomena and your own mind are without duality.

As to this point, it may be that the meaning of the inseparability of phenomena and mind is not exactly actualized as being one taste. However, here the explanation is about pointing out phenomena as mind or the coemergent nature of phenomena and mind. The manner in which phenomena and mind are inseparable is not that phenomena come and dissolve into mind or that mind goes and dissolves into phenomena, like water mixing with sand. Rather, when the unfabricated cognizance of your mind is placed on the outer perceived object, the recognition of your mind being serenely present there, both mind and object arise as an empty phenomenon without reference point. Since empty phenomena are nonreferential, mind and phenomena are certainly not something to be separated as two different things; they are the phenomena of the the natural state itself. Because the defining characteristic of the mind is its unceasing radiance, mind is like a lamp manifesting as light or water arising as waves. Unfabricated cognizance abides as the nature of indivisibility. In this connection, the precious Kagyu have described the universe and beings, as well as whatever appears, to be dharmakaya. Here follow some quotations in this regard, as in the *Heart Sutra*:

> Form is emptiness.
> Also emptiness is form.
> Emptiness is no other than form.
> Form is no other than emptiness.

In the *Vajra Dome Tantra* it is said:

> Other than the jewel of mind,
> There are no sentient beings and no buddhas.
> None of the subject and object features of consciousness
> Have the slightest external existence.

In the *Way of the Bodhisattva* it is said:

> Who made the ground of burning iron?
> From where do fire and other torments arise?
> The Muni has declared that
> All these tortures are the sinful mind.

Naropa said:

> Phenomena are naturally free, the dharmakaya.

Marpa said:

> These outer phenomena, the machinery of delusion,
> Are realized as unoriginated, mahamudra.

Lord Mila said:

> No matter what outer phenomena appear,
> When there is no realization, they are deluded perceptions.

Grasping at outer objects binds you.
To the realized ones, they appear as illusory,
And apparent phenomena arise as the mind's friends.
In ultimate truth there has never been an experience of phenomena.
Understand them to be unoriginated and dharmakaya.

Lord Rechungpa said:

Have you understood myriad phenomena?
If you don't understand myriad phenomena,
Lacking realization, they are deluded perceptions.
To the realized ones they arise as dharmakaya.

Lord Takpo said:

These forms and sounds of habitual thought,
Directly catch them as the absolute.

Phagmo Drupa said:

The nature of phenomena is emptiness.
The essence of emptiness is phenomena.

Jigten Gonpo said:

Coemergent mind essence
And coemergent phenomena,
These two have one name; by not knowing them as separate
Both are understood under one instruction.

Dharma Lord Rangjung Dorje said:

The myriad outer phenomena
Are a magical display of your mind.

They have not even an atom of truth elsewhere.
Therefore, look at your own mind!

Gyalse Togme said:

Whatever appears is all one's own mind.
Mind essence has always been free from conceptual limitations.
If you realize it, all characteristics of subject and object
Are no longer created in the mind. This is the bodhisattva practice.

Lord Barawa said:

These interdependent phenomena
Are like the shapes in a mirror—
Your mind arising as myriad forms.
However they appear, they have no existence,
So lacking true existence is their glorious victory banner.

Siddha Cher Gompa said:

All phenomena, however they appear,
Are the natural face of mind and awareness.
They have no ground, root, or essence.
Know them to be inseparable phenomena and emptiness.

Omniscient Pema Karpo said:

> If you wonder what coemerges with what, it is coemergent mind essence and coemergent phenomena. In mahamudra, which is free of bias, a biased mind designates it as the basic nature, whereby there appears to be the basic nature and its radiance. This is similar to an onlooker perceiving a person who is resting at ease as friend or foe. Therefore, in terms of the basic nature, it is deemed to be immutable great bliss, and in terms of its radiance, it is deemed to be phenomena

> endowed with the highest quality of emptiness. That is to say, the former is the absolute level, and the latter the relative level; so the relative is the cause or method, and the absolute is the result or outcome of the method.

Together with scriptural quotations, there have been many clear references to this point.

## Introduction to One's Mind through the Ordinary Mind, the Unfabricated Natural State

This consists of: (1) identifying the distinctive feature of ordinary mind, (2) how the natural state of the mind is referred to as ordinary mind, (3) identifying ordinary mind itself, and (4) explaining how not wandering from it is mahamudra meditation.

## Identifying the Distinctive Feature of Ordinary Mind

If, in the continuity of unmodified consciousness of the present moment, you are not satisfied with recognizing the essence of whatever arises or appears, you may presume that resting serenely with the vivid clarity of the presence of pure mind is mahamudra meditation. Although that is the samadhi of shamatha free from the faults of dullness and agitation, it falls short of being mahamudra meditation. Other than possessing the experience of empty clarity, the mind lacks the conviction of vipashyana. If, while all thoughts have subsided in their original place, you have experienced with conviction the lucid mind essence or awareness as being totally unidentifiable, that itself would undoubtedly be regarded as the meditation of a beginner. However, if you believe or feel that thoughts ought somehow to be absent as a result of stopping thoughts and perceptions, that would entail the fault expressed by the words: "Your ambition aims at nonthought, while you claim to be taking thoughts to be dharmakaya." It follows that this would also fall short of being the meditation of the unfabricated essence of the natural state of awareness. Therefore, it will also be difficult for such a practice to occur during postmeditation.

Similarly, when a perception of a thought occurs, some people think that it should be stopped or drawn in and eliminated, so as to rest in nonthought. There are still some who believe that once a thought has been captured in the state of lucid mindfulness, you must rest in the wakefulness of the mind's empty lucidity. If, after you have reached conclusiveness of mind essence, lucid mindfulness does not wander from the core meaning, that itself is occurring as the meditation of a beginner. However, if you haven't resolved uncertainties, then thoughts and perceptions arise predominantly as enemies. Without finding the secret of the relaxed mind nature, this is an extremely constricted and partial experience.

Nevertheless, if you know how to sustain that type of spiritual practice, once you become familiarized with it, such a meditative state of resting in composure will progress. Gradually, through meticulous care, the occurrences of thoughts and perceptions will naturally subside, and finally a definitive conclusion regarding thoughts and perceptions will arise. Yet in the beginning it happens that many thoughts arise in the mind with such feeble clarity that their natural state is not experienced. Based on this, sustaining the practice becomes extremely unpleasant and you are very concerned about whether you can endure the meditation with such irritation. Then, it is necessary to recognize, in terms of the three coemergences, the thought-free mind as well as the occurring thoughts and objects of perception, and to eliminate all uncertainties. Particularly if only nonthought is pointed out at the time of introduction, then most practitioners will think that they must always be in a version of that state. After that, their practice will become very constricted, so that is not good at all. The main point is that it is extremely important to recognize the occurrences of thoughts and perceptions.

## How the Natural State of the Mind Is Referred To as Ordinary Mind

Some certainly think that what is called ordinary mind refers to the common deluded mind with its ordinary habits, but that is not so. The

Tibetan term *thamal* (ordinary) is *prakrita* in Sanskrit, which means both "natural" and "ordinary," so it carries the meaning of "natural mind." It means that it is by nature a cognizance that is luminous, not fabricated or adulterated by anything, abiding calmly of its own accord as its own basic nature. This way of conventionally labeling the mind as "ordinary mind" (*thamal gyi shepa*) is not exclusive to the Takpo Kagyu, as others also use it. In the *Utterly Nondwelling Suchness Sutra* it is said:

> The nature of ordinary mind is the supreme fruition.
> If it is left to rest without modification, the fruition of the three kayas is attained.
> When it relaxes of its own accord, it reaches culmination, wisdom.
> Unfabricated mind essence is the state of all vajras.
> The meaning of resting in the natural state is ineffable.
> That is the mother of all the buddhas.

Glorious Shawaripa said:

> Ordinary mind, one's innate nature, of its own accord,
> Is untainted by any contrived conceptions.
> There is no need to modify the mind, which is by nature pure.
> Without holding or releasing, leave it to itself.

The Great Siddha Toktsewa said:

> Ordinary mind is awakened in the center of the heart.
> If the six senses are purified, there is uninterrupted bliss.
> All analyses are pointless, they are the cause of suffering.
> Rest in the flow of the genuine state without meditating.

The Great Jetsun [Milarepa] said:

> Sustaining ordinary mind again and again,
> The delusion of ignorance is forgotten and vanishes.

Lord Gampopa said:

> This sufficient practice of the ordinary mind
> Is found through the kindness of the Buddha in human form.

There are many quotations similar to these.

## Identifying Ordinary Mind Itself

There are a lot of discussions about ordinary mind, but few define it clearly so this topic should be explained. In the great collection of public teachings by Lord Gampopa it is said:

> If now you want to be free from samsara, you must recognize the ordinary mind because it is the root of all Dharma teachings. What is called ordinary mind is your cognizance resting in its original place, uncontaminated by any religious aspect, unsullied by any worldly consciousness, and not covered by any dullness, torpor, or thoughts. When that is recognized, it is the primordial wisdom of your awareness. Not to realize it is coemergent ignorance. If you realize it, it is called awareness, coemergent wisdom, ordinary mind, genuine nature, simplicity, luminosity, and so forth.

When the essence of ordinary mind is defined and its various synonyms are acknowledged, its special qualities have, compared to most, been extensively explained. "Uncontaminated by any religious aspect" means that the mind is not contaminated by notions derived from philosophical analyses and experiences such as bliss, clarity, and nonthought. "Unsullied by any worldly consciousness" means that it is not contaminated by the mental stains of attachment, aggression, and other afflictions, nor by immediate concepts such as "I must do this," "I'm doing that." "Not covered by any dullness, torpor, or thoughts" means that the natural condition of the mind, its mode of being, is not obscured by the haziness caused by dullness and torpor, or the distractions caused by a proliferation of thoughts as such. "Resting in its original place" means that it settles in mind essence, the basic nature, or the mode of being, however it may be, without further contamination by the effort of stopping or acquiring. It rests right on its own character. Lord Gampopa said to his disciple Gomchung:

> In brief, do not at all manipulate, block, or acquire in terms of existence and nonexistence, empty and not empty, thought and nonthought, good and bad, proper and improper, and so on. However it arises, let it arise: ordinary mind is just that, without modification.

Also Lord Gampopa said:

> Ordinary mind, nonmodification, and genuine nature; out of these three, ordinary mind is a mind that has not been influenced by other philosophical tenets, and nonmodification means not to manipulate but leave it to itself.

Lord Yangonpa said:

> In brief, this ordinary mind—this freshness not modified by anyone—that knows itself is called the birth of mahamudra meditation.

As explained before, no matter what, you must start by knowing—beyond a shadow of a doubt—what mind, thoughts, and phenomena actually are. Without this, it would be like a person with impaired vision examining the shapes of a body by staring with gaping eyes: you would not have clearly determined the meaning of ordinary mind and unmodified mind, nor have achieved certainty. But if you know them as such, the mode of being or natural condition of the mind, uncontaminated by the modifications of conceptually stopping or acquiring—however it may be—just that is how ordinary mind is. That itself is how dharmakaya is, and by reaching a deep-rooted conviction about it and accordingly putting it into practice, you will actualize it. Otherwise it has been explained that it will be difficult to realize it as it is. As Lord Yangonpa said:

> There are many teachers who classify experiences and samadhi and introduce them as meditation, but a teacher who knows how to introduce ordinary mind as meditation is even rarer than a star in the daytime.

If you realize this ordinary mind, it is equivalent to what is commonly meant by "seeing mind nature" and other expressions. Once you are very familiar with this way of seeing, finally you no longer depend on whether there are thoughts or not. The cognizance of a mind which has thoughts, and which has neither religion nor meditation—that cognizance itself, fresh and complete, will recognize its essence and be liberated. Lord Gampopa said:

> However cognizance appears, fresh, complete,
> And clearly outstanding,
> It vividly beholds the face and arms of the Buddha in person.

Lord Gomchung said:

> Original cognizance,
> Ordinary mind,
> And perceiving mind,
> Whoever recognizes these three
> Evidently recognizes their mind,
> And that seeing is primordial wisdom.
>
> The essence of the unfabricated mind, the genuine nature,
> Has been perfectly seen.
> This very mind with thoughts,

> This brilliance, is seen vividly.
> In brief, the consciousness of a layperson who never had any idea about Dharma
> Is exactly so.

Lord Gyare said:

> This cognizance, while being a common person,
> Keeps on being dharmakaya.
> There's even no need for the teacher to reveal it;
> They are supposed to know it, yet . . .

There are a great number of references such as these in the practice lineage.

## Explaining How Not Wandering from It Is Mahamudra Meditation

When ordinary mind is recognized and the mindfulness of self-knowing awareness is not distracted from it, to sustain that in its natural flow—without modifying anything that happens or arises—is what is called "meditation." It is as Lord Gampopa said:

> This undistracted ordinary mind
> Is the meditation. Now at last I understand!

Therefore, no matter how the natural flow of the mind is, sustain right there the mindfulness that recognizes your essence. In case thinking happens, if you practice making corrections and applying patches, this would go against what is meant by not modifying the mind and your practice would not be meditation on the natural state. At any rate, it would be unfitting to be distracted even for a moment into any deluded, fixating cognizance that might occur. In the *Secret Amrita King Tantra* it is said:

> The luminous empty nature
> Is not found by meditating,
> Nor is it found by not meditating.
> Meditation as such is a concept,
> And not meditating is also a concept.
> When there is not the slightest bit of meditation,
> There is no distraction even for a moment.

Also Shawaripa said:

> Without regarding anything whatsoever as a fault,
> Practice without getting distracted by anything at all.
> Don't wish for the signs of attainment, and so forth.
> Indeed what has been taught is nonmeditation,
> But don't be carried away into indifference by laziness.
> Constantly practice mindfulness.

In the *Meditation Accomplishment Scripture* it is said:

> At the time of meditating, don't meditate at all.
> To call it "meditation" is just a convention.

In this way, when you are conscious of events and phenomena—whether the mind is an immaculate emptiness or a vivid bliss, or whether whirling thoughts issue forth in agitation or phenomena appear vibrantly—do not doubt that they are all the expression of the natural state. Recognize them, don't be distracted from the very presence of your own awareness, and in particular, sustain mindfulness without making corrections regarding any of the above. The need to settle without thoughts, drawing in dispersed thoughts, or stopping perceptions that arise was called by Lord Tsangpa Gyare the "meditation hook," which slows down meditative accomplishment. The essence of the mind, thoughts, perceived phenomena, and so forth, do not exist at all as separate independent entities, so they are illustrated by the examples of the sun and its rays or water and its waves—they are the natural expression of the mind's awareness arising in myriad ways. Therefore, whatever arises or appears in the natural flow of the mind is actually neither good nor bad, so whether still, moving, or manifesting as phenomena, recognize the essence and sustain the presence of awareness exactly on stillness, thought movement, or phenomena. Other than that, there is no need to make alterations or corrections. Lord Gampopa said:

> Without putting effort into stopping or acquiring, whether no thoughts arise or a variety of thoughts keep arising, by not modifying you are free from your duality. When you feel, "Wow! Nondual wisdom is within me!" and you have understood that, then you will have recognized the essence of mind, its basic nature, its mode of being. If you have that understanding, there is no need to have a meditation object. Since you are unable to discard or settle, meditation arises by itself. Since you are unable to stop the various thoughts, they arise. And when they do so, you will also be unable to stop nondual wisdom from arising.

As Gomchung said:

> The essence of luminous awareness
> Is inseparable, undistracted, and uninterrupted.
> In that continuous state,
> All thoughts arising in myriad ways
> Have that same essence.
> If ordinary mind doesn't wander,
> All thoughts and thinking are pristine awareness.
> There is no need to regard them as faults.

You may think, "Well then, there is no need for the series of guiding instructions, since from the very beginning it would be sufficient to be conscious of what arises in the mind." In the case of some individuals of the instantaneous type, it is possible that introducing them to such a practice is sufficient. However, for the most part, unless one is guided through a series of instructions, one will not have eliminated uncertainties regarding the natural state of mind essence, thoughts, and perceptions. Since one would lack the experience and conviction of having seen their essence, it would only be a mere general mindfulness; recognition or presence of awareness would be lacking, so it would not be sufficient. In this connection Lord Gampopa said:

> Then, worldly people simply have thoughts. Yogins also simply have ordinary mind. What is the difference between these two? If there is no difference, you may wonder why worldly people do not become liberated. Since they do not have the instructions of the yogin, worldly people don't recognize nonduality, and they only have the dualistic fixation of stopping and acquiring. Even those who have received instructions, but who are uncertain about the wisdom of nonduality, have no confidence in the variety of appearances, and therefore no liberation from dualistic thought is born in them. Such Dharma practitioners also train in dualistic learning, reflection, and meditation. Yogins are free from the cause of stopping and acquiring, and for them nondual wisdom and undetermined thoughts arise as manifold great bliss. The difference between these two springs from this key point.

It is as he said, in regard to establishing the boundary.

## Introduction to One's Mind through Essence, Nature, and Characteristic

In general the natural state of mind is conventionally laid down as essence, nature, and characteristic, but in fact there is nothing else but mind essence itself. It is as said in *Leaning Below*:

> The essence of all things is emptiness.
> "Nature" and "form" have no other meaning:
> They mean one's own essence.

However, in terms of their differentiating attributes, essence, nature, and characteristic have also been taught to be distinct from one another and individually identified. Lord Gampopa said:

> As for the mind's essence, nature, and characteristic:
> The mind's essence is its concept-free lucidity;
> Its nature is its freedom from origination, abiding, and cessation;
> And its characteristic is that it manifests as both samsara and nirvana.

He also said:

> Also, the "essence" of the mind is unoriginated, unabiding, and unceasing awareness. "Nature" is that the mind is pure by nature, it is uncompounded, and it pervades all of samsara and nirvana. Mind's "characteristic" is that it manifests the diverse images of habitual patterns.

Phagmo Drupa said:

> Nonduality is mahamudra.
> Regarding essence, nature, and characteristic:
> Nature is that mind's lucidity is unimpeded;
> Essence is that it is free from the constructs of birth and cessation;
> Characteristic is that it manifests as the diversity of samsara and nirvana.

Lord Rangjung Dorje said:

> The essence is empty and the nature is lucid.
> Its forms are unimpeded and arise as all things.

The essence of the mind means that it is originally free from all substantial states of origination, abiding, and cessation. It is uncontaminated by the dualistic concepts of the *skandhas*, elements, and sensory bases.

And its nature lacking identity—abiding as emptiness—is the same as the essence of all phenomena. In the *Assemblage of Secrets* it is said:

> Because it is free from all substantiality,
> Skandhas, elements, and sensory bases;
> Has totally abandoned subject and object duality;
> And is the same as all phenomena's lack of self;
> One's mind was never born.
> It is by nature emptiness.

In the *Commentary on Bodhichitta* it is said:

> The enlightened mind of all the buddhas
> Is not veiled by the cognitive thoughts
> Of ego and skandhas.
> It is posited to always have the characteristic of emptiness.

Therefore, as mentioned earlier, if one examines and looks for the essence of the mind in a variety of ways, no basis for any characteristic whatsoever is found to exist. The seeker's mental elaboration subsides and is exhausted by itself, so the ultimate level and the primordially abiding absolute reality (*dharmata*)[8] are said to be emptiness. In the *Words Distinguishing the Two Truths Composed in a Chapter* it is said:

> On this conventional level, as things appear,
> If examined through intelligence, no diversity is found.
> Precisely this not finding is the absolute level:
> The originally abiding dharmata.

This essence of mind, emptiness, is also the empty essence of all phenomena included in the world and beings. Aryadeva said:

> One thing is the very nature of all things.
> All things are the very nature of one thing.

In the *Four Hundred Verses* it is said:

> What is the emptiness of one thing?
> It is the emptiness of everything.

In the *Words Distinguishing the Two Truths Composed in a Chapter*, it is said:

> Even the slightest distinction
> Does not exist in emptiness.

As to the nature, in the *Prajñaparamita in Eight Thousand Verses* it is said:

> The nature of the mind is luminous.

In the *Descent into Langka Sutra* it is said:

> The mind is luminous by nature;
> It is the pure tathagata essence.

In these and other quotations, it is often mentioned that the nature of the mind is luminous. The meaning of luminous has been explained as follows. Being pure of the conceptual elaborations of origination, cessation, and so forth, it is not contaminated by them. Being free from even a speck of skandhas, elements, and so forth, it is immaculate. Like space, it is immutable in all circumstances. It is nondual with the nature of space. In the *Discourse Requested by the Close Circle* it is said:

> This totally pure, luminous nature of mind
> Has been taught to be immaculate, without any speck, free from specks.

In the *Sublime Continuum* it is said:

> What is the luminous nature of mind like?
> It is unchangeable like space.

In the *Assemblage of Secrets* it is said:

> The nature of all phenomena being luminosity,
> They are originally pure and similar to space.

This being so, some claim that the luminosity of nature is signified by whatever mental visionary experiences and clarity may arise. They also claim that what is called luminosity is like the light of the sun. This is extremely wrong for the following reasons. The "nature" of the mind is a conventional term that simply entails that "luminous by nature" means uncontaminated by the stains of conceptual constructs and completely pure of these stains, as the quotations above have upheld. Also, if the luminosity of the nature of mind had a cause, such as color or light, the mind would also have the nature of color or light. And if that were so, it couldn't be said that the mind has no true nature or that it is pure by nature. You may think, "Well then, what is the yogin's self-knowing and naturally luminous cognizance, in which the visions experienced are the mind's own manifestations and brilliance transcending colors and lights?" Regarding this point, in the *Abridgement of Naropa's View* it is said:

> Because they appear and are clear,
> All these phenomena of the world and beings
> Are not apart from one's mind.
> They are, for example, like the experiences of awareness.

Also:

> One's awareness free from elaborations
> Appears while being empty, is empty while appearing;
> Therefore appearance and emptiness are inseparable,
> Like, for example, the moon reflected in water.

As Naropa said, nowadays, when talking about experiences, we see that a mere occurrence of an experience of the luminous cognizance of the mind is called "awareness" (*rigpa*). However, since such an experience is conceptual, it is neither the emptiness endowed with the supreme capacity to manifest nor the sovereign lord of everything, so it is not pristine awareness as such. In the *Great Commentary on Kalachakra* it is said:

> Well then, what is pristine awareness? "Awareness" is the inner knowing free of concepts, the emptiness in all phenomena. It is also immutability, the epitome of what is nonconceptual and undefiled. Being the epitome of cause and effect, it is cause and effect merged into one, like firelight and burning commingled and unified.

In the *Reciting the Names [of Manjushri]*:

> Sublime, all-cognizant, and all-knowing,
> It transcends the absolute reality of consciousness.

And:

> It knows itself, others, and everything.

Lord Drikungpa said:

> What is known as mahamudra
> Is precisely one's own awareness.

As indicated in these quotations, all the types of awareness that have been taught as objects of meditation should also be understood to be like that. Therefore, whatever arises as a yogin's experience, all these are precisely one's awareness, and it is totally improper to attribute them to the luminous nature. In the *Sutra That Unravels the Intent* it is said:

> The domain of precisely self-knowing awareness free of characteristics . . .

In the *Inconceivable Secret Tantra* it is said:

> Self-knowing awareness is the mind that has abandoned
> Eternalism, nihilism, origination, cessation, and other such extremes.
> It is originally free from conceptual elaboration.
> Its meaning is certainly inconceivable.

This is so because it is taught that the actuality of self-knowing awareness is inconceivable and devoid of defining characteristics, and its nature is luminous as was explained before.

Let us now consider characteristics. When the essence and nature of mind, perfect as they are, are veiled by temporary defilements, one is not aware of one's own natural state. As a result, based on the complete interdependence of afflictions, the experience of samsara as the six kinds of beings, including happiness and sorrow, takes place. After becoming free of the temporary defilements and aware of the natural state, based on the interdependence of complete purification, the absolute body of dharmakaya is actualized, and in the perception of others the array of the *rupakaya* appears as an illusion. In the *Abridgement of Naropa's View* it is said:

> *Emaho!* The defiled mind
> Magically displays the six kinds of beings, and so forth,
> And in the boundlessness of space
> The machinery of suffering is inconceivable.

Also:

> *Emaho!* The undefiled mind
> Magically displays the rupakaya
> That includes the pure visions of the buddha fields

And the diverse emanations of the mandalas.
These wondrous magical emanations
Pervade boundless space.

In the *Samputa Tantra* it is said:

The one possessing the vajra has taught that samsara
Is the mind contaminated by such stubborn stains as attachment.
Realizing the luminous nature, liberation is gained.
Free from contamination by such stains as attachment,
And without the fixation on subject and object, the mind is the supreme hero.
Precisely that is what has been taught as supreme nirvana.

Lord Dao Shonu said:

What is called samsara is by nature emptiness; it is delusion, and its characteristic is that it arises as suffering. What is called nirvana is the emptiness samadhi; it is the exhaustion and dissolution of all delusion, and its characteristic is that it is free from all suffering.

Regarding the conditions of that delusion, some say, "If it were possible for delusion to be in the ground of being, it would be a contaminated ground. If there were no stains whatsoever in the ground, the ground would be the fruit. If it were possible for delusion to arise from the path, the path would take place from the beginning of samsara. If delusion were new and not something from before, one would become deluded while in buddhahood." The incomparable Gyalwang Je said:

In the ground there is no delusion; yet, while in the ground, one becomes deluded.

All these are clear and easy to understand. In the advice of the supreme siddha Mipham Lodro we find:

> There is no delusion in the ground, but we don't recognize that there is none. This is called "coemergent ignorance." On account of this, facing outward, the conceptual mind or thoughts that generate karma are called "conceptual ignorance." For example, a rope is not a snake. Not recognizing that it is not a snake is the confusion that is similar to coemergent ignorance. Simply by confusing it with a snake, many painful thoughts arise; this is similar to conceptual ignorance, which manifests as delusion and has the characteristic of arising as suffering. Furthermore, at the very moment the rope was seen, it appeared to be a snake right from the beginning. Similarly, between coemergent ignorance and mind nature there is no before-and-after; there is no "rope" connecting factor.[9] Later on, through the pith instructions of a sublime teacher, one understands the root of delusion to be the mind. At that point, the delusion hasn't gone anywhere else; rather the delusion itself arises as wisdom. In the analogy, when one realizes through a separate condition that it is a rope, the snake hasn't gone anywhere else. By knowing that what appeared to be a snake is itself a rope, one is free from distress, all the expressions of delusion come to an end and vanish, and the characteristic is that there is freedom from all suffering.

He also provided these definitions:

> Regarding coemergent ignorance and temporary defilements, is there any difference between the two? If there isn't, what is the meaning of the terms "coemergent ignorance" and "temporary defilements"? The expanse of mind essence is by nature perfectly pure and uncompounded. "Defilement" is what is to be eliminated, and it is compounded and impermanent; being a changeable phenomenon it is called "temporary." "Coemergent ignorance" transcends temporary

> defilements and its characteristic is that it manifests as the multiplicity of samsara and nirvana.

At present, when a yogin has a meditative experience, the forms that arise in the mind are not at all predetermined and appear in myriad ways without being blocked anywhere. Due to the force of numerous past habits, although they are not external entities, they appear as being seemingly so. In other words, things will appear according to the designation and alteration brought about by the factors of karma and habits like, for example, the way in which cloth is altered by dye. Although the essence does not change, its manifestations change in myriad ways. As said in the *Descent into Langka Sutra:*

> The mind is by nature perfectly pure and luminous; it will manifest to the extent that it is designated, as for example a white cloth is altered by a colored dye.

Thus understanding the essence, nature, and characteristic of the mind according to all these explanations, you should focus on practicing from this standpoint.

## Introduction to One's Mind through Meditation and Postmeditation

This includes explanations on: (1) identifying meditation and postmeditation, (2) the common method for sustaining meditation and postmeditation, (3) the system for sustaining meditation and postmeditation, (4) how postmeditation arises as illusion, and (5) the distinction between merged and unmerged meditation and postmeditation.

## Identifying Meditation and Postmeditation

Here there are three points: meditative composure, ensuing cognizance, and postmeditation. Let us start with meditative composure.[10]

The ordinary basic nature of the mind that recognizes coemergent mind essence and coemergent thoughts is precisely the essence of mahamudra. Upon knowing that, in awareness there is neither observer nor observed object, neither something to place nor one who places. This, the self-abiding basic nature of awareness, and its radiance manifesting as manifold forms are primordially not separate. This is the sole innate nature, and by realizing this natural state there is no need to meditate conceptually, viewing and identifying as separate whatever arises and all that appears. When you are able to sustain, carefree and open, the natural flow of the recognition of this nature, this is the genuine meditative composure.

Regarding the basic way of being, if you are unable to realize the view totally free of obscurations because you are not familiar with it and haven't developed its potential, undoubtedly there will be times when you will somehow forget. However, the perfect meaning of mind essence is such that, whether you forget and are distracted or instead have mindful knowing, these two are not deliberately taken as good or bad. There is no need to meditate conceptually, evaluating mindful knowing, making corrections, and patching things up. It is sufficient to nurture and sustain the natural flow. Even if that were not the case, for as long as you rest in the basic nature of mind essence free from thinking and mental constructs and until distraction occurs due to reifying thoughts, the mind resting serenely is called "meditative composure."

In the ensuing cognizance, grasping arises to savor any experience you have had during meditative composure. However, just as in order to cross the road quickly you should not be shackled, for realization to progress to the next level you should not engage in grasping. Moreover, there is not just one kind of grasping: outer, inner, and innermost grasping should be distinguished. Outer grasping refers to clinging to this life and the things of the outer world—friends, relatives, wealth, possessions, and so forth—as being concrete. Inner grasping is to cling to attachment, aversion, and the other five poisons, as well as to situations of happiness, suffering, good, evil, and so forth. Innermost grasping is to desire to meditate and to have experiences. When these are not recognized, the ensuing cognizance is deluded. Once you experience grasping unrecognized by the determined mindfulness, you generate karma, and that would constitute the ordinary, deluded ensuing cognizance.

If, while there is grasping, it is recognized and yet you engage in it, that is the vigilant ensuing cognizance. Regarding the vigilant ensuing cognizance, it is as the sayings go: "hay that is not yet dry"[11] or "human footprints turned into dog's footprints."[12] When you are unconcerned about whatever arises and sustain the practice too loosely in a somewhat carefree way, then you are not keeping to the key point of not being distracted even for a moment. Not deeming grasping to be something critical, you think there is nothing wrong with it; this becomes a habit and you generate karma. This is what is meant by the sayings mentioned above. You should ensure that your head does not break inside your helmet. You should not consciously take poison.

Regarding postmeditation, while resting composed in the basic nature without wavering from the state of emptiness, there is no doubt that its radiance will unceasingly arise as situations and attachments. However, by naturally recognizing what arises, grasping vanishes by itself, and postmeditation is successful, so it is called "self-liberation." Moreover, when what appears does not prevail and upon recognition is completely liberated, the moment it arises would be "simultaneous arising and liberation." Just as a flying bird leaves no trace in the sky, occurring thoughts leave no trace of residual attachments and propensities.

This is what has been taught, yet over time it will seem difficult for such liberations to occur. Why is this so? Some situations are not easily self-liberated; someone may not be overcome by their sudden occurrence, yet lingering rememberances spring forth again and again. Even if you don't indulge in significant grasping during your main practice, just as the scent of musk lingers after the perfume bottle is empty, you will not be able to purify your habitual patterns no matter what. So we, ignorant meditators, in the darkness of not knowing the vital point, will amble in bewilderment. Never acknowledging that to be a fault, we would be sealing something that is not, as it were, like disregarding the slush beneath snow.[13] Knowing the key point of the meditation at the beginning, middle, and end prevents us from becoming like those who consider a mountain [bathed in golden light] actually to be gold.

To regard outer, inner, and innermost fixations as faults, to gain decisive conviction in mindful knowing of the nature—these are extremely cherished points.

## The Common Method for Sustaining Meditation and Postmeditation

According to the teachings on meditation by the great siddha Orgyenpa, there are four points, namely: rest in freshness without modifying, let thinking vanish by itself, take diversity as a friend, and let phenomena be freely open. As to the first point, "rest in freshness without modifying," by giving up all thoughts of the three poisons, the mind is unmodified. What is meant by freshness is to rest loosely on mind's fresh basic nature, however it may be, while being free of deliberate meditating and fixating. Moreover, it is crucial not to be separate from the mindful knowing that lightly recognizes your basic nature. The mind should rest without any reference point whatsoever. Apart from mindful knowing, there should be no object of meditation, that is, no targeted reference point such as thinking and thoughts.

"Let thinking vanish by itself" means that, apart from simply identifying proliferating thoughts based on the basic nature of mind, you rest right in your essence without making any adjustments. Since you are looking precisely at the essence, thinking will eventually vanish by itself beyond identification. Because that is the meaning of what will happen, this point is called "let thinking vanish by itself."

"Take diversity as a friend" means that, without rejecting or accepting the diversity of thoughts springing from the fresh unfabricated mind essence endowed with vigilance, you look at their essence. By persevering in continuously practicing in this way, the immediate signs are that your mind becomes somewhat clearer. At times thoughts dim the clarity of the mind, at other times they proliferate wildly, and so forth. When any such situations that make sustaining the practice pleasant or uncomfortable arise, don't deliberately judge what occurs to be a fault or a virtue. Neither cultivate what seems to be good and pleasant, nor stop what seems to be bad and uncomfortable; rather decide that all good and bad is the display of your own mind alone. You must rest right on the identity of whatever arises. Resting in this way, you will be taking everything as a friend, and finally everything will become a friend. This is what is meant by "take diversity as a friend." Similarly, regarding external sensory objects, don't examine them and cling to their quality, whether good or bad. Without falling under the influence of attachment or aversion, you should catch anything that appears through vigilance and rest on it. In brief, the point is not to start the modifying fixation on any perceived object of the six sensory groups, but instead take such phenomena as friends to sustain your own essence.

Fourth, to "let phenomena be freely open" means that, neither blocking external phenomena nor internal personal experiences, nor being bound by them, you rest right on the bare recognition of the essence, loosely letting the phenomena be. If we were to distill this meaning, there wouldn't be many classifications to it. No matter how the basic nature of the mind might present itself, don't modify it. In the continuous state of bare nondistraction from your essence as it naturally is, rest at ease, be effortlessly serene, and freely let be. Sustain a clearly present, undistracted mindfulness. No matter what thought movement occurs, don't manipulate it but sustain your nature. Without grasping at outer phenomena, take them as the path as they naturally are of their own accord. Since, for the most part, all these ways of sustaining apply to any kind of meditation and postmeditation, they are taught as the common way of sustaining.

## The System for Sustaining Meditation and Postmeditation

For the main part of the session, as said by Jangchub Rinpoche, "Until ensuing cognizance is extinguished, it is important not to depart from the vajra posture." Without modifying the voice, beyond thinking, speech, and description, you should practice like a mute person. Without modifying the mind, not following past or future thoughts, rest on the cognizance of the present moment, on the identity of whatever arises without making any adjustments. This is the root of all taming techniques and it is most vital that this not go wrong. Padampa Sangye said:

> The ground being the body, voice, and mind of sentient beings,
> The path consists of the yogin resting on these without modifying.
> The fruition is to be liberated into the buddha body, voice, and mind.

In the *Storehouse Tantra* it is said:

> If water is not disturbed it becomes limpid.
> If the mind is not modified it becomes clear.

Thus by resting on any perception that occurs, there is the ensuing cognizance of empty lucidity, free of grasping. Without rejecting subtle or coarse thoughts but instead by letting them dissolve in themselves, the essence of coemergent mind is luminosity, like the center of space. Practice alternating between resting one-pointedly in composure in this essence and the previous way with perceptions. If you wonder how to practice between sessions, here you must also start by exerting yourself and train in a continuous flow of mindful knowing. Lord Drikungpa said:

> If you master mindfulness, you master meditation.
> Children, regard being always mindful as crucial!

As stated in this quotation, in our case what is meant by mindfulness is mainly the experience and conviction of the previously pointed-out coemergent mind essence. Nevertheless, it does have a slight, specific difference. While keeping present the mere flavor or strength of the mindfulness of this type of practice, suddenly a circumstantial thought or a perception of a form, a sound, or any other object may occur. Clearly perceive it, but don't start to reify it by stopping or acquiring.

It is, for instance, like the cognizance of a small child seeing the frescoes in a temple. A carefree and vivid mindfulness that does not cling to the cognizant clarity, an open mind, settles. In brief, you are sustaining the continuous state of the spiritual practice of both coemergent thoughts and coemergent phenomena to which you had previously been introduced. In this context, the *Way of the Bodhisattva* says:

> Thus here, seeing, hearing, and knowing
> Are not to be stopped.
> What is to be stopped here is the cause of suffering:
> The imputation as real.

You might wonder, "Well then, what is spiritual practice to be sustained through such mindfulness like?" It should, for example, be like an experienced herder watching over his cattle. When the cattle are feeding, they are allowed to go about freely and at ease; he neither needs to drive nor follow them, nor take any such actions. All he needs to preserve them is to simply keep them within his field of vision. Here, it's not a matter of holding thoughts and perceived phenomena, blocking them, or dimming their clarity, thus actually reducing them. Conversely, by following thoughts and perceptions there is distraction, the vigor of mindfulness is lost, and you start to fixate, blocking and acquiring, whereby thoughts and perceptions solidify on their own. That too is not the point. No matter how the objects of the six sense consciousnesses arise, when, while they are clearly appearing, you are convinced that their nature is unidentifiable, all thoughts are empty movements and all phenomena are empty phenomena. Sustain this through unfixated mindfulness of its own accord without correction. Lord Gotsangpa distilled the meaning in these easy-to-understand words:

> Besides, when thought has arisen,
> Earnestly recognize it
> And rest on it loosely.
> There is no doubt it will be released.
> Look directly at outer objects;

They are like a magical illusion of your mind.
Without grasping, rest on whatever appears.
Untie spacious awareness.
Thought movement is insubstantial, like the breeze.
If you don't cling to it, movement is fine.
That is what is meant by thoughts arising as meditation.
By knowing their nature, you are free from blocking or acquiring.
Apart from simply not being distracted, there is nothing else to be cultivated.
In the continuity of nonmeditation do not be distracted!

In this way, simply embracing the four types of activity with mindfulness, properly sustain the practice. Beginners will have intense distraction initially, but when resting in composure, they will develop the strength of mindfulness on the basis of the essence. During postmeditation, relying with effort on an always present mindfulness, they will use thoughts and perceptions as the path. By sustaining continuous mindfulness of the essence through the ensuing cognizance and ensuing perception, undistracted mindfulness becomes firmly grounded and postmeditation quickens. When these two occur, each will enhance the other, and you will experience the method that will develop meditation. If you have the flow of the cognizance of awareness, whatever arises in postmeditation will be sustained naturally, and you will have found certainty on the basis of not making corrections or other alterations to phenomena. Therefore, a mindfulness that is not distracted from the core meaning in every situation is also the reason why mindfulness becomes the main point of meditation. Lord Gampopa said:

Cultivate the view of nondistraction, the mindfulness monarch.
Persevere in that, without change, through the diversity of conditions.
Don't look for anything but the path of continuous undistracted mindfulness.

And:

> Unless the tethering pole of fixation has been pulled off,
> The karma of a thought will be generated.
> So it is good to rely on the watchman of undistracted
> mindfulness.

According to the styles mentioned earlier, you should not be carried away by grasping and generating karma while employing both deluded ensuing cognizance and vigilant ensuing cognizance as the path. However, since internal stains of subject and object, residues of habits, dormant delusion, and so forth are extremely difficult to detect, you would be practicing as if a mountain bathed in golden light were gold, when in fact it is not. It is said that thoughts might linger, as in the example of slush under snow, and that the flaws of meditation dwell dormant. Therefore, it is necessary to recognize and purify them. No matter what outer conditions arise—happy or sad, good or bad—you should not be dominated by attachment or aversion, rejection or adoption. Moreover, so that outer and inner attachment, aversion, dualistic clinging, or desire do not grow in strength and mix, develop the courage of perfect mindfulness, the antidote that brings about the recognition of the essence. Always train in carefulness and with a determined mind. By knowing all that is coarse, don't be carried away by the generation of karma. Identifying everything, down to what is most subtle and dormant, you need to equalize it on the basis of mindfulness, thus using it as the path. Regarding all outer worldly conditions in this life—relatives, friends, wealth, possessions, merchandise, food—these are like last night's dream, your deluded perceptions. Don't be driven by attachment toward them but train in nonattachment and nongrasping. If outer conditions are good, don't be attached to goodness but use goodness as the path. If they are bad, don't be disheartened due to badness but cultivate mindfulness on that badness. In inner events, if angry, cultivate mindfulness on anger. If desirous and attached, develop same taste precisely on that attachment. This extends similarly to the rest of the five poisons. If your mind is happy, rest on happiness. If sad, cultivate mindfulness on sadness. In brief, don't be overtaken by good or bad outer conditions, or by inner suffering and happiness of all kinds provoked by them in your mind. It is important that everything is taken as the path on the basis of a mindfulness that does not fixate on attachment, aversion, adoption, or rejection.

Most meditators consider that it is not a mistake for vigilance to be influenced by grasping. This not only prevents meditation progress, but after regressing, while in that stubborn frame of mind, meditators and *togdens*[14] will plunge into the mire of this life's attachment. Therefore, it is important to apply every possible caution regarding this. Persevere constantly in undistracted nonmeditation. Avoid polluting whatever there is with the taste of inner or outer reification and do not fixate; instead stick to the key point of self-liberation and nonfixation. If you engage in grasping, rest precisely on the grasper without distraction and let it go into its own lucidity.

Those in whom realization has dawned don't need the meditator, object of meditation, or corrections. However, they may not have definitely understood why they don't need them. Apart from recognizing the natural flow of self-knowing awareness, ordinary mind, they don't need to practice a deliberate meditation; yet since previous retentive mindfulness is still lingering and hasn't been transformed, they harbor a desire to have something to meditate upon. Even though there is nothing to experience apart from the knowledge of the nature of the outer and inner six sense perceptions, they still have a desire for vivid clarity, bliss, and other experiences. Don't proceed in that way. Be free from any innermost fixation on desiring to meditate, and in that state, stick to the key point of nondistraction. Besides, this key point of nondistraction is such that you should sustain the natural state immaculately, of its own accord, free from fabricating or modifying mind essence or meditating on it. If you capture these key points, all stains to be purified will be cleansed like ice in summertime. This way of taking ensuing knowledge as the path has been referred to by Lord Takpo with three indications: meeting and destroying, chasing after, and insubstantial illusion.[15]

These are explained extensively by Phagmo Drupa as:

> Having used thoughts as the path
> When practicing the stage of the four sessions,
> In brief four experiences arise:
> Meeting a person known from before; snow on a hot stone;
> A burning forest; and bliss, clarity, and void.
>
> First is meeting a person known from before.
> For example, when two close friends
> Are walking on a road and meet,
> They recognize each other the moment they cross paths.
> Similarly, it happens to yogins that
> The very moment a thought arises,
> It is eliminated in their empty mind.
> This is what is meant by "meeting and destroying."
>
> Second is snow on a hot stone.
> Snow falls from clouds,
> But as soon as it falls on a hot stone,
> It immediately turns to water.
> Likewise, when thoughts arise from distraction,
> Upon arising they are cognized as mind.
> In mind essence, the simplicity of dharmakaya,
> Realization will dawn without the need for exertion.
> This is what is meant by "chasing after."
>
> Third is a burning forest.
> For example, if a forest catches fire,
> Trees, bushes, animals,
> Clean and unclean areas, and so forth
> Are burned without discrimination.
> No matter how much wind or hail there is,
> It will not extinguish the fire but instead strengthen it.

Similarly, when the flames of realization blaze,
The diversity of good and bad thoughts,
And dualistic afflictions such as attachment and aversion,
Free from adoption and rejection, stopping and acquiring,
Are burned in the state of nonorigination.
No matter how many thoughts there are,
They turn into aids to the birth of realization.
This is what is meant by "insubstantial illusion."

Thus while realization is stabilized,
Lucidity is unimpeded and free of extremes.
There is no attachment to bliss, clarity, and nonthought.
Even if pierced with a needle, there is pleasure.
Whether day or night, in between sessions, moving or sitting, and so forth,
If there is no difference at all regardless of the activity,
Or the four experiences of bliss, clarity, and the rest,[16]
It is said that this is how experiences arise at that time.

## How Postmeditation Arises as Illusion

In general, things arising as illusion are based on two factors: they must be captured by the sense consciousness, and the mind must be certain about emptiness. For instance, the vision of horses and elephants created magically by an illusionist are captured by the eye consciousness, and the mind consciousness is sure that the perceived form does not exist concretely; based on these two factors one is certain that all the perceived forms are fake appearances. Similarly, in our case, during postmeditation, apparent thoughts—as well as phenomena such as forms and sounds, based on the interdependence of cause and effect—are perceived as false by yogins through the eye and other sense consciousnesses. Mindfully sustaining the conviction and experience of having previously established the coemergence of thoughts and phenomena, and cognizing phenomena as being naturally empty, when these two factors come together, postmeditation arises as illusion. Shawaripa said:

> If its reality is examined, it is not the perfect state
> Free from the threefold focus;[17] it is like a dream.
> There is neither pleasure nor sadness that is obstructed,
> So it is like the benefit caused by an illusion created by a magician.

Also:

> All forms and sounds are like an illusion, a mirage, or a reflection;
> They do not have the characteristics of a concrete thing.
> The perceiver of the illusion is the space of mind essence.

The empty aspect is responsible for these arising in that way, and in order to realize it, the main point is that one needs to be convinced that the innate mind essence is definitely unoriginated. Therefore, during meditative composure it is important to emphasize the essence. During postmeditation it is important to emphasize the essence of both coemergent thoughts and phenomena. As to practicing with phenomena, thoughts and phenomena arise automatically, and from the strength of the corresponding interdependence of cause and effect, grasping also arises through familiarity. Although this is not something that has to be accomplished on purpose, some people are extremely attached to emptiness and, based on this, they hold that there is no interdependence of cause and effect. As this is a serious nihilistic view, it is therefore totally unacceptable. They should be clearly convinced about even the subtle interdependence of cause and effect. In brief, it is vital to bring together mastery of the understanding that cause and effect is unequivocal and the certainty that all phenomena, being devoid of true nature, are emptiness. These two together are declared to be wonderful. As said in the *Commentary on Bodhichitta*:

> Having known that all phenomena are empty,
> To have demonstrated cause and effect
> Is more wonderful than wonderful,
> More exceptional than exceptional.

In this way, upon examining the nature or essence of all phenomena, free of all conceptual elaborations, it is space-like emptiness. The scholars of the past have explained that while nature or essence is empty, forms and so forth manifest as phenomena, these being illusory on account of emptiness. Based on this, it is said that meditative composure is like the sky and postmeditation is like an illusion, and nowadays in most teachings on the true meaning these two are well known as such. Occasionally, there are explanations that refer to nonconceptual meditative composure as being supramundane wisdom and postmeditation, like an illusion, as being worldly wisdom.

## The Distinction between Merged and Unmerged Meditation and Postmeditation

Since many different experiences can occur in people's minds, it is difficult to identify the way meditation and postmeditation merge, and I have rarely seen this explained elsewhere. However, in some texts of questions and answers to Lord Gampopa we find:

> In essence what is meant by "merging meditation and postmeditation"? No matter what you do during the four types of daily activity, you are never separated from luminosity and always arrive at the essence and merge with it.
>
> Sometimes when mindfulness is lost, the mind wanders off with a thought. After regaining mindfulness it returns to the essence. Would this be "not merging"? That would be "not merging."

Also Lord Drikungpa said:

When there is meditation and postmeditation
One is called a bodhisattva.
When there is no meditation and postmeditation
One is called a siddha, a buddha.

Thus, according to these quotations, it is obvious that the perfect authentic merging of meditation and postmeditation only happens during the yogas of greater one taste and nonmeditation. It is explained that this is because, even in the ensuing cognizance of greater simplicity, thoughts do not arise solely as pure luminosity, and even in the ensuing cognizance of middling one taste, slightly dualistic reifying perceptions still arise. In the considerations of Lord Gampopa, Tashi Namgyal, and others, regarding the merging of meditation and postmeditation at the time of greater simplicity, it is easy for us to understand what is called meditation and postmeditation by distinguishing these as basic nature and radiance.

Regarding whether meditation and postmeditation are merged or not, these days there are many meditators who belong to the class of scholars, and once in a while, a slight realization is born within them. However, since they haven't captured the key point of the guru, it is also hard for them to recognize meditation and postmeditation. In fact, unmerged meditation and postmeditation is when one is somehow satisfied with the sentiment during meditative composure in the basic nature, but during the radiance of postmeditation, there is a slight discomfort so, in the ensuing cognizance, karma due to delusion is generated. Meditation and postmeditation have merged when the stains of ensuing cognizance have been purified, and there is no choice at all between meditation and postmeditation. Thus, the mind is free from the desire for meditative composure, and giving importance to basic nature or radiance vanishes. As Sherab Drukgye said:

The empty reflections of external appearances
And inner nonconceptual awareness,
By recognizing these two as being originally indivisible,
One has mastered the meaning of the view free of extremes.

And:

> Thoughts creating movement in the mind arise as meditation.
> The mind is not attached to the desire for meditative composure.
> There is no specific purpose to avoid or establish.
> Therefore, in my practice, I don't give importance to meditation and postmeditation.

Some teachers express their belief that, without any need for these considerations but simply due to the absence of a distinction between meditation and postmeditation, these are merged. I have my doubts, however: Is it that these two are simply about to merge or that they have genuinely merged?

With that I have explained briefly the division between meditative composure and postmeditation.

# 3. Introduction to One's Mind

8. Ground, Path, and Fruition
9. The Four Aspects: View, Meditation, Conduct, and Fruition
10. Mahamudra
11. Perfect Buddha
12. The Three Kayas
13. The Five Wisdoms

## Introduction to One's Mind through Ground, Path, and Fruition

First let us start by briefly explaining the natural state of ground mahamudra. The ground is the all-pervading buddha nature, the truth of absolute reality pervading the whole of samsara and nirvana. For example, like space pervaded by the void or water by wetness, from the beginning the ground is never separate from anything. In the *Abridgement of Naropa's View* it is said:

> Your own awareness free from elaborations
> Is itself the actual basis of samsara.
> Nirvana is also that.
> The great middle way is also that.
> What is to be seen is also that.
> What is to be meditated on is also that.
> What is to be attained is also that.

As said in a tantra of the great perfection (dzogchen):

> *Emaho!* It is the creator of all of samsara and nirvana.
> It is in the center of one's heart and not elsewhere.
> What brings about its realization is the kindness of the guru.

In fact, when we are down wandering in samsara, it is one's mind. When we rise up to the attainment of buddhahood, it is also one's mind. The ground is only one's awareness itself. As said in the *Enlightenment of Vairochana Tantra*:

> Thoughts are the great ignorance;
> They plunge us into the ocean of samsara.

Not knowing its own essence, the mind continuously follows negative habitual patterns, thus accumulating karma, and, while doing so, one wanders in samsara. If this very mind—knowing its own essence, not following habitual patterns of delusion—establishes the prevalence of self-knowing awareness, the binding rope is released on its own without rejecting it, and one awakens to buddhahood. In the *Two Segments* it is said:

> Sentient beings are buddhas,
> But this is veiled by temporary stains.
> When these are eliminated, that is actual buddhahood.

Therefore, all the roots of samsara and nirvana are one's mind. All the creators of the states of existence and peace are one's awareness, rootless and groundless, abiding free from limitations such as restrictions and bias, as well as origination, abiding, and cessation. Lord Gotsangpa said:

> The mind is not found by searching for it or seen by looking at it. If examined, it does not exist; if grasped at, it is not captured; if sent away, it does not leave; if settled, it does not

> stay put; if mixed, it does not merge. It is not distinguished by differentiation, split by taking it apart, known by observing it, understood through explanations, illustrated by an analogy, and nothing can be loaded onto it. No matter what name it is given, there is no contradiction.

In other words, if the mind had any concrete aspect such as color or shape, it could be found by looking for it. Similarly, indeed it could be seen by looking at it, found to exist if examined, captured by grasping, and so forth. Since it is not like that, it does not exist as a thing; it has no substance. Lacking even an existing atom of color, shape, and so forth, it is emptiness. Therefore, it is definitely not found by searching for it, seen by looking at it, and so forth. Since it has been primordially abiding as emptiness, it is not the case that it has turned into emptiness in the present. Since it transcends being an object of conceptual mind, its essence is nonconceptual and it is called spontaneously present emptiness. For this reason, all phenomena of samsara and nirvana, as well as the world and beings included in the three world spheres, abide in the state of emptiness.

If there were no emptiness, the diversity of phenomena could not possibly arise as the space of one thing would be blocked by another thing, so to speak. It is because there is emptiness that myriad things can arise. For instance, the basic nature is pure like space, but from its natural expression, ceaselessly interdependent phenomena arise and appear clearly—outer graspable things of the clinging mind such as forms and sounds, the inner subtle and coarse thoughts, the intense and feeble five poisons, happiness and sorrow, good and bad, and so forth. In other words, appearances are but the natural radiance arising in myriad ways, and in fact, they are not beyond the essence and basic nature of absolute reality, so they are nondual with emptiness. Without needing in the least to correct, eliminate, or establish, if you let them be in their own natural condition, they abide spontaneously present as luminosity or dharmakaya mahamudra from the primordial beginning. The lord of beings Zhang Rinpoche said:

> What is meant by phenomena being nothing other than mind is simply a conventional way to point to all phenomena as being mind. Like water bubbles springing from water, through the condition of mind, the diversity of phenomena such as red and white manifests and appears according to conditions. Like clouds that appear, remain, and vanish in the sky, our numerous memories and thoughts are rootless. All experiences of the karma of happiness, sorrow, or indifference are like the happiness and suffering experienced in a dream; they have no basis. All phenomena of samsara and nirvana are like all great rivers, such as the Ganges and the Pakshula, which become of one taste with the ocean; just as they become indivisible, so too samsara and nirvana are of one taste.

In brief, one's mind is originally buddha, unoriginated, emptiness, nonconceptual, primordial wisdom, the great dharmakaya, and the difference resides in whether or not the mind of a person recognizes this in thoughts and whatever arises. It is not improved by meditating and not worsened by not meditating; it never changes. The defilements consist of not understanding what it actually is and not recognizing it. To understand what it is and recognize it is to be free of defilement. It follows that defilement is not something to be eliminated, and wisdom is not something to be established. Buddhahood emanates from buddhahood, nonorigination emanates from nonorigination, emptiness emanates from emptiness, nonconceptual mind emanates from nonconceptual mind, dharmakaya emanates from dharmakaya. Therefore, perceiver and perceived are basic nature and radiance, everything to be eliminated and the antidotes that do so are nondual and not separate; they do not exist individually. You need to understand the secret key point of what it means to know that everything merges into one, because if this is not understood in a practice that hasn't discerned that there is a bias toward the natural state of the ground, delusion will arise. During the path, to practice according to this understanding and become accustomed to it is path mahamudra. Its meaning has certainly been explained in various quotations. Here follows a brief explanation. Lord Gotsangpa said:

> Look directly at your own mind.
> Nothing is seen by looking; it is not a thing.
> Rest loosely in that state of nonbeing.
> Rest without fixating, lucid, and at ease.

With the mind looking nakedly at the mind, nothing whatsoever is seen in the nature of mind; it is experienced as insubstantial, and cognizance rests loose and of its own accord. That state should not become oblivious; awareness must be clear. Without a specific reference point, it is at ease and free from the grasping of blocking or acquiring. To approach resting in this way is extremely good. Furthermore, there is no deliberate dispersion, no deliberate concentration, no resting in oblivion, no yielding to thoughts as such, no following after sensations, no distortion with discursive analysis, neither annihilation nor reification of external objects, no regarding a lack of an inner self as nothingness, no holding as a fault the rootless thought movement, no tending toward fixating on phenomena or fixating on emptiness, no chasing after the past, no anticipating the future, no fixating on the present as a thing. Instead cognizance is left uninterruptedly unaltered, effortlessly loose, aimlessly uncontrolled, free of clinging, silent in its nonorigination, transparently unimpeded, and clearly lucid. All external things become simplified as one, and internally everything boils down to only mind. This is how to rest in unfettered composure. Saraha said:

> This mind tightened by busy thoughts
> Once let loose will no doubt be released.

And:

> Let unmodified cognizance rest in its freshness.
> The sublime path will not be attained through a fabricated mind.

What he means is that you rest taking as the main practice being barely undistracted from your own mind. Other than that, you must be free of ambition and not think of anything at all. Moreover, the essence of your mind is free from conceptual elaborations and primordially familiarized, so don't deliberately meditate conceptually. It naturally flows, so don't deliberately modify it. Arising thoughts are its natural expression, so don't deliberately reject or direct them, but rather you should rest composed in the continuity of simply recognizing their original face.

Furthermore, there is no specific way to rest composed in nondistraction. The practice is sustained having clearly determined the experience and realization in one's own stream of consciousness. Superior practitioners in whom realization has dawned and who have mastered meditation will relax at this point in the expanse of thoroughly knowing the basic nature. Actually, in "rest composed in the essence," "rest" is just a word. Through the recognition of the realized essence, in one's awareness, the innate, the flow of the basic nature, there is no one who rests nor anything resting, no meditator nor meditation object. There is just an apparent resting without anything that is being placed, a mere seeming meditation while there is no meditator. Furthermore, without depending on a dualistic meditation that splits into two deliberately being mindful or not, meditating or not, it is sufficient to naturally keep present the spirit of nonmeditation of its own accord without interruptions. The flow of one's awareness—the basic nature of mind knowing its own essence—and the mind of the guru are inseparable, and this is what is meant by the nonduality of the guru and one's mind, or the guru yoga of devotion; it is also called the ultimate guru yoga. This is the style of practice of a realized individual with superior faculties.

If such a realization hasn't dawned in your experience, deliberately recall its features—high or low, stable or unstable—and sustain that; otherwise it would entail a somewhat retentive mindfulness. Yet if this mindfulness is quite stable and is capable of sustaining the recognition of anything that arises or appears, then deliberately keep in mind that flow. Persevere in sustaining the natural flow of recognizing thoughts—whether it is a thought that judges resting calmly in the basic nature of your mind as good or not doing so as bad—as well as recognizing through mindfulness any outer phenomena that arise.

Otherwise, for those who have not attained stability in retentive mindfulness, forget a lot, are very distracted, and need to apply great effort to be mindful, at this point also they should rest in the expanse of unfabricated awareness in order to prevent struggling with distraction and falling into gloom. Undistracted mindful knowing should be clearly focused. While being firmly determined to be mindful, if awareness stays still, rest on that stillness; if it moves, rest on that movement; and if you perceive external objects, rest on them. Thus, rest right on these by deliberately having the intention to catch awareness.

Thus apart from sustaining the identity of any stillness or movement that may arise, don't involve yourself with dualistic blocking or acquiring, such as to like deliberate stillness, dislike movement, acquire the former, or block the latter. Sustain the nature in its natural flow, of its own accord. If it happens that every now and then you wander, don't continue being distracted; recognize that instance of distraction and again, through determination, persevere in constantly fostering the practice.

Actual meditation is all about emphasizing undistracted mindfulness. If, within the mind, you are not sustaining the recognition of the true nature through undistracted mindfulness, or despite having some knowledge of how to do so, you are unable to sustain it through effort, outwardly your body may seem to be in the right posture and eye gaze, but your mind is dominated by delusion. That is useless; it is what is meant by "sitting like a dummy" and is not meditative composure. Therefore, apply as much effort as possible to undistracted mindfulness while in a meditation, unlike the distracted meditation just described.

As to just the general way of meditating, Lord Gampopa said in relation to beginners:

> Regarding what is commonly known as the three skills, the first one is the skill at the beginning of the meditation. After adopting the right physical posture in line with the earlier explanations on shamatha, you arouse a fervent confidence

> and determination through seeing the qualities of samadhi, and having eliminated all other mental discomforts, you enter the practice. Then follows the skill in stabilizing the practice. You correct the faults of dullness and agitation affecting cognizance, and free yourself from the moisture of intense experiences. Having done that, you sustain the naked mind essence. Finally, you are skilled in discontinuing. Having sustained clarity again and again for short periods at a time, break the meditation in a friendly spirit, without being irritated.

Lord Yangonpa said:

> First, free from effort, relax body and mind.

Letting the body be natural without tensing it up, the mind devoid of a specific object of ambition, without exertion, carefree, and lucid, let go into the basic nature of the mind. He also said:

> Then, without hesitation rest in freshness of its own accord.

Abandoning doubts such as "it is" and "it isn't," you don't further modify the freshness of reality, the primordial natural state, however it is. And he concluded:

> Know all occurrences of sensations to be unoriginated.

As soon as mindfulness recognizes all sensations arising from situations and phenomena, liberate them in the state of the innate, where they lack any originated, abiding, or ceasing essence.

Also Lord Gampopa said:

> Open and lofty like the sky.

Let phenomena be like that: carefree and lucid.

> Extended like the earth.

Extensively embraced by mindful knowing.

> Massively steady like a mountain.

Rest the mind without moving.

> Brilliant like a butter lamp.

Arouse the brightness of the essence of awareness.

> Free of stains like a crystal.

Not covered by meditative experiences, let cognizance rest as vividly lucid. Also, Gyalwa Yangonpa said:

> Fervently supplicate the lord guru. To supplicate one-pointedly to the authentic guru is what is meant by "devotion is the head of meditation."

By this, he means to supplicate not as lip service, but instead from the center of your heart and the marrow of your bones, with the hairs of your body standing on end and tears rolling down your face, and with such strength that it is able to block all six sense perceptions. This will give rise to meditation that hasn't yet dawned, enhance the meditation you have already developed, and finally bring about the merging of mother and child absolute reality. Precisely this is the principal task performed by the tradition of this lineage. Just as no sewing can be done with a two-pointed needle, the purpose of the Dharma will be hard to fulfill through an ambivalent mind.

As has been taught, "completely discard the mundane mind!" Therefore, totally clear away the involvements and dualistic thoughts of this life like cleaning the dust off a conch shell. Renunciation is called the feet of meditation. In that state, let your mind look at itself. While your mind looks at itself—like one's eye looking at itself—all past thoughts have already ceased, future thoughts haven't yet arisen, and present mind is a vividly brilliant awareness whose essence has no identifying characteristic whatsoever. Rest there continuously as long as you can; this is what is meant by "look directly at your mind!" To look at this unfabricated natural mind is to recognize mind essence, mahamudra. In that state, no matter what kind of thought—bad, good, neutral—arises, don't follow it like an ordinary person; don't reject it through a battery of antidotes like *shravakas* and *pratyeka buddhas*; don't establish emptiness through analyzing whether it is one or many as in the sutra path; and don't transform it through mantra like in the outer tantras. Since its natural mode is mahamudra, recognize precisely whatever arises and rest loosely. This is what is meant by "recognize the identity of everything that arises."

Without giving any thought free rein but instead by recognizing it, the world and beings are the enhancement of mahamudra. Therefore, by one-pointedly sustaining nondistraction, in time you will not need to chase mindfulness or hold it. Without being distracted, you proceed in the continuity of practice, and even if you were distracted, it would make no difference. Based on defining characteristics, noncharacteristics are born, and based on reference points, the nonreference is born. This is the basic nature. When you are accustomed to these, there is no difference between distraction and nondistraction, mindful and unmindful, meditation and postmeditation, and there is no specific session of practice. Any perception, any thought, and any action during daily activities, they all point out the dharmakaya. The original face of the three kayas is revealed. Let us take water as an example: Even when swirling it still is water; when calm it still is water; agitated by waves it still is water; flowing gently it still is water; cold, warm, or frozen it still is water. It never transcends being water. Similarly, for the mahamudra yogin who lets the meditation be of its own accord—while being mindful it is meditation, and while thinking it is also meditation. At that time, the yogin does not consider even a hair tip of any phenomenon of the world and beings, or samsara and nirvana, as something to cast away or reject. Everything has become completely unified in the vast expanse of primordial wisdom, the sun of absolute reality dawns, great bliss spreads out extensively, and the fruit of spontaneous presence ripens.

Thus has been taught, including a description of the fruition. Accordingly, the thicket of temporary delusion on the naturally pure ground mahamudra—the inner space of awareness—is burnt away by familiarization with path mahamudra through the fire of wisdom. Therefore, pure from even the subtlest dualistic perception, like an immaculate sky, the ground is rendered evident as it is, and all becomes exclusively primordial wisdom endowed with the twofold purity.[18] This is the fruition mahamudra, the attainment of the level of buddhahood.

## Introduction to One's Mind through the Four Aspects of View, Meditation, Conduct, and Fruition

As said by the masters of the past, what is needed is a view that masters situations, a meditation that overcomes distraction, and a conduct that controls wandering about. If these three were to be explained extensively, then generally it would indeed require a lot of discussion, but here we will approach it in a concise way. People like us seek out the causes and conditions for the Dharma and collect them. Then we exert ourselves in the methods that make the Dharma become the path, particularly the path of the profound true meaning in which we properly carry out the specific meditation of undistracted mindfulness. Hence, the essence of the view is "initially the view that masters situations." Theoretical views, such as views of words and the thinking process, and the presumptuousness derived from them, are hollow so don't incur these, and at all times sustain mind essence. With great devotion incessantly supplicate a qualified guru about whom you are convinced. Then, without adulterating the absolute view of the basic nature with anything conceptual or intellectual, you must see the essence of your naturally luminous awareness.

Furthermore, the nature, essence, or characteristic of the mind is like the sky, an unidentifiable lucid emptiness free from all conceptual elaborations, without the duality of observer and observed, and beyond words, thoughts, and description. This itself is the root of all of samsara and nirvana, the source of all phenomena, the foundation of all philosophical tenets, the subject matter of all main texts, and the sap of all pith instructions. At first it is the topmost view, then it is what is settled as the basis of the meditation and maintained during conduct, and lastly it is the final destination of the fruition. Ultimately, what is meant by "realizing the view" is—without falling into extremes or bias—to recognize the mode of being of our naked ordinary mind as it is, to realize exactly the natural state of awareness, and to cognize the way of delusion as it is: the natural radiance of awareness. This is also called "seeing mind essence" and "realizing the nature of awareness."

However, except for those karmically destined ones, it is certainly very difficult for such a genuine view, which has suddenly eliminated misconceptions about all phenomena, to be born from the outset in the mind of most individuals. Nonetheless, at the beginning we learn how to engage in the realization of the view. Then, regardless of whether one's realization of the identity of the view has been high, medium, or low, this must be followed by becoming familiarized with it. To integrate this with all dualistic phenomena of one's activity and sustain it in all situations—good, bad, neutral—as well as during meditative composure, postmeditation, and ensuing cognizance (whether these are with or without characteristics) will finally bring about liberation into nonduality. We need to become free of the stains of acceptance, rejection, and evaluation.

Second, they taught the "meditation that overcomes distraction." What is called meditation is to become familiarized with the view explained earlier: the realization of the nondual essence of the mind, unoriginated and unceasing. No matter what perception of external objects arises, sustain awareness on it. This immaculate naked awareness—uncontaminated by rationalizations and fixations, totally open and free in the nonduality of meditator and object of meditation, of undesirable and antidote—is complete within undistracted effortless mindfulness. It is consummate perfection in which outer and inner are inseparable and there is nothing to keep or let go. What is needed is that it becomes a continuous cycle of luminosity beyond bright and dim.

Third, they taught the "conduct that controls wandering about." While in the meditation that is familiar with the flow of the realized view mentioned earlier, one develops its potential and must merge it with the variety of situations one finds oneself in. In other words, in the continuity of the sky-like realized view of the natural state, one carries out one's spontaneous activities unhindered, without the stain of hypocrisy or attachment in the mind. Whether the situations that take place are positive, negative, or neutral, transparent wisdom must flow without the view being obstructed or the meditation discontinued. There are many classifications in this regard. Those of the instantaneous type who possess the highest faculties will have the view, meditation, conduct, and fruition from the beginning, these four being perfected at the same time as they arise. The middling type will have "perfected view and meditation." Having seen the view, it remains present without distraction, but they do not integrate it with other situations, so they haven't perfected the conduct. For the lower type, in our tradition, at first to see mind essence is the view; it is to perceive observer and observed in the mind as nondual. However, it is hard for it to flow continuously like a major river, so to become familiar with that is the meditation. Further, even when one is familiarized with it and neither forgets nor is distracted, it is difficult to integrate it with the variety of apparent objects and situations. In this case, what is meant by conduct is to sustain everything in the state of undistracted meditation. This is the way it should be understood.

Culmination is what I think is meant by fruition. I have roughly explained view, meditation, and conduct in this way. Approaching this subject in the way of definitions, the masters of the past have referred to view, meditation, conduct, and fruition, including samaya, on numerous occasions. However, here it will be more useful to approach it according to what is needed. Let us discuss Lord Milarepa's teaching on view, meditation, conduct, and fruition, including samaya.

First, regarding certainty about the view he said:

> While in nonorigination, manifestations flow ceaselessly;
> The characteristics of birth and cessation vanish within themselves.
> How good it feels to be certain about the view!

This means that by seeing mind essence, we realize the basic nature of the mind as being unoriginated. While in that state, the natural radiance flows ceaselessly as the myriad things but, no matter how they occur, they are realized as not transcending the basic nature. These two, basic nature and radiance, do not become separated; they do not exist as distinct entities. Since we realize that they are a unity, Milarepa refers to the characteristics of birth and cessation. In other words, at the beginning, when not realizing that in the basic nature its radiance is ceaseless, we need forceful mindfulness. Regarding thoughts, there are characteristics of birth and cessation. Upon the arising or birth of a thought, first it is identified by mindfulness, then it stays, and finally it ceases. This has the stains of conceptual attention and fixation on defining characteristics.

Nevertheless, here we are realizing the nondual essence or nature, so there are no stains of conceptual attention and fixation on characteristics regarding the origination, abiding, and cessation of any arising thought, as these vanish into themselves. From the unoriginated basic nature, its radiance arises without obstructions. Since one's awareness recognizes its own essence, these fixations are certainly self-liberated. Likewise, the view of vajra mind—one's essence—is not to be searched for elsewhere. You are certain that it is your mind itself. Milarepa then says how good it feels to have this certainty.

Second, regarding meditation he said:

> While in the state of nonmeditation, the mind flows undistractedly.
> The characteristics of concentration vanish within themselves.
> How good it feels to be certain about the meditation!

What he means is that the essence of the view of the nonduality of undesirable and antidote, observer and observed, basic nature and radiance is one's naturally luminous awareness. So, apart from awareness, there is indeed no need whatsoever to deliberately meditate on anything through the conceptual division of meditator and object of meditation. Nevertheless, it is very important for us not to be distracted. While one is flowing undistractedly in the expanse of thoroughly knowing the nature and in continuous undistracted nonmeditation, the characteristics of thoughts being held by a deliberate retaining mindfulness as something other than that natural state definitely vanish within themselves. Thus, the flow of undistracted nonmeditation is itself the essence of meditation and, as before, he says that being certain about the meditation feels good.

Third, regarding conduct he said:

> While in the spontaneous state, one flows ceaselessly.
> The characteristics of hypocrisy vanish within themselves.
> How good it feels to be certain about the conduct!

Thus, while we are in the state of the view of nonduality and undistracted meditation, various activities, such as moving and sitting, are also carried out in the state of spontaneous alertness. In this conduct there is no contamination by the stains of the characteristics of intentionally pretending to be perfect, as these vanish within themselves. Spontaneous alertness of its own accord, that itself is the nature of conduct, so he mentions this certainty.

Fourth, regarding samaya he said:

> While in the state of not being on guard, nondistraction flows.
> The characteristics of vows to be observed vanish within
> themselves.
> How good it feels to be certain about the samaya!

Being certain about the view, meditation, and conduct, one is in a state in which, in turn, the samaya is free of the duality of guarding and guarded. Since there is no distraction from the nature of mind even for a moment, there is no samaya to be observed, yet it is not violated even for an instant. This being the case, there is no conventional keeping of vows involving concepts as these characteristics vanish within themselves. This ultimate samaya and observance of vows, free of characteristics, is the very nature of samaya. The certainty that it is so is what Milarepa refers to.

Fifth, regarding the fruition he said:

> While in the state of nonattainment, nothing to be accomplished flows.
> The characteristics of hope and fear vanish within themselves.
> How good it feels to be certain about the fruition!

One realizes the essence of the view of one's mind, attains meditative stability, develops the potential of the conduct, and is free from the stain of samaya. Therefore, apart from this, there is no other buddhahood to attain. As said in the *Sutra of the Wisdom at the Moment of Death*:

> If you realize the mind, that is buddha. Cultivate the clear understanding that buddhahood is not to be searched for elsewhere.[19]

As taught here by the Tathagata, you should indeed gain certainty within the state in which the attitude of accomplishment does not exist even for a moment. Hence, these conceptual characteristics—hopes for something good called nirvana and fears of something bad called samsara—vanish within themselves. Such is the fruition of nothing to be eliminated, nothing to be obtained. To have this certainty about the fruition is what Milarepa says is delightful.

At that point, since the equality of samsara and nirvana has been realized, there is no hope or fear and nothing to be eliminated or obtained; one has finally reached fruition. Although it is quite rare for us to attain that much, in reality one's self-luminous mind has no cause itself for wandering below in samsara. Since it has no transition or change from this ground itself, even the name nirvana does not exist, so samsara and nirvana mean the same. I feel that we need to realize that kind of fruition.

Otherwise, if we are to further discuss the view, meditation, conduct, and fruition, let us quote the replies that Lord Lhatsewa gave to his circle of realized yogins upon their request regarding the final conclusion about view, meditation, and conduct:

> Glorious embodiment of all the buddhas, dharmakaya,
> You manifest in the faithful eyes of your disciples.
> Your name is exceedingly famous, glorious Drukpa.
> Kind father, I supplicate to you.

With this first stanza he precedes the explanation with a supplication to his kind guru. The guru embodies the essence of all the buddhas. The glorious guru is the dharmakaya or the ancestor of all the buddhas. For Lhatsewa this was Lord Pema Karpo, so he continues with his praise:

> The basis of manifestation of all the conquerors who came in the past,
> The source of all the buddhas to appear in the future,
> Inseparable from all present protectors,
> At the feet of the Dharma king, I supplicate.

Being the great ancestor of all the conquerors, the guru is the supreme basis, abiding as the essence of the dharmakaya. From that state he reveals himself as the rupakaya, manifesting as such generally before all beings—our mothers in numbers as limitless as space—and in particular in the perception of all those disciples who have faith and virtuous karmic destiny and who are to be trained.

Lord Lhatsewa praises his guru, Pema Karpo, who has various other highly renowned names, saying that his name is exceedingly famous. Regarding "glorious Drukpa," this is to identify him with the common name [given to the Drukchen].[20] Then, calling his guru "Father," he implies that since he delivers him and other beings from the ocean of samsara, sets them onto the path of nirvana, and what is truly important, introduces them to the naked nature of mind, the inseparability of samsara and nirvana, he is much kinder than others. Pondering his guru's kindness, he made this supplication.

Now, regarding the certainty about the very essence of view, meditation, and conduct, starting with the view, he said:

> Because there is no falling into the extreme of insubstantiality,
> Beyond extremes there isn't even the term "view."
> Intellectual views have withdrawn.
> Now I have reached the final conclusion about the view.

This means that based on receiving the authentic guru's blessing, the nature of the mind is definitely realized as emptiness, insubstantial. "Falling into the extremes" indicates that one does not hold the mind as real, thereby falling into the extreme of materialism. The mind is empty, yet this emptiness does not entail falling into the nihilistic extreme of being nothing. The radiance of emptiness manifests as the myriad things, empty yet appearing. In other words, the emptiness of mind essence and its variegated natural radiance are inseparable and are realized as a unity. Since the basic nature and radiance have merged, there is no alternative whatsoever: the realization is of emptiness itself. If you are considering whether it is or isn't emptiness, that would be a biased view, instead of the genuine view which is free of extremes. Here the view is free of extremes, for there is no bias regarding whether it is or isn't emptiness. Since freedom from extremes is like space, one cannot measure it by saying "this," and one is incapable of describing it verbally. Based on this meaning, the natural radiance of the view is called "view" only at the mere conventional level; ultimately there is not even the label "view," for there is neither viewer nor viewed. Thus, by realizing the genuine ultimate view, one does not hope for the verbal or theoretical views, or intellectual "ultimate" views, and there are no doubts about absolute reality, so whatever is mind-made and impure is banished. Not only has Lord Lhatsewa simply realized such a view but also at that time, based on this human existence, he swiftly came to the final conclusion about the view free of extremes.

Second, regarding meditation he said:

> In primordial meditation, conceptual fabrications do not exist,
> So perfect mindfulness is seduced as a friend.
> All that arises is cognized as mind essence itself.
> I have now reached the final conclusion about meditation.

Since one has realized the emptiness of the mind, the nonconceptual view, this is how to practice within it through meditation. Since the meditation is primordial, he says not to meditate conceptually, so the view should be sustained through nonmeditation. Apart from that, what is meant by "perfect mindfulness" is a meditation that is not a product of one's conceptual modifications. Although the view has been realized, stains haven't been purified, and the potential hasn't developed. Once the subtle stains of feeling pleasure in the empty aspect and attachment to that experience, as well as the lack of development of the potential based on phenomena, have all been purified, these are "seduced" (so to speak) as friends toward progress in perfect mindfulness. This implies that all attachments to the experience of emptiness are radically purified as well. In particular, the development of the potential on the basis of phenomena is also such that all that arises is "mind essence itself." One knows it to be simply the unceasing display of the mind and is convinced about it. Hence, he says that he has "reached the final conclusion about meditation."

When connecting this view and meditation to the yogas of mahamudra, the view—or seeing mind essence—is genuine simplicity itself. Primordial meditation on that, "unfabricated by the mind," is to sustain the essence of that view with undistracted nonmeditation. Then "perfect mindfulness" is what sustains the essence of the realization of simplicity; therefore, what is called perfect mindfulness has advanced to one taste. Furthermore, the essence of one taste being that "whatever arises is cognized as mind essence itself" is similar to what has been taught as mingling phenomena and mind. What is meant by "whatever arises" would commonly be taken to be any thought that arises; however, this is not what we mean here, so we must specify that it means whatever phenomena take place.

Third, regarding conduct he said:

> Naturally flowing activity turns into Dharma.
> Fixation on acceptance and rejection collapses by itself.
> Non-dharmic actions automatically cease.
> Today I have reached the final conclusion about conduct.

In the jargon of the stages of the four yogas, it has been taught that during simplicity, one has revulsion for this life. During one taste, one equalizes the eight worldly preoccupations. Furthermore, since one has reached the final conclusion about view and meditation, the eight worldly preoccupations have definitely come to an end. Therefore, activity flows naturally instead of the deliberate actions of the eight worldly preoccupations. Since there is no clinging to selfish interests, whatever one does is embraced by such means as bodhichitta and altruistic aspirations, in which case everything one does turns into Dharma, as said by Lord Lhatsewa.

Thus, since one's actions are carried as a practice, they have become Dharma. Clinging to acceptance or rejection resulting from a deliberate intention collapses by itself. Nonetheless, this does not apply to other acceptances or rejections belonging to cause and effect, because regarding cause and effect, one must be extremely meticulous about accepting and rejecting. Therefore, since internally the eight worldly preoccupations are purified and externally one is free from acceptance and rejection, non-dharmic actions automatically cease. This then is the nature of conduct for there is no selfishness, and whatever one does is embraced by skillful means. Thus, Lord Lhatsewa says that since he has reached the final conclusion about conduct, it spontaneously happens of its own accord.

Fourth, regarding fruition he said:

> Uncompounded mind is dharmakaya.
> I understand that its radiance based on other factors is the nirmanakaya.
> I realize that ultimately these two are indivisible; that is the sambhogakaya.
> Today I have arrived at the final conclusion about fruition.

In this way, when the potential of view, meditation, and conduct has been developed, one has arrived at the fruition. At that point, one's mind is "uncompounded." Objects, mind, awareness, and phenomena, all being inseparable (apart from being individually distinct and clear) they are not compounded, so mind is uncompounded. Precisely this is the ground dharmakaya, which he has realized as it is. Fruition is arrived at on the basis of the ground. From the radiance of the dharmakaya, based on other positive or negative factors, all kinds of happiness and suffering take place, which he has understood to be the nirmanakaya, the dance of the appearances of dharmakaya. Ground and radiance merely appear separate at present, for ultimately they are "indivisible sambhogakaya." Thus he said that he realized the essence of indivisibility. In other words, he attained the three kayas; so then he reached the final conclusion about the fruition by having correctly realized the ground.

Furthermore, previously the view was simplicity and meditation one taste. The multiplicity of inseparable mind and phenomena indeed arose as one taste, yet one taste did not really arise as multiplicity. Now, in our case the term "uncompounded" implies one taste as multiplicity. Before, phenomena were the same as mind, in which case the fixation on phenomena collapsed. Thereafter, fresh phenomena and natural lucidity were inseparable. That is to say, the dependent origination stemming from knowing that all phenomena of samsara and nirvana arise from one's mind has been accomplished. Lord Lhatsewa says this uncompounded state is known as dharmakaya; therefore, one taste as multiplicity also upgrades to nonmeditation. Of course, dharmakaya is present in the yogas of simplicity, one taste, and so on, but that is not the dharmakaya free of all kinds of obscurations. It is during nonmeditation that the genuine dharmakaya occurs, notwithstanding that subtle stains are still to be purified in accordance with the great, middling, and lesser levels. This is the common colloquial way of referring to nonmeditation. Now, it is extremely important to have the realization through understanding, knowing, and experiencing the described view, meditation, conduct, and fruition.

## Introduction to One's Mind as Mahamudra

The term *mahamudra* has been defined in many ways, but according to the Great Brahmin, mahamudra is free from the three conditions, transcends the four joys, and is especially luminous. It does not depend on the conditions of bliss, clarity, or nonthought. These conditions have attachment, fixation, and mental constructs, so they are not free from these three factors. Regarding the four joys, these are joy, supreme joy, special joy, and coemergent joy. Here there is an introduction by the guru and an understanding by the disciple, which constitute example wisdom that involves something shown and someone showing it.

In mahamudra there is nothing to be shown by the guru and nothing to be understood by the disciple; there is no mixing with meditative moods or experiences; there is no contamination by concept or reification; there is no division into view, meditation, and conduct. Without arbitrarily dividing it into ground, path, and fruition, in all phenomena throughout samsara and nirvana, or the world and beings, there is nothing to remove or add, fetter or release, and no alteration whatsoever to be made by a remedy. What is meant by mahamudra is liberation by recognizing the natural condition. Similarly, in the *Utterly Nondwelling Mahamudra Tantra* it is said:

> This is mahamudra.
> It is not contaminated by stains.
> In this, there is nothing to block or achieve.
> It is not found through paths and remedies.
> This is the body of all the buddhas.

> This is the basis of all sublime qualities.
> This is spontaneously present.

Regarding mahamudra being especially luminous, in phenomena that are without reference points and free from conceptual elaborations, mahamudra is fresh phenomena and elaborations are self-liberated. Therefore, luminosity is special. Thus, in the forms of deities or demons, beautiful or ugly, blissful or miserable, manifest or empty arising within luminosity, there is no object whatsoever that is generated or appears, be it lucid, conceptualized with or without attributes, or so forth. By thinking that there is a form that is definitely divine, demonic, beautiful, ugly, blissful, miserable, manifest, or empty, one would be blocking or acquiring luminosity by conceptualizing it or not, with attributes. Without engaging in this acceptance or rejection, it is sufficient to let it rest in its own condition. As said in the *Ornament of Clear Realization*:

> In this, there is nothing to remove
> And not the slightest thing to add.
> Perfectly look at what is sublime.
> If you see perfectly, you will be completely liberated.

As to this, any adulteration of removing or adding is a perception, a temporary experience, a defining characteristic, or a reference point. In fact, just as a bird flying in any direction in the sky never goes beyond the sky, in one's mahamudra mind whatever arises is mahamudra: quiescence is mahamudra; movement and dispersion is mahamudra; manifestation is mahamudra; and every experience is mahamudra. In short, no matter how it abides, or however it occurs, nothing happens beyond the seal of mahamudra.

In the term *mahamudra* or *chag gya chenpo*, *mudra* (*chag gya*) means that the whole world and beings, samsara and nirvana, are in their natural state. From there, totally fresh and unfaded, they are always innate wisdom in the past, present, future, and beyond time. *Maha* (*chenpo*) means that nothing is apart from or higher than that. *Mudra* can be partially applied to a moment of cognizance as follows. When a thought suddenly arises and is neither blocked nor acquired, since that thought is actually innate wisdom—regardless of whether it is realized as such or not—the fact that it is not beyond innate wisdom is mudra. *Maha* means that what is called primordial wisdom or buddha's enlightened mind is not to be sought elsewhere. In the *Mahamudra Bindu* we find:

> *Chag* is the wisdom of emptiness.
> *Gya* is freedom from samsaric phenomena.
> *Chenpo* is indivisibility.

Whether manifested, realized, or deluded, there is nowhere beyond mahamudra, nowhere to settle beyond mahamudra, nowhere to wander off from the mandala of mahamudra, and no way for innate awareness to be either forgotten or deluded. Nevertheless, innate awareness appears as if obscured. This is similar to the sun itself being free from obscurations while its luminosity is dimmed by clouds. In truth, it manifests in everyone from buddha to sentient beings. At the lower extreme, even when experiencing being burned in the fire of Incessant Hell, that raw perception of hell is still abiding upright in the essence of the three kayas. There is nowhere for that itself to be deluded, it doesn't originate as something substantial, it is not blocked as something insubstantial, and it does not appear to be something separate from these two. Actually, on the basis of realization, the eight extremes are self-liberated. Since extremes are not annulled by one another, realization is originally free from extremes, and there is nowhere to deviate to. When not recognized in this way, distraction, delusion, strayings, and so forth happen in the perspective of the mind, which makes conceptual designations. In brief, what is meant by mahamudra realization is this raw natural mode of ordinary cognizance, which hasn't been created by anyone, recognizing itself. As clearly expressed by Lord Rangjung Dorje, including references to meditation:

> The enlightened mind of all buddhas of the three times, the striving of all sublime beings, the renowned and illustrious term *dharmakaya mahamudra*, these are names for one's

own mind. If you don't recognize your own mind, the cognizance that thinks all kinds of thoughts is called the ego mind. All phenomena of samsara and nirvana also are not beyond this. The quintessence of the collections of scriptures (*pitaka*), sutras, and tantras are also this. When you put this into practice, since there is nothing to meditate upon, let awareness rest wide awake in its original condition. There is no need to doubt, wondering whether it is mahamudra or not. Don't expect it to be correct or fear it being faulty. Don't follow many kinds of thoughts. Rest right on this wide-awake awareness itself. Loosen up and rest relaxed. Don't have anything at all to meditate upon. By meditating repeatedly in this way, at some point it will happen that on recognizing a thought, it is automatically realized to be groundless and rootless, whereby all attachments vanish into themselves, so that, in an instant, all habitual patterns without exception are uprooted. Precisely that is what is called "awakening to buddhahood."

## Introduction to One's Mind as Perfect Buddha

Once the elaborations of the three times have been severed, while in the state in which there are no longer any preconceived beliefs or objectives, resting loosely in undistracted nonmeditation, you may wonder what the essence is like. There is no specific essence to arise from anywhere else. This present natural mode of the naked, resplendent cognizance of nowness, the wide-awake lucidity, the emptiness of mentally created ignorance, is given many names, such as nature of mind, mandala of mind essence, essence of the innate ground, natural luminosity, buddha nature, or dharmakaya as it is. Although many synonyms are used, in actual fact it is this one thing: one's own mind. The incomparable Buddha Shri elucidated this point as follows:

To pursue the past is the root of regret and attachment, so let it go. Since thinking about the future is the ground for hopes

> and fears, let it go. This experience of the present is the continuous state of attachment and aversion, so let it go. Awareness that looks inward is buddha's enlightened mind, so practice it. In other words, the naked, resplendent, and wide-awake essence of your mind is the enlightened mind of the buddhas, the buddha nature, and the vivid primordial wisdom of the dharmakaya present in yourself. This has many names. When lacking realization it is called self, I, all-ground (*alaya*), the mind that thinks all kinds of thoughts, cognition that knows all kinds of things, intellect that ponders in all sorts of ways, and memory that has all kinds of recollections. If it is recognized, it is also called buddha, as said:
>
> After purifying all ego-fixations,
> The all-pervading wisdom of selflessness blooms.
> This is what is called buddha.
> Once all the darkness of ignorance has been cleared away,
> The wisdom of awareness blooms.
> This is what is called buddha.
> After removing all adventitious fixations,
> The wisdom of nongrasping blooms.
> This is what is called buddha.
>
> Furthermore, there is no end to the number of names given to mahamudra, such as: sugatagarbha, immaculate luminosity, ordinary mind, self-existing wisdom, spontaneous presence, five kayas, primordial purity, vast expanse, indivisibility, and coemergence. However, in short, mahamudra is the present mind, this essence of awareness.

You may think that these are of the same essence as the habitual patterns of delusion and thoughts, but this is not so. Perceptions are adulterated by mistaken cognizance, so because of the habits resulting from being unaware of one's own original condition, defiling stains of temporary delusion and conceptual imputations are accumulated. This being so, these are capable of being separated through an antidote, like the tarnish on gold or the rock encasing a jewel. Due to these stains the obscuration of not knowing adulterates the nature, radiance, and expression of emptiness, yet in reality these three cannot be reached or touched, like clouds forming in the sky. The *Sublime Continuum* says:

> Distorted thinking
> Resides in the purity of mind.

And Naropa said:

> However, through adventitious thoughts and stains
> The mind is afflicted;
> It is like water, gold, or the sky,
> Which may presently be pure or impure.

Lord Rangjung Dorje said:

> We already have purity itself,
> But due to the conceptualization of ignorance
> It is not realized, so this is samsara.
> If these are removed, that is nirvana.

Thus it is because the temporary stains are capable of being purified that he speaks of removing them, rather than saying that the radiance stops. He also said:

> The mind consciousness
> That possesses defilements is alaya.
> Undefiled, that is called the essence of buddha.
> From pure thoughts the faculty of sublime knowledge is born.
> It vanquishes impure discursive thoughts.
> Holding on to it is taught to be the truth of the path.

And also:

When reaching final fruition,
Thought formations are momentarily born and cease.
Their pure aspect is similar to the impure formations.
If this were not the case,
The activity of rupakaya would be interrupted.
Nonetheless, they are referred to as thought formations.

Also:

Well then, you might think that it was not taught
That the moving conceptual mind is unchanging.
However, it has three types of permanence.
While the three types of impermanence are stains,
The three types of permanence are wisdom.

And:

The mind that abides in purity from the three obscurations
Is equality and also peace.
It possesses great love and compassion.
The perfect buddhas have acknowledged so.

Gyalwang Chodrak Gyatso said:

> By purifying the stains on the unoriginated basic nature of mind, the ground, one realizes one's benefit, the dharmakaya. By purifying the stains on what appears as thoughts, the benefit of others manifests as the rupakaya. Therefore, it is said that there is no conflict if thoughts are referred to as being the rupakaya.

Nevertheless, all these are ways of explanation taken from the texts on awareness and vajrayana, and one may wonder how it is explained in the middle way (*madhyamaka*). Nagarjuna referred to this in many ways, such as:

All stains arising from mind
Are removed by mind essence.
Homage to one's mind
Which is what dispels the ignorance of the mind.

Also:

No phenomenon
Is not originated dependently.
Therefore, no phenomenon
Is not emptiness.

Therefore, all temporary stains have no existence, either in the essence of the mind, apart from the mind, or in both, so in reality they have no existence. Yet, while not existing they manifest as what are known as temporary stains or deluded perceptions. On thorough examination they are not beyond the mind, so it is said that the root of samsara and nirvana should be acknowledged as the mind. Whatever phenomena arise in conjunction with their emptiness, which establishes that they have no existence, in an instant of the wisdom of one's awareness these two are not separate, so they are equal. That is also buddha's enlightened mind. The masters of the past have said that once one has awakened to buddhahood, at first the fresh phenomena and cognizance that occur while a sentient being do not emerge as concrete things, do not cease as nonexistent things, and do not remain as a variety of different things. The cognizance that occurs by itself within its original condition has been primordially free of the eight extremes. This is the way it is.

Lord Tilopa said:

All phenomena, however they appear,
Are nondual with inner space and wisdom.
Within the numerous samsaric thoughts
Arise the kayas and wisdoms of the buddhas.
Their nature is unoriginated, the mother expanse,

And the unimpeded lucidity is the father sky;
Their nonduality is great bliss.
These should be present in the lucidity of the yogins.
All the purifying efforts of awareness
Include method and wisdom in union.

At that point, since all misconceptions about both samsara and nirvana have been resolved in the mind, this is called "misconceptions resolved from within." In the absence of realization, since samsara and nirvana are held to be separate, this is called "dualistic mind." If realized, since there is no bondage, this is called "stripping the deceiving dualistic fixation." Since it knows itself, it is called "self-knowing awareness-wisdom." Since there is no deliberate meditation, it is called "nonmeditation." Since it is liberated within itself without rejection, it is called "effortless." Since it is not adulterated by the cognition of good and bad, it is called "fresh." Since it is the primordial basic nature, it is called "unfabricated." Since it is not to be sought from anywhere else, it is called "self-occurring." Since it does not need to depend on anything else, it is called "awareness." Since samsara is pure in the ground, it is called "primordial purity." Since samsara is purified in its own nature, it is called "natural purity." Since ultimately it is pure in the inner space, it is called "transmuted." Since the essence does not change into anything else, it is called "natural." Since it arises as any form, it is called "manifestation." Since these two are inseparable, this is called "the inseparable two truths." And this very same meaning is what is referred to by "inseparable samsara and nirvana."[21] Similarly, Vajradhara said:

Samsara and nirvana arise in the single mind essence.
If you realize mind essence without rejecting samsara,
Nirvana is not sought; it is spontaneously present.
In the dharmadhatu, samsara and nirvana are indivisible.

Orgyen Rinpoche [Padmasambhava] said:

> If you realize mind essence, that is buddhahood.
> Buddha is not to be sought anywhere else apart from the mind.
> Buddhahood is not something accomplished; it is originally present.
> Without searching for it, the natural state is captured by resting.

The *Descent into Langka Sutra* says:

> This mind essence freed from concepts
> Reverses from mind consciousness.
> Because it knows all phenomena,
> I declare this mind is buddha.

In the *Kalachakra Root Tantra* it is said:

> The mind of beings is luminous
> And originally free from origination, abiding, and cessation.
> From beginningless time
> They are supreme buddhas from the start,
> Without a cause and not contaminated by any factor.

In the *Condensed Tantra* it is said:

> Sentient beings are buddhas. In this world no other great buddha will be found. The mind is the perfect Buddha himself. No buddha has been revealed elsewhere.

Manjushri said:

> The chief of all things is your mind.
> If you realize its essence,
> That itself is buddhahood and enlightenment.

There are a lot of citations such as these.

## Introduction to One's Mind through the Three Kayas

The authentic ground—mind essence abiding in simplicity free of conceptual elaborations—is ground dharmakaya. The lucid nature stably remaining unobstructed is ground sambhogakaya. The attributes arising in myriad forms is ground nirmanakaya. These three abiding inseparably is the ground svabhavikakaya. Thus, the ground is nondual, coemergent samsara and nirvana. In it, good and bad, being and nonbeing, are indivisible, so letting the mind flow in its unfabricated freshness is what is understood to be meditation. Its unceasing radiance arises as strong or weak thoughts, and without adopting or rejecting them, they are let loose of their own accord.

By placing outer appearances in the care of the main practice, one never lapses into delusion, and then the realization of mind's simplicity is path dharmakaya. To experience the ceaselessness of the lucid nature is path sambhogakaya. The unpredictable cognizance arising in myriad ways and abiding rootless and without ground is the thought movement that turns into manifest emptiness, and this is path nirmanakaya. The realization that mind's essence and its nature are indivisible is path svabhavikakaya.

Otherwise, while the essence of one's mind is arising as nonconceptual lucid emptiness, its identity has no existence whatsoever as a form, shape, color, substance, or distinguishing characteristics. That it rests immaculately as outer emptiness, inner emptiness, and essence emptiness is dharmakaya. That this emptiness is not a blank vacancy, but its nature is a vivid clear lucidity, is sambhogakaya. Emptiness and lucidity are inseparable—the nature of emptiness being lucidity and the essence of lucidity being emptiness—and precisely that awareness, in which emptiness and lucidity are indivisible, arising in all kinds of ways, is the compassionate nirmanakaya. Thus, the *Brilliant Expanse* states:

> The empty essence is dharmakaya.
> The vivid features are sambhogakaya.
> These unceasingly arising as everything is nirmanakaya.

Orgyen Rinpoche said:

> The empty essence is dharmakaya.
> Unceasing natural luminosity is sambhogakaya.
> Unobstructed expression of awareness is nirmanakaya.
> The innate three kayas are realized without accomplishing them.

Lord Rangjung Dorje said:

> The emptiness is enlightened body.
> The lucidity is enlightened voice.
> These two resting without duality in composure is enlightened mind.
> This is the introduction to the enlightened body, voice, and mind.

Not leaving the meaning of this approach as just theory, but instead through the strength of sustaining it and receiving the blessings of the venerable guru, the conceptual veils are removed and the naked ordinary mind itself properly recognizes its own essence. Thus, the fixation on the undesirable and antidote as being two entities is destroyed. Since there is a complete pervasiveness within the essence of nonconceptual mind, where interruptions created by gain and loss have ceased, everything is indivisibly occurring in the vast expanse of absolute reality. Like not finding an ordinary stone in a land of gold, one has fully awakened to the supreme three kayas. Therefore, while being in the simplicity of the dharmadhatu free of fixated concepts, all movements occur in the transparency of primordial wisdom. This is fruition dharmakaya. The form adorned with the major and minor marks of excellence that appears before the pure beings that are to be trained, and benefits them, is fruition sambhogakaya. Manifesting emanations according to the trainings that correspond to beings whose mind stream is impure, and benefiting them, is fruition nirmanakaya. That the essence of these three kayas is inseparable is the fruition svabhavikakaya. The two purposes—the shower of all that is wished for or needed, and all excellence—arise spontaneously.

## Introduction to One's Mind through the Five Wisdoms

In the originally pure, fundamental nature of one's mind, there are no veils of conceptual fabrications. Its essence of emptiness and natural luminosity abides as spontaneously present wisdom. Its radiance manifests from the essence in numerous ways, yet it does not go beyond it but remains as wisdom. From the unoriginated mind essence, in the deluded perception the conceptual mind seems to be born from causes and conditions. Yet although it appears to be born, in fact it neither is born nor exists in that way; this is the dharmadhatu wisdom of the all-ground.

Likewise, in the very obstruction of all phenomena, ultimately this indivisible, thought-free natural luminosity is unobstructed, and this is the mirrorlike wisdom of the all-ground consciousness (*alaya vijñana*). It dwells on any support, yet it does so only seemingly, for in reality it is a nondwelling indivisibility: inseparable from and unbiased toward the basic nature of things. This is the equality wisdom of the afflictive consciousness. Things are objectified as separate, yet ultimately they are a nonobjectifiable indivisibility where subject and object are a nondual discerning lucidity, this being the discerning wisdom of the mind consciousness. Any coming and going is none other than a seeming occurrence; in actuality these are an indivisibility devoid of coming and going. Mind essence that is not sought because it is spontaneously present is the all-accomplishing wisdom of the five sensory consciousnesses.[22]

One's mind resting in great bliss and wisdom, the essence of the ground, has never been separate from oneself for even a moment. Loosely letting it be of its own accord, free from reference points and fixation, immersed in all-embracing nondistraction, is what is understood as the body of meditation. This meditation is sustained through the key point of nongrasping and self-liberation, without contaminating the manifestations of unceasing natural expression of the six senses with acceptance or rejection. The lucidity present in its inseparability with postmeditation is mirrorlike wisdom. The empty essence of that lucidity is the dharmadhatu wisdom. Inseparable lucidity and emptiness is the wisdom of equality. Lucidity and emptiness— these two not being mixed but distinct from each other—is discerning wisdom. That the essence of precisely this empty lucidity has been spontaneously present from primordial time is the all-accomplishing wisdom. The *Realms and Transformations of Sound* says:

> The essence of awareness is the five wisdoms:
> Mirror, equality, discerning,
> All-accomplishing, and dharmadhatu wisdoms.

Lord Rangjung Dorje said:

> Emptiness is the dharmadhatu wisdom. Lucidity is mirrorlike wisdom. These two abiding equally is the wisdom of equality. These two not mixed but abiding distinct from each other is discerning wisdom. That all these are spontaneously present and not sought is the all-accomplishing wisdom. This has been the introduction to the five wisdoms.

If the meaning of such a type of meditation is not left in the realm of the intellect but is diligently put into practice, having rid the originally pure mind of the temporary obscurations of conceptualizing, one reaches the very ground itself. Actualizing the dharmakaya, the unfabricated, primordially pure basic nature, one realizes that the myriad natural manifestations of its radiance are self-liberated. Since all outer and inner phenomena have merged, one attains the glories of the great vast expanse of indivisibility, the equality of existence and peace, the wisdom of consummated great bliss. Having acquired the one Dharma that liberates all, self-liberation becomes spontaneous. At that time, the total absence of reference points is the dharmadhatu wisdom. The thought-free lucidity is the mirrorlike wisdom. Not dwelling in the extremes of samsara or nirvana is the wisdom of equality. The evident clear seeing of every single phenomenon is the discerning wisdom. Engaging in the unimpeded activity of bringing benefit to beings is the all-accomplishing wisdom.

Furthermore, these are subsumed under two wisdoms: the dharmadhatu wisdom is the "wisdom of knowing things as they are," and the other four constitute the "wisdom of knowing everything in existence." One attains the sublime, unsurpassable level of having completely accomplished the two precious purposes.

# 4. Eliminating Obstacles

- C. Eliminating the Obstacles and Narrow Paths of Experiences and Realizations
  1. Removing External and Internal Obstacles
  2. Removing Common Hindrances and Faults on the Path
  3. Eliminating the Path's Common Mistakes and Different Strayings

## Eliminating the Obstacles and Narrow Paths of Experiences and Realizations

This explanation has five parts: (1) removing external and internal obstacles; (2) removing common hindrances and faults on the path; (3) eliminating the path's common mistakes and different strayings; (4) specific narrow paths, strayings, deviations, and obstacles; and (5) general discussion about different kinds of mistakes.

## Removing External and Internal Obstacles

In the *Enlightenment of Vairochana Tantra* we find:

> For this there are two obstacles:
> In the external and internal spheres.

As to external obstacles, being led by such people as a chieftain or a relative, your frame of mind is driven to hanker for worldly experiences.

You are unable to cast away expectations for long. Endangered by enemies, thieves, and the like, you abandon your dedication to spiritual practice. You should avoid proceeding in that way by whatever means and focus on the Dharma for the purpose of everlasting well-being. In particular, postponing the practice of samadhi, attached and clinging to this life, you become very busy. As the workings of Mara, this is an even greater confusion than delusion. Lord Lhatsewa said:

> It is not difficult to give birth to meditation.
> What is hard is to bring it to culmination.
> You yogins do not recognize the obstacles.
> Don't conform your mind to that of ordinary worldly people.

Don't become like that. Know that the experiences of this present life are like last night's meaningless dream, and be determined to renounce them. If your mind forms the intention to acquire this life's food, clothing, and so on, knowing this to be an obstacle, drop attachment. Our ideals are the liberating lives of the victorious Kagyu masters of the past, so always practice in isolated places and apply yourself straightforwardly to your practice. If in these places there are too many distractions created by sponsors and the like, this too will easily become an obstacle, so in all outer and inner situations, stick well to the norm: Sit and rely on simply the basic food and clothing that happens to come along. You must set about practicing with great diligence, not relenting even for a moment. Still when doing so, all kinds of good and bad situations will occur; that is just the nature of things. Obstacles might arise like magical manifestations brought about by immaterial beings such as obstructing spirits, gods, and demons, as well as by wild men, savage beasts, and so forth. However, these are habitual patterns residing in your mind stream from beginningless time. Everything that comes up is meant to test you; hence knowing them to be so, use them as the path. Without deviating from the essence, the spiritual practice consists of training in recognizing everything to be its radiance. Perceiving gods and demons as parents, cultivate compassion. Seeing them as the yidam, ask for the siddhis. Perceiving them as the guru, supplicate. Knowing them to be your own mind, enhance the strength of your realization. Practicing as if it were secret conduct, you should completely attain stability in the natural state.

As to internal obstacles, these occur due to the disturbance of the body's four elements resulting in an unbalanced combination of factors. The diversity of diseases arising from the combination of wind-energy, bile, and phlegm should be cured through such methods as physical exercises and *rishi* medicinal treatment, or by placing the disease itself in the care of the main practice and using it as the path. Also, there are obstacles created by thoughts, making you slip into the five afflictive emotions without control. You may have given birth to some meager qualities of the spiritual practice, experience, or realization, but unable to keep them to yourself, you speak out, show off, wish others to notice them, appreciate others' praises, and so forth, and are carried away by the eight worldly preoccupations. As Padampa Sangye said:

> In those whose attributes are noticeable, many obstacles may occur.
> Keep your practice secret, people of Tingri.

Learn the meaning of the following teaching: without wishing for this life's fame or gain, on the basis of mindfulness, use all thoughts of the five poisons as the path. Practice without hypocrisy, regardless of whether or not people notice, are impressed, praise or criticize, or it makes you happy. Hide all your qualities and expose all your faults. The realized scholar Kyer Gangpa said:

> "The fogginess mara invading your head" is the unclear experience of your spiritual practice. "The speech mara invading your tongue" is to delight in talk and be unable to keep your practice secret. "The dispersion mara invading your heart" is your cognizance being dispersed in objects and unable to remain calm. "The movement mara invading your limbs" is

> your hands moving actively and legs moving from place to place, so you are unable to remain in solitude and are full of desire to leave.

For this, meditate step by step on the guru at the top of your head, throat, heart, navel, and so forth, and aim at pacifying these obstacles by fervently supplicating that each of these maras is subdued in turn.

Similarly, your retreat also may have become such that it is not striking the key point, and as time passes your mind becomes more impervious, the retreat more lax, occupations multiply, and practice deteriorates. The great obstacle created by laziness becomes more prominent, so you lose sensitivity toward Dharma. Determined to avoid this, apply yourself only to the Dharma of true meaning. If, having practiced for months or years, you wonder if some sublime quality has come about and somehow expect it, as Zhang Rinpoche said, the following will happen:

> Immediately wishing to have a sign of accomplishment
> Is a premonition that you are about to lose it.

Don't have a feeble type of perseverance that is only concerned with immediate results. Avoid having an attitude that neglects distancing yourself from the pursuits of this life. With great diligence apply yourself extensively to genuine accomplishment, endeavoring to practice without concern for this life. In brief, if they impede the development of the qualities of view and meditation, then even the creation of merit and ordinary siddhis is considered to be an obstacle to supreme attainment. Until you have actualized the fact that samsara and nirvana are neither good nor bad, there will remain individual maras of attachment and fixation. Therefore, since the roots of samsara and nirvana lie in the present worldly occupations, you should eliminate these flaws in any way necessary: by applying the antidote of not being carried away by them, by observing the all-sufficient preservation of the essence, or by using them as the path.

## Removing Common Hindrances and Faults on the Path

It is important to remove obstacles to the essential practice. Having previously resolved misconceptions through your guru, when practicing accordingly, you indeed need to know which and whose are the flaws without leaving them to do as they please, unrestricted, in the dark, and without appraisal. It is not possible to give here a complete explanation that covers all these points as there are so many different ways in which experiences and realizations occur in people according to their various capacities. This point cannot be covered by one explanation alone, so we are unable to explain it completely. What follows is a synthesis of the key points in a nutshell.

Again, from the standpoint of not blocking or acquiring thoughts, or analyzing and fixating on perceptions, no matter how the unfabricated mind essence rests, or what arises or appears, it is important to stick to undistracted mindfulness without losing track of knowing your own nature. This is definitely the root of meditation. In this regard, if the meditation faults of torpor, dullness, and agitation occur to a beginner, although there are many techniques to eliminate them, in short, don't fixate dualistically in regarding them as good or bad, but instead be convinced that whatever takes place is the radiance of your own mind. So if you sustain this in whatever occurs, it will itself finally be released without a trace. Jetsun Milarepa said:

> This certainly being the true meditation,
> Don't eliminate the faults of dullness and agitation.
> If you try to clear away these faults of dispersion, dullness, torpor, or agitation,
> It would be like lighting a butter lamp in daylight, O physician monk!

Also Gampopa said:

> If dullness and agitation occur, look straight at them!

Signs of meditative experiences are unpredictable: unpleasant, such as feeling unhappy, or pleasant, such as a calm mind, bliss, clarity, or nonthought. No matter what experiences occur, don't deliberately cling to them or have dualistic preferences regarding them as good or bad. Instead, convinced that all of them are but expressions of your mind alone, entrust the core of your meditation, the body of your practice, onto whatever occurs: if feeling sad, on sadness itself; if feeling good and clear, on your well-being and clarity itself. Lay bare your own nature and sustain it with alertness; this is the way it should be understood.

Don't give importance to the good or bad meditative experiences. If you happen to strike the key point and rest accordingly right on the face of whatever arises, it all becomes simple and you are called a meditator for whom whatever arises or occurs is sufficient. No obstacles, deviations, or mistakes will occur. All you need to know is this key point. You are not sure whether many other restless modifying actions are sufficient or not, so understand it in that way. Thus, apply yourself to sustaining the unfabricated essence and the thorough knowing of the nature of anything that arises. If you exert yourself in supplicating your authentic guru, at some point this will purify your obscurations and the blessings will enter you, whereby you will perceive mind essence. From then on, this naked, ordinary cognizance of nowness, unmodified by the concepts of good thoughts and unadulterated by the stains of bad thoughts—the original face of the primordial natural state—will be seen by itself in the manner of "nothing to see," and ultimately you will understand that everything is mahamudra. The essence transcends mentally created attributes; therefore you will become certain about the essence being beyond concepts, and a trusting conviction will arise from within. All these will make you feel happy. This is what is called "seeing the coemergent essence of natural mind."

Since you have recognized the natural face of coemergent mind essence, the undesirable and antidote merge into one, and any occurring thought—the manifold natural radiance—arises without basis or root within the essence of empty lucidity. As it is released into that absence of basis and root, the main part of meditation arrives at the thought itself, and there is no need to give importance to whether it is the basic nature or its radiance. This is what is called "seeing the original face of coemergent thoughts." Furthermore, having become familiarized with this and developed its potential, finally all objects appearing to the five senses arise without fixation as insubstantial, and there is no need to cling dualistically to subject and object. This is what is called "the realization of the nature of coemergent phenomena." In fact, the meditating mind and the variety of perceived objects of meditation are all realized to be an inseparable unity. In other words, all meditations and meditation objects are free from the basis and root of fixation. All thinking and distractions also turn into one uninterrupted limitless sphere. This is the supreme meditation. Thereafter, whatever is encountered is used as the path, and apart from this conduct there is no other training to be carried out. However, it is important to bring all phenomena of samsara and nirvana into your own natural state. Then, after integrating them with your own natural state, to expand it in all directions is a profound key point.

## Eliminating the Path's Common Mistakes and Different Strayings

The infinitely vast and profound pith meditation instructions of mahamudra, dzogchen, cutting, pacifying, and so forth, all agree on the main point: it is all about letting one's mind rest without modification. However, in accordance with people's individual ways of understanding, this has been presented in different ways. In this regard, some practitioners hold meditation as being solely thought-free cognizance that has blocked the entire range of perceptions from coarse to subtle, but that is a deviation into blank shamatha. Some others desire a meditative stability of dull oblivion not embraced by awareness, and they stray into deluded stupid meditation. There are others who, attached to such experiences as the mind's bright clarity, vivid bliss, or utter void, hold these to be the meditation. And some feel that only a blank cognizance between a past thought that has ceased and the next thought that hasn't yet arisen is what is required, so their meditation is split into pieces. Yet there are some who will intellectually grasp at thoughts such as "mind essence is dharmakaya," "it's empty," "it's unidentifiable." Similarly they think in such terms as, "everything lacks true existence," "it's like an illusion," "it's like space." Considering those beliefs to be the meditation, they fall into the extreme of conceptual fabrication. Some people say that whatever they think or anything that arises is of the nature of meditation, so they are carried away by ordinary thoughts and stray into insanity. For the most part, the rest view thought movement as a fault and block it, and believe that meditation consists of settling by constricting that movement. By tensing thoughts and thinking, they rigidly bind themselves. Many situations such as these occur.

In brief, whether the mind is still or moving, resting with any thought or emotion, or remaining calmly in bliss, clarity, or nonthought, whichever it may be, those who know how to sustain the coemergent innate nature of its own accord, without needing to reject, manipulate, or make corrections on precisely whatever appears, are extremely scarce.

Furthermore, the supreme root of all outer, inner, secret, and heart true meaning teachings, the significance of all key points in a nutshell, is exactly the undistracted mindfulness of one's own mind, and indeed this is spontaneously present. However, it happens to some that, even though they have experienced nondistraction, while they are in the essence, they do not notice that they have become distracted. How is this? Since the nature of mind is beyond the field of theoretical knowledge, if one conceptualizes what has been realized and mentally construes it, there is a slight distraction. As the truth of mind is beyond cultural knowledge, to mentally construct a true meaning out of such knowledge is also to slightly wander from the essence. The truth of mind is not an object of meticulous examination, so to analyze and investigate through theory and mentally construe that it is empty, unoriginated, and so forth is also to slightly wander from the essence. The truth of mind is not something that can be objectified; therefore to deliberately aim one's focus through theory on experiences, such as those of bliss, clarity, and nonthought, is also to waver slightly from the essence. In brief, whereas the nature of mind is beyond all mental constructs, any mentally construed alteration, as well as practices with or without characteristics, is a mental construction. Even though people may think that they are not engaging in any mental construction, still they are slightly wandering from the essence. The Great Brahmin said:

> If the stain of the intellect is purified, there is coemergence.
> At that time there will be no involvement with what is incompatible.
> If the intellect is made to not be the intellect,
> That will result in the attainment of unsurpassable enlightenment.

Virupa said:

> If suchness is mentally construed and you fall into the extreme of dualism,
> That is the root of existence and cycling in samsara;
> Therefore, look at the ground and root of all, the essence of mind.
> If by looking you don't see and are free from mental constructs, you are definitely liberated.

Shawaripa said:

> Look, look, don't look at anything!
> Meditate, meditate, don't meditate at all!

Thus, what is needed is to sustain the key point of undistracted nonmeditation.

# 5. Narrow Paths and Strayings

4. Specific Narrow Paths, Strayings, Deviations, and Obstacles
   a. The Five Narrow Paths
      i. Phenomena Arising as Enemies
      ii. Thoughts Arising as Enemies
      iii. Emptiness Arising as an Enemy
      iv. Cause and Effect Arising as an Enemy
      v. Compassion Arising as an Enemy
   b. The Three or Eight Strayings Including Supplementary Explanations
      i. Straying to the Three Spheres through Bliss, Clarity, or Nonthought
      ii. Straying to the Four Concentrations through an Outward-Looking Samadhi
      iii. Straying to the Four Formless Spheres of Perception through Mind-Constructed Concepts
   c. The Four Deviations
      i. The Basic Nature
         A) Timeless Deviation to the Nature of Knowables
         B) Temporary Deviation to the Basic Nature
      ii. The Path
         A) Timeless Deviation to the Path
         B) Temporary Deviation to the Path
      iii. The Antidote
         A) Timeless Deviation to the Antidote
         B) Temporary Deviation to the Antidote
      iv. A Label

A) Timeless Deviation to a Label
B) Temporary Deviation to a Label
d. Removing Common Obstacles
5. General Discussion about Different Kinds of Mistakes

---

## Specific Narrow Paths, Strayings, Deviations, and Obstacles

This explanation has four parts: (1) the five narrow paths, (2) the three or eight strayings including supplementary explanations, (3) the four deviations, and (4) removing common obstacles.

## The Five Narrow Paths

The five narrow paths are as follows.

## The Narrow Path of Phenomena Arising as Enemies

When we are sustaining meditative composure, if we don't integrate the five objects of perception from the outset, they will not mingle with the meditation. Actually, right now when we sit in meditation free of adversities or foes, we enjoy it, but then if we don't integrate it into perceptions when nice or disgusting forms appear in our visual field, sweet or harsh sounds arise to the ears, or any of the other sensory objects appear, we will be carried away and slip into fixating on good or bad, attachment or aversion. Some people would consider it to be intolerable if that happens. Considering forms, sounds, and so forth as being harmful to the mind, they might become irritated, thinking, "If only these weren't there, or didn't happen." So phenomena would be arising as enemies. Here you should be cautious from the outset and use them as the path. Padampa Sangye said:

> Phenomena arising as enemies is like a thief in an empty house.
> In reality there is nothing gained nor lost, people of Tingri.

While sustaining the essence during meditative composure, all kinds of beautiful or ugly forms may arise in your visual field, yet neither deliberately fixate on or examine them as beautiful or ugly, nor engage in attachment or aversion; rather rest loosely on the perception itself and sustain it while being aware of your own nature. The same applies to whatever sounds are heard by the ears—human or animal, loud or quiet, sweet or harsh. Don't deliberately examine the sound. For example, in the case of something someone has said, don't ponder over the meaning or analyze it; instead identify the sound and rest loosely on it, while recognizing your own nature. Similarly, avoid deliberately analyzing the array of fragrant or foul smells in the field of the nose, as well as the diversity of tastes in the mouth—delicious, disgusting, sweet, bitter, and so forth—becoming attached to the tasty ones and feeling distaste for the opposite. However they happen to be, recognize them, and right there relax and sustain that knowingly. As to the sensation of such things as clothes in the field of the body, don't be carried away by attraction and rejection, liking the soft ones and disliking the rough ones. You need to know how to sustain the meditation right on it. In fact, don't deliberately fixate on the five sense objects; no matter what appears or arises, recognize that itself and loosen up on it, sustaining the meditative composure while being alert and mindful. In case a thought of good or bad, like or dislike, arises, you should recognize that thought and sustain your nature.

In regard to phenomena appearing as enemies, it is not okay for anger to arise. If we take ourselves as an example, generally speaking we are continually caught in the cycle of attachment and aversion in this life. But that is not all. Particularly, for those of us who have a bad temper and are always cursing, irritated, angry, and mean, if some external situation takes place which we don't want or like, we will surely all become angry. We are very accustomed to thoughts of anger and the other poisons: Our habits are thick and strong, and these concepts are powerful and dominating, so they do not stop. In other cases, when facing benign situations, one is carried away by anger, cruelty, or rage, and harsh insults. For example, any damage done to oneself by an inanimate thing such as the earth is surely not deliberate, yet one reacts angrily and barks words such as, "This land is finished! This place is the worst!" Empty external space is harmless, yet one shouts, "The weather is horrible! This is a disaster!" For no reason, one also angrily curses the land, stones, mountains, rocks, plants, and forests, as well as the elements of water, air, space, and so forth. Particularly by being angry and cruel, one creates a lot of bad karma by insulting, hitting, and beating people and animals. Besides that, we too become angry for no reason and curse our important necessities such as food, wealth, and good circumstances, calling our clothes "burial shrouds" and our food "food for the dead." If we have this train of thought, there is nothing that isn't harmful to our minds, and it is nearly impossible to avoid triggering our anger. We imbue all outer and inner things with the nature of anger and cruelty, and all our words are naturally harsh and insulting. Since the fruition of the common affliction of anger is hell, its ripening has profound effect. Of all three poisons, anger is the most negative. As said, "There is no greater negativity than anger." So this anger is one's ruin and others' harm, it causes unhappiness in oneself and others, and for this reason it is taught that this wrongdoing is the greatest.

While this topic is found in the general explanations regarding karmic cause and effect, there is more to it, as what is called "phenomena arising as enemies" entails that even a slight aversion arising toward a perception has a ripening effect. For instance, during the time of Buddha Kashyapa, the tip of a monk's robe got stuck in a piece of wood while he was walking on a path. He became angry and broke the wood. Due to his earlier observance of the monastic discipline, he was born as a naga king named Ele Dabma; however, angrily breaking the piece of wood resulted in him having a tree trunk on top of his head. His head oozed lots of blood and pus and was extremely painful whenever it was buffeted by the wind. Such ripening is fearful. At present, many of us get angry and curse appearances, with or without reason. The ripening will be similar, so if you can give it up, you should. Geshe Potowa said:

> To be angry at things is similar to hitting a rock with your fist; if you hit a rock with your fist, the rock will not be harmed, but you will hurt your hand and have a headache. Likewise, by getting angry and cursing things you don't harm them, but you do hurt yourself with the ripening of anger and abusive words.

The actual utilization of anger at phenomena as the path is illustrated by the following story of Naropa and Tilopa. Once they went to a town of blacksmiths and stayed there for a few days. Just after midnight, a blacksmith struck a single blow of his hammer, after which all the other blacksmiths got up and followed suit, making a very loud noise. Not liking this sound, at first a form of anger arose in Naropa's mind, but at that moment he identified the thought of anger and uprooted it, and rested in meditation on the hammer's sound. Thus, he actualized phenomena and mind as inseparable, as equivalent. In the same way, while we are in meditation, people or other beings could disturb it by moving, sitting, doing things, chatting, or making loud noises. If by thinking, "If only they weren't there," you feel irritated, ill at ease, or any other discomfort, then don't be carried away by it. In reality all phenomena are the same within the mind and it is only a matter of recognizing it or not. So considering it to be that way and understanding that phenomena themselves must be used as the path—whether it is a perceived object or especially a mind troubled by an angry thought—recognize that discomfort. Having recognized it, you must know how to sustain it without modification. Lord Gotsangpa said:

> All these phenomena are one's mind; although they appear, they have no true nature. Since they are like a reflection in a mirror or the moon in water, rest openly without grasping. There is no need to block appearances; if you remain without grasping, that is mahamudra. Sustain just that without distraction.

If you understand it in this way, phenomena will be harmless and the narrow path of them arising as irritating will be removed. This will also create the conditions for the final integration of phenomena and mind. In other words, regarding any object of perception that may appear, as well as anything else that you may deliberately manifest, you should relax right on it and, aware of your own nature, use it as the path.

## The Narrow Path of Thoughts Arising as Enemies

For some of us, to sustain mental stillness feels good. If so, when a lot of thoughts and mental agitation occur, we experience discomfort. Many corrections, stopping, acquiring, disturbance, hopes, and fears well up. It will not do to consider thoughts as enemies and react in that way. In reality, to want the mind to remain still and feel good about it is itself a strong thought of desire. There is no difference between a still mind and a moving mind, so to grasp at it and engage in acquiring and stopping is itself the greatest dualistic thought. The Indian Padampa Sangye said:

> To reject bad thoughts is like gushing water—
> You can't stop them by blocking, people of Tingri.

Lord Milarepa said:

> Even if you nail a thought with nine iron pegs, it will not stay still.

We should not proceed in that way. From the start there is no difference between a still and a moving mind. No matter how it stays still or how it manifests, you should know that these are the display or magical show of the basic nature of none other than your own mind. Lord Mila gave many analogies to the maiden Peldarbum and sent her off to gain certainty about mind essence. She then told him:

> At first I indeed asked for many examples.
> Actually meditating on mind essence was all right,
> But meditating on thoughts felt a bit uneasy.

Jetsun Mila replied:

> If meditating on mind essence was fine
> But meditating on thoughts felt uncomfortable,
> Thoughts being the magical display of the mind,
> You should still ascertain that magical display.

And:

> Once thoughts are recognized to be dharmakaya, by letting them be, they will be liberated.

Having this understanding, you will be content with whatever occurs. If the mind is still, recognize the nature of just that, and when a thought is produced, also identify that itself. You should relax loosely on that very nature, sustaining it by merely remaining undistracted. In a tantra it is said:

> Thoughts are purified by thoughts themselves.
> Existence is purified by existence itself.

And:

> That which is binding a person,
> Thoroughly knowing it will liberate the yogin.

Lord Gampopa said:

> Don't reject thoughts, for they are the display of dharmakaya.

Lord Gotsangpa said:

> If a hundred thoughts arise, they are a hundred dharmakayas.

There are many quotations such as these. In general "thoughts are dharmakaya" means that thoughts themselves are the essence of the realized, self-knowing awareness-wisdom.[23] While realizing them as such, without the identity of whatever arises losing its freshness or becoming faded, naked empty lucidity manifests as the nondual basic nature and radiance. Nonetheless, when experiences and realizations take place, obscurations are at that moment dispelled, as a result of simply having recognized the actual state as it is. Other than that, there hasn't been an ensuing realization that has caused lucidity and emptiness to become inseparable. From the primordial beginning, dharmakaya has always been lucidity and emptiness abiding without duality, but at the moment, due to our negative karmic habitual patterns, this fact has been clouded. It is only a matter of not having recognized that; yet on the ultimate level they have always been nondual, all-pervading, and perfectly pure. So what is the point of recollecting whether thoughts are or are not dharmakaya, applying corrections, or meditating with manipulations? Therefore, consider the basic nature and radiance as not different. Avoid the attitude of rejection that regards thoughts as a fault. Instead having recognized the original face of any thought that occurs as it is, rest on it loose and easy, whereby the thought will be liberated by itself as it arises, like a snake undoing its coils. For that reason, without regarding thoughts as a fault, it is profound to simply rest loosely on them, resting barely undistracted. Orgyen Rinpoche said:

> Without modifying the manifestation of the myriad phenomena,
> Whatever appears is recognized to be the display of
> dharmakaya.

And:

> By leaving thought movement to itself, it will be liberated into dharmakaya.

Lord Gyalwang said:

When the nature of thoughts is known,
Whatever arises chimes and tinkles in dharmakaya.
Situations sway and whirl in self-liberation.

When giving an introduction to the nature of mind, considering that thoughts are the basis for all karma and afflictions, the sacred masters teach as is mentioned in the *Enlightenment of Vairochana Tantra:*

Thoughts are the great ignorance.

Once the sacred master has given the introduction, all kinds of mixed pure and impure experiences arise in those who practice. Not reifying these experiences, but by just recognizing them and letting go, all paths and *bhumis* will be included in that. Zhang Rinpoche said:

When the manifestation of the variety of phenomena
Is not blocked but its nature is recognized,
Devotion, compassion, suppleness, and so forth
Are effortlessly and spontaneously accomplished.
Thus thoughts are not to be rejected.
To recognize their nature is the supreme path.

Also at the time of awakening to perfect buddhahood, kayas, deeds, activity, and wisdom are all innately present in thoughts. Lord Phagmo Drupa said:

Pure thoughts are the expression of dharmakaya.
The ten powers, the eighteen distinct qualities,
The fearlessnesses, the three classes of miracles, and so forth
Are all spontaneously present from beginningless time.

If you know how to see thoughts as the original face of dharmakaya, you will know how to act in the openness of dharmakaya, so mahamudra becomes your good harvest.

## The Narrow Path of Emptiness Arising as an Enemy

Here there are two instances: lower and higher. The lower instance happens during meditative experiences. If you trust the mind abiding in empty lucidity and are content with that, it would be greater one-pointedness. If that empty lucidity becomes somewhat continuous during day and night, there is a danger that, thinking that your meditation is good, you feel self-important and become proud. If this happens, don't cling to that feeling or be attached, presumptuous, or proud, but rather establish the level of your experience and sustain your essence.

For instance, Gampopa told Lord Mila, "I have a good samadhi that continues unbroken for about twelve days." "Ha ha," laughed Milarepa. "That is a meditative experience of samadhi which does not result in anything higher than the three worldly spheres. Not only that, you cannot obtain oil from pressing sand: oil comes from pressing mustard or black sesame seeds. Therefore, practice my *tummo*." Gampopa then practiced, whereby he saw buddha fields and had divine visions and other various wonderful experiences. When he reported this, Milarepa said, "These are neither faults nor qualities, continue practicing." Then he added, "These are said to be mere signs of meditative experiences. They are similar to the liquids oozing out when burning wet firewood. In time, the realization of primordial wisdom will arise from the ground. At that time, a devotion to me, this old man, different from the one you have now, will well up."

Having gained certainty about all these points, and without being satisfied with the experience of empty lucidity, one must sustain one's essence and eventually persist in cultivating devotion, and so on. All this refers to the phase of meditative experiences.

Regarding emptiness arising as an enemy during the phase of realization, to see emptiness as a void happens at the time of simplicity, constituting an obstacle to simplicity. It is what is meant by "to be carried away by attachment to emptiness lacking the realization of simplicity." You see the emptiness of the mind in the sense that it has no existence whatsoever, and moreover, that all phenomena are empty as they do not dwell anywhere. Having understood their lack of a true nature, or emptiness as a whole, you might also conclude that what is called "cause and effect" has no existence: There is no undesirable nor antidote; in the mind's emptiness there is no virtue that benefits or negativity that harms; and in it no karmic fruition ripens as all these would be like planting a seed in space. If you behave by mixing up virtue and vice without considering cause and effect, view and conduct are bound to become perverted. This is the great straying of everything turning black.[24] In his *Fundamental Wisdom of the Middle Way,* the teacher Nagarjuna said:

> If emptiness is wrongly approached,
> Those of lower intelligence will be ruined,
> Just like wrongly holding a snake
> Or wrongly accomplishing knowledge mantras.

All Kagyu masters of the past refer to that as "the view of everything turning black." We don't follow that path but instead practice in the following way on the absolute nature as it is. The nature of the mind is nonexistent; it is emptiness and the nature of all phenomena. Although we already know that, we must understand that in its unimpeded radiance manifesting as phenomena on the relative level, cause and effect, virtue and vice, interdependence, and so forth are infallible. Therefore, in practice, it is important to meticulously take cause and effect into account. Lord Milarepa said:

> Although you have realized the truth of nonduality
> And recognized mind essence to be dharmakaya,
> You should be meticulously careful about cause and effect.

Lord Drikungpa said:

> When conviction about cause and effect is born,
> Careless and outrageous behavior is a sham.
> Consider whether it is worth
> Being carried away by negativity.

Lord Gyaltsen Palzang said:

> The variety of phenomena arises interdependently.
> Without taking only emptiness into account,
> It is profound to train in all the methods,
> Such as altruistic love, faith, and devotion.

If you understand the above without wavering from the state of the basic nature, emptiness, and you understand that its radiance as all kinds of phenomena arises interdependently, you will be free from the bondage of exclusive emptiness. In his exegesis of mahamudra, Lord Pema Karpo says:

> Although you may be spending all your time practicing generosity and the rest of the six paramitas, understanding emptiness should be the purifier of attachment.

Accordingly, the sutras and tantras taught by the Buddha say, from many points of view, that buddhahood is attained only through the indivisibility of the two truths. They haven't taught that buddhahood is attained through a Dharma that separates means and knowledge. In line with the teaching in the *Mother of the Conquerors* (*Prajñaparamita*) that mentions the example of a bird with clipped wings, by not separating means and knowledge, one develops the radiance of emptiness: altruistic love, compassion, pure perception, and devotion, as well as the elaborate generation-stage practices, and so forth. In short, by training on all dualistic phenomena within the supreme capacity of awareness, one must come to realize them all as nondual. From the perspective of the indivisibility of emptiness and its radiance arising as great compassion, having generated a vast aspiration toward supreme enlightenment, you should distribute all compounded and uncompounded merit among all beings, who have been your mothers, and make aspirations. Saraha said:

> Those who have entered emptiness without compassion
> Have not found the supreme path.

But if they meditate only on compassion,
They will remain here in samsara and will not attain liberation.
Whoever is able to indivisibly merge these two
Will dwell neither in samsara nor in nirvana.

Similarly, once the radiance of emptiness emerges as faith and pure perception, one trains on the buddha fields without preferences. Once the radiance of emptiness emerges as uncontrived devotion, one endeavors to view the world and beings as the display of the great mandala of the guru's three kayas. The radiance of emptiness also emerges as the elaborate practices of the generation stage of the deity's form—by training in the skandhas, elements, and so forth as the deity's mandala—in harmony with the path of all the buddhas. When that happens, one attains the inseparability of phenomena and emptiness, as indivisible as the moon reflected in water. Thus, without deviations, one enters the great avenue of the conquerors. Related to these points, siddha Shawaripa gave Maitripa instructions on nineteen key points:

Although you know phenomena as mind, don't discontinue generating compounded merit.
Although you know your mind as buddha, don't abandon your root guru.
Although you have no hopes for buddhahood, don't belittle the Buddha.
Although you are not afraid of hell, give up negative actions from the smallest up.
Although you are not afraid of the *preta* state, don't discontinue generosity down to the smallest act.
Although you are not afraid of going astray, keep your physical and verbal vows.
Although you have realized that gods and demons have no reality, don't abandon your yidam.
Although you have realized that birth and death have no reality, since you are still dependent on the body of this sentient being, familiarize yourself with view and conduct.

> Although you have realized nonorigination, don't stop behaving virtuously.
> Although you have realized equality, don't be irritated with ordinary beings.
> Although you know forms and sounds as dharmakaya, persevere in cleansing your own mind.
> Although you know that everything is mind, don't kill even the smallest being.
> Although you never part from the continuity of the innate, always keep your samayas and vows.
> Although you have realized the nonconceptual view, meditate on the view free from bias.
> Although you know how to meditate without distraction, don't be attached to the mind.
> Although your conduct may be without anxiety, behave in conformity with beings.
> Although you have realized your own mind, keep the samayas without deception.
> Although you have realized that awareness is beyond birth and death, meditate on your body skandha as impermanent.
> Although awareness wells forth from within, hold your sublime guru on the crown of your head.

Tilopa said:

> Until you have realized as unoriginated
> These interdependent phenomena,
> Don't separate the two accumulations.
> They are like the wheels of a cart, Naropa.

Lopon Rinpoche and the Dharma king Songtsen Gampo also taught this point many times. Also, Virupa said:

> On the relative level, even if you are confident that you don't expect to become a buddha,

> Don't give up the great generation of merit, but exert yourself in it as much as you can.
> Although you may be fearless and have no anxiety about all of samsara,
> Be cautious about even the smallest negative action.
> Although you have realized that all phenomena are empty like space,
> Completely abandon all likes, dislikes, and attachments.
> Although you have realized the great transparency of limitless absolute reality,
> Until you have attained stability, keep your experience and realizations to yourself.
> Although you have realized that ultimately self and other are not two,
> On the conventional level, think about the great purpose of benefiting beings.
> Although you don't depend on other guidance because you possess great confidence,
> Keep your kind guru on the crown of your head.

These were citations by Indian mahasiddhas. There are also many other references by Kagyupa masters. To quote a few, Lord Mila said:

> Having realized nonduality,
> Although you know mind essence as dharmakaya,
> Be cautious about the subtlest cause and effect.
>
> Having realized spontaneous presence,
> Although there is no interruption to luminosity,
> Keep your sublime guru on the crown of your head.
>
> Having realized equality,
> Although free from both hope and fear,
> Don't irritate mundane people.

Having realized the ineffable,
Although you abide beyond acceptance and rejection,
Make vast altruistic aspirations.

Lord Rechungpa said:

Although you have realized mahamudra,
While you are not free from your body of ripened karma,
Cherish making offerings to the guru and the dakinis.
Although you have no desire for nirvana,
Cherish Dharma activities and the practice of the ten virtues.
Although all phenomena are mind by nature,
Don't pretend you aren't harming others.
Although you have realized inseparability,
Cherish wandering in mountain solitudes and being accustomed to them.
Although you have no qualms about falling into samsara,
Cherish avoiding to commit the slightest negative action.
Although you have realized the equality of self and others,
Through compassion, cherish not giving up the six kinds of beings.
Although you don't cling to your own philosophical tradition,
Cherish possessing bodhichitta.
Within the various dispositions of beings,
Cherish harmony with the views and actions of others.
The profound instructions and practices,
Cherish keeping them both secret from unsuitable recipients.
This body of a yogin,
Cherish making it stay extremely isolated.
These are the nine things to cherish.
You meditators, keep them in mind.

In the *Jewel Garland of the Supreme Path:*[25]

These are the four common points of Dharma. You may have realized everything as mahamudra, yet meditate on your guru

> on the top of your head and apply yourself to compounded merit. All you do may become Dharma, yet be cautious of subtle negative actions. Solitude and the village may be the same to you, yet meditate while living in solitude. Sitting straight may not be different from lying down, yet meditate sitting straight.

There are many more similar citations by Tsangpa Gyare and other masters. By focusing on the key points of the practice thus explained, you will be free from emptiness arising as an enemy.

## The Narrow Path of Cause and Effect Arising as an Enemy

By holding cause and effect to be paramount but not understanding the absolute-level teaching as it is, you adhere to defining characteristics and concrete reality as supreme. Then, rather than the mind being calm and empty, you are attracted to elaborate diversions such as distracting activities and Dharma practices done between sessions, and so underestimate the natural state or else you reify it. If so, this would be the narrowest path. Moreover, it has been said that what is needed more than anything else is emptiness and mahamudra. Saraha said:

> Ordained monks (*bante*),
> Called bhikshu, novice or elder,
> Some explain the sutras,
> Some see one taste as conceived by dualistic mind,
> And some take the mahayana as the cause.
> However, all these are scriptural treatises on characteristics.
> Others meditate on every single mandala circle,
> Some engage in explanations on the meaning of the fourth
> empowerment,
> Some conceptualize the sphere of space,
> And others make emptiness into a view.
> Most of them have headed in an incompatible direction.
> Others who lack coemergence

May meditate on nirvana.
They may reach cessation,
But none will accomplish the other one: absolute truth.
Those who are inclined to do certain practices
By resting serenely in concentration, how will they attain liberation?
What is the need of butter lamps? What is the need of ritual cakes?
What is the point of that? What is the need of secret mantra?
What is the need of pilgrimage and austerities?
How can you be liberated by dipping in water?

Shawaripa said:

Some deluded people are bound by making conceptual distinctions.
Placing the landlord in the home, they search for him elsewhere.
Some hold reflections as real things.
Some leave aside the root and cut the leaves.
No matter what they do, do they not notice the deception?

Tilopa said:

From bathing and ritual purity, bliss is not found.
Although offerings are made to the deities, freedom is not gained.

And:

Through mantra recitation, the paramitas,
Ethics, sutra, the baskets of teachings, and so forth
Corresponding to your own scriptures and philosophical school,
You will not see luminous mahamudra.
The emergence of desire veils luminosity so it is not seen.

Virupa said:

> Some cause pain by conferring empowerments.
> Some say "Hung" and "Phet" and count complete *malas.*
> Some ingest urine, sperm, and blood.
> Some meditate on the yoga of channels and energies, and
> become completely deluded.

There are many references such as these. Therefore, in general we should reflect on karma, cause and effect, and on that basis, unify it within ourselves with the true meaning teachings of the profound shortcut. Moreover, apart from the preliminary practices, we should not emphasize other elaborate activities and practices done between sessions, but rather sustain mind essence, the truth of emptiness. Jetsun Milarepa told Takpo:

> At the time of mahamudra meditation,
> Don't carry on physical and verbal spiritual practices,
> Lest nonconceptual wisdom decline.

For instance, when Takpo joined the Kadampas in their Dharma activities, his nonconceptual wisdom waned just as his teacher had said. He had doubted, but later he became convinced of his guru's words and from then on he persevered in emptiness itself, whereby eventually the wisdom of realization dawned, as mentioned in his life story. Lord Jowo [Atisha] said:

> If your mind relies totally on meditative composure,
> Don't emphasize physical and verbal spiritual practices.

There are other references such as this one, but once you have arrived at the mind, and developed conviction in the practice of emptiness itself, that is exactly the meditation to be emphasized. Then, after your realization has dawned, and you are on the verge of attaining stability, you need to train in all Dharma teachings. Once you understand this point, train in all elaborate practices. Then consummating them together while in the view that is like the sky, carry out the Dharma activities as an illusion. Having understood this teaching, you must exert yourself in the phase of benefiting others day and night without respite. This is how the sequence should be understood.

## The Narrow Path of Compassion Arising as Enemy

Generally, thinking about this present life, to look for gain on the pretext of benefiting beings indeed does not go along with the Dharma. Otherwise, a slightly more well-known situation may happen. Even though you have not attained stability in emptiness, compassion for beings dawns in you. Thus, you feel compelled to help them, and you wish to get up from practice thinking to exhort yourself toward merit. In that case, compassion is arising as an enemy, and if you proceed in that way, while your untimely altruism will mildly benefit others, the harm to yourself will be extremely serious. So avoid this. If you narrow-mindedly think that, since compassion is urgently needed, you must engage in benefiting others before you have accomplished your own purpose, you should know that it is an obstacle. In the *Self-Existing Bliss Tantra* it is said:

> Without oneself having knowledge, to liberate others
> Is to fall into the gateway of Rudra and continue circling.

The *Wisdom Equal to Space* points out this fault:

> Without realizing one's mind as dharmakaya,
> One may know how to explain many sutras and tantras,
> But will fall into Rudra's gateway and wander in samsara.

Orgyen Rinpoche said:

> To benefit beings without having supernormal perception is unsuitable.
> First exert yourself in practice and develop that level.

The Indian Dampa [Padampa Sangye] gave good advice:

> The first entrance to Mara is activity; what is the point of leaving water at home and moving to a dry place? At that time, you interrupt the progress of your own spiritual practice and aren't able to benefit others, so be careful.

And:

> During practice it is inappropriate to engage in altruism.
> The progress of your spiritual practice will be interrupted,
> people of Tingri.

Lord Jowo [Atisha] said:

> Without first taming yourself,
> How will you be able to tame others?

The Dharma Lord Marpa Rinpoche said:

> Not accepting in your mind that you are a disciple,
> You act as others' teacher.
> Not being acquainted with the road to a certain destination,
> You are like the blind leading the blind.
>
> Without having realized your own mind,
> To introduce others to their minds
> Is like a blind person showing a small child
> The colors of the moon.
>
> Without having tamed your own mind,
> To explain the Dharma to others
> Is like a leper conducting a healing rite
> For a sick person possessed by an evil spirit.

> While your mind doesn't stay still for even an instant,
> To give instructions to others
> Is like a person exhausted and without any resources,
> Planting a seed in a rock.
>
> Generally, if you sincerely wish to attain enlightenment,
> Give busyness a rest and stick to solitude.
> Abandon disciples that hinder your practice.

Lord Yangonpa said:

> Unless meditation is arising as one taste, the benefit of beings will not be vast. Whatever benefit there is will be distorted.

Remember these and other similar quotations, and let them influence you. Attain high stability in emptiness endowed with the heart of compassion, and rather than worshiping the demon of simulated altruism, avoid working for the benefit of beings before the time is right. Don't give up love, compassion, and bodhichitta. Focus on making altruistic aspirations and genuinely accomplish them to a great extent. It is important to plant the seed of altruism from the very beginning.

## The Three or Eight Strayings Including Supplementary Explanations

The three strayings are: (1) straying to the three spheres through bliss, clarity, or nonthought; (2) straying to the four concentrations through an outward-looking samadhi; and (3) straying to the four formless spheres of perception through mind-constructed concepts. These explanations will include supplementary discussions.

## Straying to the Three Spheres through Bliss, Clarity, or Nonthought

Although these modes of deviations have already been explained at the time of shamatha, here they will be briefly discussed according to the stage of removing obstacles. Having practiced meditation and become attached to shamatha, any of the experiences of bliss, clarity, or nonthought may have occurred to us. Accordingly, during a very intense experience of bliss, unless we differentiate between contaminated or uncontaminated bliss, we generally examine the bliss that is being experienced through our intelligence. If we meditate on that very bliss and cling to that as perfect meditation, we will stray to the desire sphere because we would be completely ensnared by desire. After being attached to that, although we do stray, we would not be reborn in the ten lower states of existence, belonging to the twenty realms of the desire sphere. By being attached to an experience of clarity alone, we would stray to the seventeen realms of the form sphere. If we are attached to nonthought, we would stray to the four formless spheres of perception. Lord Phagmo Drupa said:

> Having gone to where the guru is,
> And practiced the appropriate instructions,
> Body and mind well up with bliss.
> By sustaining that with preferential attachment,
> One will stray and go to a realm in the desire sphere.
>
> Pristine clarity like the sky,
> In and out like the rising moon,[26]
> Whether with open or closed eyes,
> If practitioners sustain that clarity,
> Clinging and being attached to it,
> They will stray to the form sphere.
>
> When, having looked inside and outside,
> There is not even the subtlest thought,
> And one regards that flawlessness to be the dharmakaya
> With feelings of hope and fear,[27]
> If one sustains that experience with certainty,
> One will stray to the formless sphere.

For instance, if one dies while the experience is stable and clings to it, one will stray to any of the three spheres as explained. On the other hand, if the experience occurs momentarily for just a short while, only one or two months, or every year, and then it is finished, there would be no straying. Moreover, Lord Yangonpa believed that:

> Having attachment to bliss, or clinging to clarity, or having conceptualized nonthought, if you fixate on these three, you will stray to the three spheres. If you have no desire or attachment, but you have not seen the original face of the natural state, you will stray to the fruition of a shravaka or pratyeka buddha.

Lord Gampopa's teachings say that by practicing an analytical emptiness, without love and compassion, one strays to merely the hinayana path. However, it has been explained that to attain the fruition of a shravaka or pratyeka buddha, both shamatha and a vipashyana aimed at egolessness, as well as the elimination of afflictions, are required. Merely sustaining bliss, clarity, and nonthought without attachment but devoid of vipashyana insight would be an ordinary worldly concentration. Therefore, I think that the attainment of arhatship of the shravaka or pratyeka buddha by those means is objectionable. "Well then," you may think, "how is it that Lord Gampopa warns about the danger of an unascertained perception becoming the cause of cessation?" As to that, it is said in the *Open Teachings of Auspiciousness and Prosperity*:

> A teacher who possesses the Dharma eyes and has actualized mind as emptiness starts to ascertain that bliss, clarity, and nonthought are unoriginated. If he is not convinced that they are unoriginated, it is called "unascertained perception," and he will proceed to a nondiscerned cessation. Since this is an ordinary path, there is no way to know where he will be reborn.

As said in the quotation, this would be a nondiscerned cessation, and the *Abhidharmakosha* says in connection to this:

> What is meant by cessation is that it forever blocks the birth [of afflictions],
> And it happens through nondiscernment.

And in its self-commentary it is said:

> Future births [of afflictions] are forever blocked. Cessation is none other than that separation [of afflictions], and that is the nondiscerned cessation. Here, since what was obtained is the result of discernment, it is not the case.

As explained in this citation, incomplete conditions will result in an everlastingly blockage of any future birth of pure and defiled mental phenomena. This is a cessation different from the discerned one. The reason it results in the impossibility of knowing where the rebirth will take place has been mentioned in the *Way of the Bodhisattva*:

> In a mind separated from emptiness
> [Afflictions] may be blocked but they will be born again.
> This is similar to the perception-free meditative absorption.

Thus, "perception-free" indicates rebirth into the realm of the conception-less gods, which causes mental events to be blocked. "Conception-free meditative absorption" indicates that in the fourth concentration, through perceiving the enduring nonperception as freedom, the meditative absorption is such that mind and mental events are stopped. The meditative absorption of cessation entails an absence of conceptions; based on the concentration of neither conception nor nonperception, perception and sensation are warded off. Since these are perceived as actualized peace, mind and mental events subside, and it consists in an appeasing meditative absorption. At this point, this is why they are considered to be a straying. All these absorptions lack the truth of egolessness, so they are incapable of subduing the root of samsara, ego-fixation, and because of this, once karma and afflictions emerge, one again circles in samsara. As Chandrakirti said:

> If there is I, there is a cognition of other.
> From self and other arise attachment and aversion.
> From being completely linked to these,
> All evils take place.

This meaning is analogous to the example of Udraka[28] who did not transcend samsara, although his mind had reached the pinnacle of this existence.

Regarding the discerned cessation, this has been explained as being the cessation free from contaminating factors, attained through the discerning intelligence of the unhindered path of the four joys.

Thus, the experiences of bliss, clarity, and nonthought arise based on the immediate interdependence with the body's channels, energies, and bindu, and once we reify these habitual meditative moods, by holding them as true, we stray. If we don't deeply revert from attachment, it will be as said, "Meditative experience may be good but it is weak like watery lentil soup." Hence, don't deliberately consider, be attached to, or cling to the experiences of bliss, clarity, and nonthought, but look to the nature of mind as it is and equalize the taste of all cognized perceptions in the dharmadhatu. In order to avoid heading toward the state of shravakas and pratyeka buddhas through nonattachment to bliss, clarity, and nonthought, again supplicate your guru with devotion, whereby blessings will enter. You must see the original face of the mind wherein experience and realization have merged.

## Straying to the Four Concentrations through an Outward-Looking Samadhi

Through the power of the samadhi of shamatha including bliss, clarity, and nonthought, the samadhi is sustained without apprehension and with expansive delight. This brings forth at the outset a complete training that makes the mind pliable. Through that power, the energy that becomes the cause for physical pliability moves in the body, and when it has pervaded the body, the complete training of physical pliability takes place. There are various ways in which this happens. According to the

*Shravaka Levels*, once that complete training is born, one possesses the six mental engagements: understanding the meanings individually, isolation derived from interest, joy, collection, discernment, and ultimate engagement. When one possesses them, this state becomes the preparation for the first concentration of the form realm. Then, one gradually accomplishes the meditative absorptions of the concentrations, the formless realms, and so forth. In the *Stages of Meditation* it is clearly said:

> Endowed with a neutral feeling, the mind becomes conceptual and analytical. At that moment it is called "not unmanageable." This is a mind that is connecting with the first concentration. At that time, free from craving and vicious propensities, one possesses concept, discernment, joy, and bliss; that is called the "first concentration." The mere absence of thought from the first concentration is called "special concentration." When, free from concept and discernment, one becomes free from the craving of the first concentration, one comes to possess joy, bliss, and a complete inner limpidness; that is called the "second concentration." Then, once one becomes free from the craving of the second concentration, one comes to possess bliss, equanimity, mindfulness, and vigilance; that is called the "third concentration." Eventually, when one is free from the craving of the third concentration, there is neither suffering nor happiness, and one becomes endowed with equanimity and mindfulness; that is called the "fourth concentration."

If one attains these complete trainings, one may rest in the meditative equanimity of samadhi for many days, and during that time, since negative karmic consequences on the state of body and mind have been interrupted, joy and bliss are attained, whereby one is able to enter samadhi. For instance, having placed a butter lamp on his head, Takpo was able to remain in samadhi for thirteen days.

The complete trainings have been deemed by the masters of the past as the basis or legs of meditation. Held to be paramount, if they were sustained, it would be unsuitable for the purpose of the natural state, for it is a cognizance that looks outward. If holding them as real, you practice for a long time and die—since this creates the cause for rebirth in the realm of the concentration gods—you will not rise above the higher worldly realms. Once you sustain the practice of turning within and not looking outward as explained, don't desire or cling to the experiences of bliss, but know your own nature without fixating. Then you should see the genuine wisdom to be realized.

## Straying to the Four Formless Spheres of Perception through Mind-Constructed Concepts

It is said that since all phenomena have no color, shape, center, perimeter, and so forth, they are similar to space. After analyzing all phenomena through intelligence in terms of being like space, if we hold that as being perfection and become attached, we stray to the perception sphere of infinite space. In this regard the Bhagavan said:

> *Kye!* Sons of the victorious ones! These three worlds are merely mind.

That said, we reflect on it as follows. Consider that all phenomena are merely consciousness or mind; if we reify it and are attached, we will be reborn in the perception sphere of infinite consciousness. If we think that nothing exists and are attached to that, we will be reborn in the perception sphere of nothing whatsoever. If, by thinking that nothing exists or is nonexistent, we reify it, we will be reborn in the perception sphere of neither perception or nonperception.

Hence, all phenomena are viewed as space, held as merely mind, considered to be nothing whatsoever, and regarded as neither existent nor nonexistent, barely free from these two extremes. However, these are still just intellectual understandings and are of no benefit at all, so don't have that intention. Instead, exert yourself from the outset in undistracted mindfulness of unfabricated mind, and then see the nature of mind. Later, you should reach the conclusive certainty that the single absolute sphere of all phenomena is awareness.

As to the supplementary explanations in this connection, it is said that having generally taken hold of the ground of nondistraction of mind itself, we conclude that whatever arises is its radiance or manifestation. Toward all that, we need precisely a flow that is free from evaluation, blocking, or acquiring and that brings us to the recognition of their nature. The eminent teachers remain in this mind itself, the originally pure essence. They are beyond the field of all constructs and conceptual meditations, and in the presence of the wisdom of great bliss, anything that takes place is the display of perfect wisdom, apart from which it does not occur, abide, or exist anywhere else. Nevertheless, as Lord Yangonpa scolded:

> Being densely obscured by extremely intense samsaric habitual patterns, we may evidently see it but fail to recognize it. Even though it is within ourselves, we are still undecided; it is innate yet we haven't seen its face. We have become blind like a statue.

That is true. We are indeed wandering in delusion, reverie, and fantasy. Then at the very moment we somehow contrive that we are sustaining the essence of mind, we are also conceptually fabricating the essence of mind. We like it when mind stays still and dislike it when it doesn't, thus incurring a lot of adoption and rejection in these and other ways. This is not the way to overcome present misunderstandings. The masters of the past used the analogy of a bird flying in the sky: no matter in which direction the bird flies, it never goes beyond the sky. In fact, no matter what arises in one's own mind—the originally perfect great dharmakaya—its nature is dharmakaya. However it changes, its essence is dharmakaya. If it stays still, it is the original face of dharmakaya. If it doesn't stay but projects, it is the radiance of dharmakaya. And the whole of phenomena is the light of dharmakaya. In brief, they say that no matter what you think or what arises, its nature is the perfect dharmakaya. It does not exist, is not born, does not dwell, and does not cease anywhere else apart from mahamudra.

Therefore, since that is the way the ground abides, right now when our mind stays still it is all right, when it moves it is all right, when it is cognizant it is all right, when it is lucid it is all right, when it is mindful it is all right, when it is well it is all right. Nothing is beyond the display of the mind; so by understanding it in that way, the style of sustaining is such that whether the basic nature of your mind appears clearly or not, blissful or not, rest right in that. Avoid desiring to dwell in bliss and clarity; instead loosen your mind and rest effortlessly. Don't hope to rest comfortably in empty clarity. Barely undistracted from the natural face of the mind, rest entrusting the very heart of meditation to precisely this point. In an open and free bare nondistraction, identify any thought that arises and rest on it. In short, no matter what takes place, completely avoid fixating, blocking, acquiring, or contaminating with alterations. Whatever it may be, having decided that all has the same nondual nature, relax and rest on anything that takes place. By doing so, no obstacles or deviations whatsoever will occur. As Lord Gampopa said:

> Generally all strayings are deviations through attachment or fixation, so get rid of all attachments and fixations, and rest relaxed in the absence of these two. Rest relaxed in nonaction, in the absence of adopting and rejecting. To rest like that without modifications is what is conventionally called "meditation."

Also as is said in the *Illuminating Lamp Tantra*:

> If one rests in the state of bare equanimity without modifying,
> That is what is commonly said to be "meditation."

Besides, one approaches bliss, clarity, and nonthought convinced that they are unoriginated. If one is undecided about their being unoriginated, that is called "unascertained phenomena." This was explained before. In general, the explanations about straying to the three spheres, the four concentrations, and the four spheres of perception indicate that the deviation is based on just a slight fixation. Straying to the shravakas and pratyeka buddhas is to deviate to the discerned emptiness. There is no straying in resting in the essence without fixation. Lord Gotsangpa said:

> If we are to condense the practice, since in the innate, which is ineffable and beyond thought, there is no deviation, while meditating don't reify and don't grasp at the void, but rest in nonaction. If pleasant, let it be so. If unpleasant, let it be so. If lucid, let it be so. If unclear, let it be so. By resting without attachment, free from blocking and acquiring, no deviation will happen. Should it occur, I will take the blame!
>
> You may wonder, "Well then, to be certain about nonorigination alone is all right, so why would there be any need for the experiences of bliss, clarity, and nonthought?" That also is not entirely so. Although Lord Gampopa said that, in the absence of bliss, clarity, and nonthought, it is definitely correct to just rest in the unoriginated nature of mind, guru Milarepa stated, "That is true, but not quite so. There is a trunk, but empty of fruit. These are qualities if they are nonconceptual."[29]

The great Jowo brought up this point as follows:

> The yogin who hasn't seen that he is not habituated to
> renouncing [the god realms]
> Is like a bee sucking from a sky-flower.[30]

So he mentions that both experience and realization are necessary. Then, how is this so? What is called "the view connected with realization" means not to leave the limitlessness or simplicity of the essence of mind, the natural state, at a mere conceptual understanding or some mental fabrication. Instead, by looking with intelligence, one will evidently realize that mind does not possess any nature whatsoever, and transcends words, thoughts, knowledge, and description. What is called "meditation connected with experience" means not to leave the true meaning thus realized as intellectual understanding, but instead to experience it lucidly in awareness. It is taught that this is the experience that is needed. Also, as Lord Gampopa said:

> At the beginning, while you are learning, you should train in a vivid lucid awareness. Furthermore, train cognizance not to be distracted. And moreover, never be distracted from the essence of awareness. Once you have become accustomed to it, conviction is born.

And:

> Vivid lucid awareness is a meditative experience. Not wandering from it is resting. Looking with intelligence to see that it does not possess any nature whatsoever is realization.

To call such an experience "the self-experience of realization" or "the self-experience of the essence" is accepted. It is also accepted that the meditation in which experience and realization are inseparable is free from deviations. Lord Gampopa said:

> Then, how is a meditation coupled to experience? It is called the self-experience of the essence, the self-experience of coemergence, the self-experience of mahamudra. What does this apply to? It applies to the essence of one's mind. How is that? It is not existent and does not have even as much as one-hundredth of a sliced hair tip of something identifiable. It is also not nonexistent because there is something that is experienced and realized. Such mind essence, which is an unidentifiable empty lucidity, must arise as an uninterrupted flow of empty lucidity. If it does arise in that way, it would

> also be called a meditation that is coupled to experience, and would also be said to be the coincidence of experience and realization.

If you see and recognize the essence of naturally luminous self-awareness, this is called "the basic nature having no true existence whatsoever." To say that the radiance of the nonconceptual nature is unimpeded means that all self-occurring diversity also abides, arises, and dissolves in the expanse of indivisibility.

## The Four Deviations

This discussion has four points: emptiness deviating to (1) the basic nature, (2) the path, (3) the antidote, and (4) a label. Each of these is divided into two types of deviation, timeless and temporary, and so the four deviations are subdivided into eight. In this regard, what is normally called "timeless deviation" is considered to be the aspect of a mental image straying (to theoretical knowledge), and "temporary deviation" is when the system of practice strays to delusion.

## Emptiness Deviating to the Basic Nature

### *Timeless Deviation to the Nature of Knowables*

The meditation of inseparable phenomena and emptiness is called "emptiness endowed with the supreme aspect." Not knowing how emptiness and interdependence abide in nonduality, you decide that emptiness is a nothingness that has never existed and that is not influenced at all by qualities or defects. Then you underestimate the cause and effect of virtue and vice, or else lapse exclusively into the nature of all things being originally pure, primordially free, and so forth. Bearing such emptiness, the relative level of interdependence is not mastered. In this respect, this is what is known as mahamudra: one's basic nature is unoriginated and, since it is neither existent nor nonexistent, eternal nor nil, true nor false, nor any other such aspects, it has no existence whatsoever. Nonetheless, its unceasing radiance arises as the relative level of all kinds of interdependence, so it is known as emptiness having the core of interdependence and interdependence having the nature of emptiness. Therefore, emptiness does not stray to the nature of knowables. In the *Fundamental Wisdom of the Middle Way* it is said:

> Anything that doesn't arise dependently
> Is a phenomenon that has no existence.
> Therefore anything that is not empty
> Is a phenomenon that has no existence.

And as said in the *Commentary on Bodhichitta*:

> It is taught that the relative plane is emptiness,
> And emptiness alone is the relative plane.

### *Temporary Deviation to the Basic Nature*

Having studied the scriptures considerably, from a conventional point of view, you think that what is called the absolute level, mahamudra, or the natural state of things, is in such and such a way. Even though your guru has given you instructions, you consider that to be your meditation, say it is simply not something to be meditated upon, and leave it at the theoretical level. You may even know how to teach that style to others, yet it hasn't integrated with your mind stream, so it becomes something belonging to others. Not recognizing the natural condition itself in your own awareness, you are not carrying it into your experience, so the mind remains hard and solid. This is called being stubborn and impervious to the Dharma. Even though you lack previous knowledge, you prefer to adopt a conviction right away. It should not be that way; you should develop conviction in the Dharma and sustain the practices, bringing them together into your mind. Tilopa said:

> Conceptual Dharma does not realize what is beyond concept.
> The Dharma of action does not find the meaning of nonaction.

If you want to realize what transcends concept and action,
Delve into awareness and rest in raw mind essence.

## Emptiness Deviating to the Path
### *Timeless Deviation to the Path*

Wishing to realize all the paths through emptiness alone, you do not take into account the aspect of skillful means. In emptiness, path and fruition are not two. In that respect, you think that by meditating now on emptiness and taking that as the path, in the future you will attain the fruition of buddhahood endowed with the three kayas and the five wisdoms, and also that from your meditating on emptiness you will attain the fruit of the ten bhumis, the five paths, the four yogas, and so forth. Then emptiness deviates to the path. You must abandon that.

In truth, if you realize your mind, that itself is dharmakaya. Since all phenomena are from the beginning the spontaneous presence of the four kayas and the five wisdoms, you should not look for buddhahood as something new, and instead remain in the continuity of great equality. The Great Brahmin said:

Since bhumis, paths, and all buddhas are of one taste,
This innate wisdom . . . let the mind ask the mind.

Also:

The unattainable fruition abides primordially within yourself.
There is no need to fasten it through antidotes of hope and fear.

Lord Gampopa said:

This empty lucidity, the essence of my own awareness,
At last I know it to be the dharmakaya!
This perfect beginningless mind,
At last I know it to be the fruition!

> *Ema!* The expanse of this mind jewel,
> At the time of the cause it is actually the result!

### *Temporary Deviation to the Path*

You may manage to sustain the truth of the natural state as it is, yet you are not sure that you are free of grasping or that you have carefree trust. Having expectations such as, "Isn't there something else? Is there something higher?" you are not satisfied with the ordinary cognizance and look for something else. Or alternatively, you apply patches such as, "The natural state of mind is something quite blissful or lucid," and accordingly settle in meditation. In that case, you would be temporarily deviating to the path. Don't proceed in that way. Cutting off the production of desired alterations, you must avoid affixing conceptual meditative patches to the innate natural state without lapsing into wandering from it. Lord Gampopa said:

> As long as there is concept, there is the seed of concretizing attributes.
> Not grasping at anything at all, arising and liberation coincide.

And:

> Don't grasp at anything at all. No matter what manifests,
> Don't pollute your mind stream with the stains of elaborations.

## Emptiness Deviating to the Antidote

### *Timeless Deviation to the Antidote*

In the meditation, undesirable and antidote are inseparable, and due to being aware of your own essence, the innate nature of the afflictions that are to be abandoned abides as emptiness, their antidote. By being aware of its natural face, the very undesirable affliction arises as wisdom, the antidote. Not understanding this to be so, when negative thoughts of the three poisons and the like are born, they are seen as something impure, and the life force of liberation is snatched. Thinking that you must defeat them through emptiness, you conceptually examine the afflictions as emptiness and meditate on their nonexistence. In addition, by practicing the meditation taught by your teacher, you may have had a slight realization of emptiness, and taking that as an antidote you think that by rejecting afflictions and thoughts you are attaining ultimate buddhahood. Then, you meditate in nonthought as the antidote to thoughts, and so forth, in which case emptiness has deviated as an antidote. So don't meditate deliberately rejecting afflictions and thoughts. Without clinging dualistically to the harm, that which harms, the object being harmed, and so forth, with undistracted nonmodification you should sustain your nature and whatever arises as nondual. In the *Two Segments* it is said:

> Embodied perfect wisdom
> And conceptual samsara
> Haven't the slightest difference.

And:

> Samsara, anger, and so forth,
> These phenomena are nirvana.

Maitripa said:

> Afflictions are the great primordial wisdom . . .

### *Temporary Deviation to the Antidote*

Without knowing how to rely on perfect mindfulness that recognizes the nature of all that appears, be it thoughts, situations, or phenomena, you meditate on emptiness as the antidote to thoughts, destroying them or, as it were, drawing them in with a hook. When meditating on emptiness as the antidote to thoughts, it is a temporary deviation to need to pull in emptiness and settle it on the thought. As to this, you should look at the undesirables themselves and look effortlessly at anything that arises. As said by Maitripa:

> In nonorigination, the adventitious thought
> And emptiness itself, the essence of space,
> From the beginning these two have not been separate.

## Emptiness Deviating to a Label

### *Timeless Deviation to a Label*

Not being aware in meditation of the inseparability of method and knowledge, conceptual and nonconceptual, and so forth (all these points dwelling inseparably in the very nature of all phenomena), you have been accomplishing physical and verbal compounded merit. You now think that through profound unconditioned meditation on emptiness, you enter the expanse of the perfectly pure three spheres.[31] You reify the characteristics of all positive qualities and are attached to them. Taking them as an antidote, you analyze with concepts from scriptures, reasoning, and so forth; you think that things don't exist, and consequently you train in emptiness. This is a limited emptiness. If the perfect three spheres were embraced by wisdom, to establish the lack of true nature would be acceptable. But first you have a reference that things possess defining attributes, and then you label them as empty and lacking true nature or label phenomena as being empty. Basing your meditation on that, practices such as the generation stage would also be labeled as empty, and you would think that they have become empty. In that case, in all your meditations emptiness has strayed to a label. The method for correcting this is not to persist in annulling these phenomena. Don't block perceptions. At the very moment of manifestation, phenomena appear as emptiness. Therefore, you should know that phenomena and emptiness are inseparable, devoid of true nature, and indivisible. The Great Brahmin said:

> This phenomenon established by concept is empty by itself.
> Since it has no support, it is devoid of all analyses.

> If you know its nature to be intrinsically free suchness,
> Nothing is there to be seen, heard, nor any such perception. It is free from having a nature.

Shawaripa said:

> All composite actions are primordially the dharmadhatu.

Maitripa said:

> For someone who realizes suchness,
> The whole world and beings are mahamudra,
> The great pervasiveness of dharmakaya.

## *Temporary Deviation to a Label*

When sustaining the meditation, all becomes a mess and you cease to be in control. At first you have a good understanding, but later no more than a vague idea lingers. Then, you look back meditatively in your mind and think that your meditation is nonreferential—it is meditation or it is nonthought—thus assigning different labels. You are stubbornly just labeling. As soon as awareness is becoming dispersed, notice it and avoid following that course. Don't stray in that way. Don't affix any patches of conceptual meditation onto anything that arises, and recognizing with undistracted mindfulness, sustain the recognized essence without forgetting. As the masters of the past said:

> In the absence of even an atom of meditation,
> Sustain without a moment of distraction.

Without recognizing meditation and postmeditation to be of one taste, and with ensuing cognizance not arising as the path, previously your mind wandered and you didn't do any practice. Once in a while you thought, "Oh I must meditate," and you somehow cut the continuity of thoughts through the meditation. This was lapsing into the labeling of a small mind. At all times, during all four activities, rely on an uninterrupted flow of undistracted mindfulness, and if you forget, train to restore the continuity of the intention to meditate. Don't differentiate between meditating and not meditating; make use of both and carry on in that way. As the Great Brahmin said:

> Seeing, hearing, thinking, touching,
> Eating, meditating, walking, moving, staying,
> Talking, conversing, and replying,
> If you recognize these to be your mind, none will generate karma.

Of all these deviations, the timeless straying as to the nature of knowables is an extreme fault and a great wrong belief. Saraha said:

> To fixate on nonexistence is even more stupid than that . . .

The result of this impervious nihilistic view is the miserable realms. Nagarjuna said:

> The nihilist will go to a miserable realm.

And Gampopa said:

> The void of the nature of knowables
> Is free of attachment but lacks the realization of the true meaning.

As mentioned earlier, one becomes an impervious practitioner. As the saying goes, "Buddha's compassion toward the insensitive practitioner is ineffective." Since that is a great loss, it is important for us not to deviate toward that. The other three deviations are not wrong beliefs, but they are not the actual absolute level of the natural state, so don't stray there. It is important that you sustain the self-occurring awareness itself without contaminating it with anything conceptual. However, the emptiness of the four deviations, which are conceptual meditations, is not something inappropriate at all times. As said, "In fact, to beginners all phenomena are by nature empty and quiescent," which is a concept. If beginners don't practice a conceptualized meditation, it is said that they will be afraid of emptiness, so they will not enter it. Therefore, through the knowledge of scriptural reference and reason, and so forth, there is no conflict to be led skillfully and meditated upon. Likewise, it is admissible to apply meditation as an antidote to karma and afflictions, to use that as the path, and to meditate having sealed all elaborations with the label of simplicity. Gradually you would start to become familiarized, but nevertheless it means that you would be rejecting. Therefore, the meditation object of a beginner and that of someone of the highest capacities are not comparable at the beginning. For instance, it is said that food for a youth is unfit for a baby. In short, it is important to practice according to the level of the individual's mind. Finally, without slipping into these four deviations, if you actualize unequivocally the view of the natural state, this will be the highest enhancement of the practice.

## Removing Common Obstacles

There are many obstacles. The obstacle to the accumulation of merit is wrong beliefs, and to deal with that, train in an unbiased pure perception without underestimating the subtlety of interdependence. Since doubt is the obstacle to the practice of the pith instructions and the realization of siddhis, develop conviction. As having many options regarding what to accept and reject is the obstacle to a swift dawning of sublime qualities, focus on whatever conviction you may have and don't harbor many hopes and fears. Since the obstacle to the quick purification of the obscurations is to remain inactive and indifferent, apply yourself to the generation of merit and the profound path of means. The obstacle to completing the generation of wisdom is fixation on dualistic subject and object, so stick to the fundamental texts on the illusory nature and the freedom of extremes of all phenomena. The obstacle to benefiting others is self-centered cherishing; therefore abandon cherishing yourself, and instead train in impartial compassion and make vast altruistic aspirations. In general, the source of removing obstacles is up to us, so keep this in mind. With this I have explained a few ways to remove obstacles.

## General Discussion about Different Kinds of Mistakes

There are many levels of deviations apart from those related to experience and thinking that have been mentioned. In the *Mound of Gemstones* it is said:

> If you think that the conceptual view
> Is the ultimate, you are mistaken.
> If you think that the experiences of bliss, clarity, and nonthought
> Are the dharmakaya, you are mistaken.
> If you think that in primordial wisdom, which is self-abiding and not intentionally settled,
> There is distraction, you are mistaken.
> If you think that a contrived disdainful conduct
> Destroys delusion, you are mistaken.
> If you think that a desire-free, not-assessed action
> Is a moral downfall, you are mistaken.
> If you think that compassion, the conduct of skillful means,
> Is something low, you are mistaken.
> If, lacking realization, you think that outrageous actions
> Are the ultimate, you are mistaken.
> If you think that to benefit others with vested interest
> Is bodhichitta, you are mistaken.
> If we were to classify them, mistakes would be inconceivable.
> If we summarized them, they would boil down to dualistic reification.
> If you realized the lack of identity in reified things
> And became free from all reification,
> Even the term "mistake" would not exist.

The meaning of all these has been clearly presented in this citation, in which it says that the root of mistakes is dualistic reification.

Let us discuss this point a little. In the *Way of the Bodhisattva* it is said:

> Whatever harm there is in all the worlds,
> As well as all fear and suffering that exist,
> All these arise from ego-fixation.
> What is the use for me of this great demon!

As said, the fixation of clinging to self and others is the root of samsara, so unless this ego-fixation subsides, fixation will consequently develop over and over again, whereby one is not free from samsaric existence and circles around like a wheel. In this regard, some people who wish to be free do not identify ego-fixation as being the root of karma and afflictions and do not know how to eliminate it. With the wish to eliminate suffering, which is the fruition of karma and afflictions, they abandon negative deeds and accomplish conditioned virtuous actions such as learning and reflection. But if intention and action go wrong, there is no way to know how this will turn out. Some meditators say one must meditate on egolessness as the means to actually subdue ego-fixation, but after stopping fixation on existence, they develop a strong conviction that clings to nonexistence. This results in an even stronger fixation that plunges them into the nihilistic view. Also, to some people who want to have good meditation it happens that, on having the experience of meditation, attachment ensues, so instead of going straight they deviate from the path; they wander off to the four mistakes, the three strayings, and so forth. In other words, because they cling to the meditative state, they create the cause for mistakes and deviations, and by clinging to ensuing cognizance, karma is accumulated. This becomes the cause for going around in samsara over and over again.

Therefore, all faults arise from attachment entering the mind, so it is important not to indulge in attachment. As said by the Great Brahmin:

> If the thought "This is beautiful"
> Touches your heart and you cherish it,
> All it will ever cause is suffering.
> Pain inflicted by a simple sesame husk is still pain.

And:

> While those who fixate on substantiality are like cows,
> Those who fixate on insubstantiality are even more stupid.

And:

> No matter what you are attached to, give that up as well!

Because of this, it has been taught that the supreme path for yogins is to rest without holding on to anything that arises, such as visionary meditative experiences (with or without characteristics), or phenomena as they appear based on ordinary habitual patterns. Lord Gampopa said:

> There is no higher path than this supreme path
> Wherein no matter what occurs, there is no grasping at all.

If you become accustomed to sustaining the continuity of nonfixation, karmic perceptions and habitual patterns will be purified, and the birth and liberation of all thoughts will be simultaneous. At that time, your mind stream will cease to be contaminated by the stains of elaborations, whatever appears becomes the display of dharmakaya, and many other sublime qualities such as these have been said to occur. Lord Gampopa said:

> All kinds of phenomena solidified by habitual patterns,
> By being accustomed to nonfixation, without rejecting them, they are naturally pure.
> Everything grasped by the conceptual mind is the seed of concretizing attributes.
> Not grasping at anything at all, birth and liberation happen simultaneously.

And:

> Without conceptually fixating at all on anything that appears,
> The stains of elaborations cease to contaminate the mind stream.

And:

> If you are not polluted by the stains of dualistic clinging for a moment,
> Every single thing is the dharmakaya itself.

And:

> If there is no evaluation, the birth and liberation of thoughts are simultaneous.
> If there is no ambition, everything is the same.
> If you realize it like that, there is no interruption to meditation.
> Since there is neither birth nor death, this is the king *phowa* transference.
> Since there are no concretizing characteristics, luminosity is uninterrupted.

If fixation subsides, one gains liberation. If internal fixation on "I" and external fixation on "mine" come to an end, the perpetuating aggregates no longer transmigrate. When that happens, rebirth is finished, whereby karma and afflictions are exhausted and liberation is gained. As said in the *Fundamental Wisdom of the Middle Way:*

> Upon purifying inner and outer,
> If both I and mine come to an end,
> The aggregates cease.
> Because they wear out, rebirth ends.
> When karma and afflictions end, there is freedom.

Thus, nonfixation, nonattachment, no reference point, no concretizing attributes, no aim, no stopping and acquiring, no adoption and rejection, no hope and fear, no ambition, and so forth, all have the same key point. Therefore, gain an accurate certainty in your mind about the manner of all these. At the time of each training such as the four yogas, based on your practice and in a state of bare nondistraction, know that not to fixate is very important at all times.

# 6. Enhancement

D. Enhancement in the Manner of Developing the Potential
   1. General Enhancement
   2. Distinct Enhancement

## Enhancement in the Manner of Developing the Potential

This explanation has six parts: (1) general enhancement, (2) distinct enhancement, (3) conclusiveness about nonorigination and transparency, (4) enhancement of the realized essence in meditation, and (5) development of the potential of unceasing appearances.

## General Enhancement

If you are attached to the sensual objects of this life, meditate on the preliminary practice of impermanence. If conviction in cause and effect diminishes, reflect on the negative consequences of samsara. If compassion toward beings weakens, meditate on altruistic love, compassion, and bodhichitta. If you are attached to the ordinary body, you need to meditate on the yidam deity. As to the enhancement for all these, don't forget your main authentic teacher, whoever they may be, and at all times and in every situation practice guru yoga. From the standpoint of the great devotion that perceives them as Buddha in person, have complete trust in this life, the next one, and all future lives. Always exert yourself in supplicating without breaks in practice. Think of nothing else apart from your teacher, do nothing else apart from devotion, and say nothing else apart from supplications. This is important. Tilopa said:

> The sole teaching of all enhancements
> Is the guru, O yogin.

Naropa said:

> In everything, guru yoga is auspicious.

Furthermore, rely on perfect mindfulness as the antidote to fixation on concretizing characteristics. For sickness and negative influences, practice the secret conduct of using these as the path. Also, in accordance with the masters of the past, enhance skillful means through knowledge and knowledge through skillful means, emptiness through compassion and compassion through emptiness, bliss through emptiness and emptiness through bliss. In other words, referring to practitioners of standard intelligence, they said that yogins who fall into the limitations of method uphold as supreme a practice possessing characteristics and desire to attain fruition through them. If they do not realize the natural state of reality, they do not transcend the root of samsara, so they fall into the extremes of eternalism and samsara. They must focus on knowledge and emptiness. Yogins who fall into the extreme of knowledge are delighted with bliss and the luminosity of their minds, and underestimate the aspect of method and interdependence. Since they will fall into the level of nihilism and quiescent nirvana, they must focus on skillful means and interdependence. To yogins who practice indivisible unity, from the ground of being the expression of emptiness arises as interdependence, which in turn is an unceasing illusion free from extremes. Therefore, these are somehow never separate, and the path is the practice of method and knowledge indivisibly united.

For beginners, there is an emphasis on the practices of method. Once they are introduced to all methods and phenomena being illusory and lacking identity, and emptiness being free from extremes, they become aware of the profound nature of reality. Until they attain stability in that, they focus on knowledge without disregarding the importance of the interdependence of method and knowledge. Attaining stability in the natural state and practicing method and knowledge inseparably as one taste, they constantly learn about the key point of the interrelationship between method and knowledge. Through this, the fruition is spontaneously perfected, this being the great significance of interdependence. Therefore, profound emptiness and interdependent mahamudra must be practiced inseparably. This is why it is taught that all biased grasping on to view, meditation, and conduct as separate and individual must be abandoned.

"Enhancing skillful means through knowledge" means as follows. At first you may have a glimmer of the recognition of mind essence, but you are distracted by practice with characteristics. If you do not progress in meditation, this is a sign that you are grasping at the characteristics of things and you are only practicing method. So be free from all desire-based conceptual characteristics and know that the method itself is devoid of true nature. By exerting yourself in the truth of the natural state, enhancement will happen.

What is meant by "enhancing knowledge through skillful means" is that if you sustain the wisdom that knows emptiness for a long time but make no progress, this is a sign that you have strayed one-sidedly to the empty aspect. Therefore, persevere in interdependence, and by extending your knowledge about it, enhancement will take place.

If the nature of mind abides well but there is no progress, this is a sign that you have lapsed one-sidedly into stillness, so rely on the undistracted mindfulness of meditative composure.

To "enhance bliss through emptiness" refers to the case in which there is no enhancement of bliss, which indicates that you are attached to it. So meditate on both wind-energy and mind, and bring forth the radiance of lucidity, thus developing knowledge of the natural state.

To "enhance emptiness through bliss" refers to when there is no progress in emptiness; you are attached to solely the experience of voidness. So practice a yoga of bliss such as tummo meditation and arouse the strength of compassion toward all beings who lack the realization of emptiness.

Furthermore, when good experiences involving concepts of altruistic love, compassion, renunciation, and devotion arise, if you are attached to and follow them, a fault will come about, so make the essence of emptiness prevail. In particular, it is said that until the roots of faults are dug out, the enhancement of sublime qualities will be difficult. Therefore, subdue the head of ego and don't be carried away by the negative concepts of the five poisons; instead, you must subjugate them and take them as the path.

In brief, until you have captured the stronghold of emptiness, don't feel satisfied with meditation, don't be lazy, and don't even for an instant take into account the meaningless experiences of this life. You should concentrate on what lifetime you still have and extend the presence of the natural condition, regardless of happiness or suffering. We all want to eat the fruit without having cultivated it. Similarly, without practicing, we intend to be a good, realized yogin, but that is hard for the mind to cope with. Therefore, don't act in that way. Don't be carried away by the experience of this life, the troublemaker. Place your residence in an isolated area, rely for sustenance on immediate sufficient food, bear hardships sitting on your cushion while keeping the awareness of death present in your heart, consider properly having no wants, establish a sense of urgency in your being, uphold the ground of devotion to your teacher, earnestly sustain the practice of supplications and emptiness, without attachment let experience be, without desire let go of pleasure and pain, and sustain the nature of your mind. In other words, take your time, don't be in a hurry, and make this the main system. Through this, realization will gradually dawn, the potential will be developed, and stability will be gained. Whether or not we succeed, this is the way. If you make mistakes, enhancement will not come about in this life, the next one, and all lives to come, so avoid erring and instead exert yourself.

The masters of the past have said that renunciation is the feet of meditation, devotion is the head of meditation, and mindfulness is the heart of meditation, so it is very important to consolidate these three.

As to renunciation being the feet of meditation, we, Dharma practitioners, should not spend this petty, hollow human life wandering about. After properly reflecting on the excellent Dharma key points of the cause and effect of karma, impermanence and death, and the consequences of samsara, we should decisively cut samsaric ties. Then we must completely set our thoughts and actions toward the perfect sublime Dharma. What is the sublime pure Dharma? If you practice without having any attraction to such things as the eight worldly preoccupations of this life, wealth, possessions, or food, and are unmoved in any way whatsoever by anything unrelated to practice, then that is it. This being the type of practice that we need, it is also relevant to consider this life, the next one, and between these two. If we take into account the samsaric deceptive seductions of this life, when we go tomorrow to a different world, it is certain that it will be worse. Unlike what we now call misfortunes, they will definitely be a million times more intense there. We need not consider just the world of tomorrow as we would be inserting our head in the constant misfortune of endless samsaric lives. After reflecting on this, we will no longer be attracted and attached to the experience of this life, and the great deception of this world will not trick us anymore. You must strive to gain the everlasting well-being of the pure sacred Dharma in all your lives. Tilopa said:

> Alas! On properly comprehending worldly phenomena
> As not being permanent, they are like a dream.
> There is no reality in a dream,
> So develop weariness and abandon worldly activities.
> Having cut off all connections to attraction and aversion to
> samsaric things,
> Practice alone in forests and mountain solitudes.

As to devotion being the head of meditation, we should supplicate our guru with great devotion blooming from the center of our heart. Whether or not meditation dawns in us depends on the blessing of the guru. Therefore, recite supplications uninterruptedly, not paying lip service but with fervent heartfelt longing and devotion from the core of your bones, shedding tears, and with your body bowed down. The blessings of an authentic teacher remove the obstacles to meditation, give birth to meditation where it hasn't yet dawned and enhance the meditation that has already been born, develop the potential that hasn't yet developed, accomplish the precious fruition, and give birth to the sublime qualities that haven't dawned.

In general, the teaching of the precious practice lineage is to take one's mind, mahamudra, as meditation. Here there will be realization only through the supplications of a devoted disciple to an authentic teacher; other than that, it does not occur from being knowledgeable about the things of this life, having scholarly knowledge of the theory of Dharma, strength, wealth, or power. Making huge offerings to the teacher will not bring it about. Once you have established the foundation by means of the devotion that sees the teacher as Buddha in person and have placed your complete trust in them, by having your practice be just to supplicate, realization will happen. Understanding it in this way, in a nutshell, the Dharma is devotion and supplication alone, with constant dedication and not restricted to sessions or sporadic instances. In other words, Barawa Gyaltsen Pal Zangpo said:

> If you don't supplicate to the teacher, even if you make efforts for the sake of the Dharma through action, word, and thought, it will not benefit your mind, like a ceramic vegetable. Therefore, this lineage of the great scholar Naropa's children was liberated solely through devotion. As to others, realization will not happen through eloquence in telling numerous stories; the verbose husk of many explanations; learnedness, righteousness, and importance; the horn of pride type of confidence that thinks, "This is the accomplishment."
>
> It is not the domain of those impervious practitioners familiar with the Dharma like yak herders too familiar with yak. And neither is it the sphere of those who bemoan thinking about hardships and exertions for the sake of the Dharma. Through devotion alone, think that although this

teacher abides as the essence of all the buddhas of the three times, they adopt an ordinary form in order to tame those like myself who have wrong beliefs. Consider that their being a practitioner training in the path is only a show because in fact they are the all-pervading Vajrasattva, and with fierce devotion and yearning, supplicate them with longing from the center of your heart and the core of your bones. Receive the four empowerments over and over again, after which the teacher dissolves into you. This is what gives birth to meditation that hasn't yet occurred, enhances that which has already arisen, calms the mind that hasn't yet become still, completes whatever hasn't been completed, and also liberates thoughts and emotions that aren't yet free. Because of this you should persistently develop devotion.

As to mindfulness being the heart of meditation, whether general learning, reflection, and meditation, or specifically when sustaining meditation, you should meditate remaining in mindful knowing and carefulness. In the sutras it is said:

> If you always rely on mindfulness and vigilance,[32]
> The marks of wrong beliefs will not be able to approach you.

In the *Way of the Bodhisattva* one finds:

> All of you who want to protect your minds
> I beseech you with folded hands:
> Guard mindfulness and vigilant knowing
> Even at the cost of your lives.

Here mindfulness means not to forget a subject one is familiar with. As said in the *Higher Abhidharma*:

> Not to forget an object of one's acquaintance is the function of a mind that is totally undistracted.

Based on it knowing arises. In the *Way of the Bodhisattva* it is said:

> For as long as mindfulness remains at the doorway of the mind
> For the purpose of guarding it,
> Knowing will come.

Anyway, here the main point is to sustain the natural state of the mind and to act in a way that brings enhancement. For that, it is important to rely on mindful knowing that will follow properly what is to be abandoned and adopted. The faults of not having such mindful knowing are, as mentioned in the *Way of the Bodhisattva*:

> By having a mind that lacks vigilance,
> Like a water jug with a side hole,
> Learning, reflection, and meditation
> Will not be settled in memory.
>
> Those who possess learning and faith,
> And engage in numerous diligent exertions,
> Because of the fault of lacking vigilance,
> Will be stained by moral downfall.
>
> Lack of vigilance is like a thief
> Who hides behind a weakened mindfulness.
> Even if one has accumulated merit,
> As if stolen by a thief, down one goes to the lower realms.

In possession of such mindful knowing, carefulness arises. Its nature is such that it utterly guards the mind from afflictive phenomena and makes one accomplish both worldly and transcendent virtues. As said in the *Secret Sutra of the Tathagata*:

> Furthermore, regarding carefulness, it tames one's mind, guards the minds of others, removes attraction to the afflic-

> tions, and introduces one to a mind that is pleased with the Dharma.

Then:

> There is no movement of improper thoughts, or thoughts about negativities and unvirtuous things. This is what is called carefulness.

Therefore, no matter what spiritual practice we are to maintain, from then on it is the heart of the path to sustain the nature of that practice without distraction at all times and in every situation. So what we need is not to be separated from the mindfulness of one's uncontrived awareness. This is because, if we lose mindfulness, we would be losing the very meaning of the practice. Thus, Nagarjuna said:

> Lord, it has been taught exhaustively that mindfulness focused on the body
> Is the common path walked by the sugatas.
> Adhere to this and guard it.
> When mindfulness is impaired, the whole Dharma is destroyed.

And Lord Gampopa said:

> Meditate on the view of nondistraction, the mindfulness king.
> Persevere in it without alterations caused by various conditions.
> Don't look for anything but the flow of undistracted mindfulness.

And Lord Phagmo Drupa said:

> When you don't apply the mindfulness sentinel,
> That will be the time for the four maras to surround you.
> You will be in danger of losing the jewel of wisdom.

Lord Drikungpa said:

> The highway of the buddhas of the three times
> Is constant uninterrupted mindfulness.
> If you don't know undistracted mindfulness,
> There is no use in being careful about body and mind.

Some who aren't very stable on the nature of nonthought should diligently sustain the main practice holding mindfulness itself as its heart. Based on the realized essence, if a mindfulness that doesn't forget appears as if consolidated, at that point, of course you should not deliberately meditate labeling that conceptually as "mindfulness." If you do so, that would be what is called a "meditation patch," and it is a stain. At any rate, nondistraction wherein there is no meditator and meditation object is important. As said in many references, "In the absence of even an atom of meditation, sustain without even a moment of distraction."

As to mindful knowing, the need for its application on each individual occasion and its purposes and classification will be explained later. In our case, as was mentioned before quoting from the sutras and tantras, sometimes mental activity is advised, but many object saying that there is no need of mindfulness and no need of mental activity. However, they were referring to a specific level of capacity of an individual. For instance, a ship is indispensable to cross water, yet one discards it upon reaching the other shore. Similarly, to cleanse the defilements on the path, it is said that conceptual mindfulness is indispensable, but at the end it is also to be purified.[33]

## Distinct Enhancement

There is no way to express all the teachings of the buddhas of the past, so at this point we'll mention a verse in which they all agree:

> For the enhancement of meditation, entrust yourself to devotion.
> For vigilance in meditation, entrust yourself to mindfulness.

For meditation activity, entrust yourself to compassion.
For the way to sustain meditation, entrust yourself to decency.

Let us discuss each line. First, they say that to enhance the meditation we should entrust ourselves to devotion. Having an authentic guru, we start to have devotion in him. If we do a practice that results in experience and realization, this will arouse whatever meditation we haven't managed to arouse initially. Even when it has arisen, if we haven't later stabilized it, this will do so. Although meditation has stabilized, if we don't entrust ourselves to the great expanse of the fruition, this will do it. For all these reasons, we must supplicate one-pointedly to the guru as being the essence of the buddhas. This is the most important point of all. In other words, at all times and in every situation never cut off your devotion to the guru. This devotion should not be nominal or superficial. Arouse a fervent yearning and supplicate from the core of your bones and the center of your heart. To find a fault in the guru, however tiny, hinders the emergence of sublime qualities, so don't regard it as a fault. If you think it is a fault, understand that it is an impure perception of yours. Then recalling his qualities, concentrate on devotion. Primarily, imagine the guru above your head and supplicate. Particularly, supplicate imagining him in your heart. Merge your mind indivisibly with the guru's mind and persevere in sustaining the essence of your spiritual practice. If you do that, enhancements such as devotion reaching its culmination, stability of your spiritual practice, and knowing that your mind and the guru's mind are nondual will come about.

In addition, don't be prejudiced about teachers or biased in your devotion, but cultivate what is called an "all-embracing devotion." Without dividing them into good and bad, meditate on all beings of the six kinds, or the three realms of existence, as being your guru. Consider them as emanations of your guru and practice devotion one-pointedly. Give away your body, wealth, and all the roots of merit of the three times as offerings, as well as a mandala composed of all the offerings of samsara and nirvana. With one-pointed devotion, supplicate correctly. By following this, all the three worlds, which are the guru by nature, dissolve into yourself. Rest your mind without duality and sustain the essence of the practice.

Persevering in this way at all times, the samaya is never to part from the empty essence. Always perceive the universe—countries, mountains, and so forth—as the pure realm of the guru. And for the rest, since they appear wherever there are beings to tame, and it is said that buddhas emanate in forms to train them, perceive the guru as such. Don't hold attachment and aversion toward good and bad. Turn everything into the expanse of purity. Then, whatever beings you see inhabiting the world, such as humans, other male or female beings, and animals from the smallest insect or bee upward, vividly perceive them as the guru and arouse yearning devotion. Don't hold even a hair's breadth of malevolence or contempt toward them, regarding them in terms of good and bad, attachment and aversion. Always meditate on them as the guru, and persevere in devotion. Likewise, when hearing the various sounds these beings make, don't indulge in attachment and aversion, in pleasant and unpleasant. Instead regard them as the display of your guru's voice, the sound of the Dharma. In brief, practice the devotion that experiences sights, sounds, and cognitions as the body, voice, and mind of your guru.

It is said that devotion is such that all thinking is taken as the mind of the guru. However, those who haven't recognized the essence of mind should meditate on that deliberately and conceptually. If the manner of practicing is correctly identified, the emptiness of all that appears is itself the mind of the guru. Apart from the natural flow of that, there is no need for a deliberate manner of practicing. All objects and perceptions are a manifestation of the pure realm of your guru. All beings are in essence your guru. All sounds are the voice of your guru. Meditating on the nature of phenomena in this way, you must generate devotion.

Furthermore, once you are practicing in the manner of seeing the world and beings as pure, it is important not to have attachment or aversion. If close relatives and other kinfolk feel a special love for you, don't become attached but purify your perception at once. Particularly when people such as enemies cause you harm, don't be angry. Above all meditate on this very person as being your guru; with devotion make offerings, supplicate, dissolve them into yourself, and rest in this nonduality. Even if there is a direct evil action, don't react with aggression but rather think that its nature is an emanation of your guru. All evil actions are the blessings of the guru and an admittance to enter the door to empowerment, so be pleased and take all verbal abuse as Dharma instructions. All malicious thoughts are compassionate and loving blessings to yourself, so arouse devotion considering them as such. Taking these as examples and adjusting them accordingly, meditate on all goodness and evil as being the guru and arouse devotion. From the harm caused by the smallest insect upward, consider everything as the display of the body, voice, and mind of the guru who possesses the doorway to blessings. Train like this without the slightest animosity. Constantly have the devotion that reflects the world and beings as the guru, make offerings, and supplicate as explained. If you exert yourself in this way, eventually all the world and beings will appear as the body, voice, and mind of the guru. You will have arrived at the realm of infinite purity and "mastered the great all-encompassing devotion," an excellent place to reach.

In what way is purity infinite? First, regarding the pure world there are many references expressed by the Kagyu masters of the past. However, here the supreme siddha Sherab Drukgye was asked by his disciples to compose a song of realization that included words of defense against negative forces,[34] to which he replied,

> The actual defense is here, in the lineage of the children of Ngawang Zangpo. My body is, without difficulty, a buddha field. Because of that, this is my defense. I don't need to look for a "buddha field" apart from it. My living place itself is precisely a buddha field. Even if I burn in the hot iron ground of the hells, I have the confidence that it would be no different than a buddha field.

As to the mastery of the purity of the world's inhabitants, the Indian

Padampa Sangye was asked by Kunga if he had had the vision of the ocean-like tathagatas, to which he replied, "Whether I see a buddha or an ant, what is the difference between these two?" Kunga asked, "Is it better to have the sight of a tathagata?" And the guru said, "Thinking 'is it better to see?' actually demonstrates that you have not seen." That is the way it goes. With this approach, it is indeed extremely hard to cultivate pure perception of our vajra brothers and sisters. As said, that which possesses all the key points of the Dharma is compassion for all beings. It will not do to feel you are superior while regarding beings as somewhat lower. If you reified this feeling, you would be contradicting all the samayas of the vase empowerment of the vajrayana whereby all beings are to be seen as deities by nature, and you would be at odds with the devotion of infinite purity.

What would be required instead? You need to have pure perception of everything. Mainly considering all beings with love and compassion, you certainly need to practice vast merit imbued with bodhichitta. Yet aside from that, pure perception is also important because by keeping this, you will not be deteriorating the samaya of the vase empowerment and will bring about the guru devotion to infinite purity. So apply yourself to the relevant practices.

As said, for vigilance in meditation entrust yourself to mindfulness. In general, for an ordinary person—from the time of being a beginner, throughout the ten bhumis, and until completion of the path—it is mindfulness that is capable of eliminating all that needs to be abandoned. This has been taught in the common Dharma expositions and by the Buddha himself. Normally, it is also said in specific meditation terminology that mindfulness is needed from the one-pointedness sustained by the beginner up to nonmeditation, where concepts and phenomena come to an end. Yet we should understand that in mindfulness there is not a single level, but rather many successive levels. Otherwise, one might wonder whether the initial mindfulness when one starts the practice of stillness and movement would be exactly the same afterward. The term is the same but it is necessary to distinguish its confusing meanings. Generally, there are a great number of classifications of mindfulness, and according to the four yogas, they are classified as follows.

For beginners and middling practitioners who have training and experience, mindfulness is the indispensable root of the practice. Furthermore, those in whom experience and realization haven't dawned but are still hoped for should always have a one-pointed determination to be mindful, without wavering from it. It is taught that if there is mindfulness, there is meditation, and if there is no determination to be mindful, meditation is destroyed. These are points to be contemplated. Even those in whom shamatha has taken place need mindfulness.

If in the experience of stillness there is no mindfulness that recognizes its identity, that would be vacant shamatha, so no matter how intense the experience of shamatha, it would not pertain to meditation, and it would not become a way to buddhahood. When, in that experience of stillness, there is an experience of clarity and a mindfulness that recognizes its identity, that would belong to meditation and become the path to buddhahood. On the basis of shamatha, mindfulness is also needed for the meditative experiences such as bliss, clarity, and nonthought to arise. In the absence of a mindfulness that recognizes their identity, after savoring the taste of bliss, clarity, and nonthought, if you desire them and become attached, they would not pertain to meditation. This would not become a way to enlightenment even for a moment; it would be a deviation. Toward bliss, clarity, nonthought, and any other experience, neither savor their taste, nor desire them, nor become attached. If there is bliss, it is delightful. If there is clarity, it is lucid. And if resting in nonthought, the mind remains still. The whole point is that whatever experience arises, you are mindful of just that. Recognize it and sustain the recognition of its identity. If you do so, you will not deviate to the three spheres of existence, but instead you will be on the path to buddhahood. Meditation is like a stepping-stone to the main point: the dawn of realization.

Also in the case of an experience that is not so pleasant, in which the mind is extremely dispersed and agitated, mindfulness is needed. When you are not mindful and are dominated by that unpleasantness, the practice has been taken over by an obstacle and fruition has gone far away. So then, know it to be simply a bad experience. Ultimately both pleasant and unpleasant are no more than mind experiences. Be sure about that and don't regard unpleasantness as a fault.

Then if discursive thoughts proliferate, and that proliferation produces discomfort, recognize that itself through mindfulness. If it results in suffering, also recognize that itself. If, no matter what arises, you sustain knowing it as it is in itself, the bad experience will not cause harm. Finally, since it is self-liberated, the obstacle becomes an acquired quality. The same applies to the other defects of meditation: dullness, excitation, and torpor. In those cases again, if mindfulness is absent, you will be carried away by that fault. Instead, don't regard dullness and excitation as faults. In the immediate present, simply consider whether there is clarity or not; and if toward any dullness and excitation you sustain with mindfulness on their specific identity and continue on that, a good quality will arise from these faults. Therefore, mindfulness is also important in the case of faults.

Thus, at the time of one-pointedness, mindfulness is very important. If you know how to sustain good mindfulness, you will avoid obstacles or misunderstandings. Once these arise as qualities, enhancements from each of these will take place. So you must know these differences. Then, supplicating your authentic guru with one-pointed devotion constantly and in every situation, if you sustain the practice of persevering in your mindfulness, eventually your obscurations will be purified, the blessings of your guru will enter your being, and without any other meditation you will become certain about your own mind. Since all thoughts will have merged with mindfulness, what was to be eliminated arises as an antidote. Whether we say basic nature and radiance, mindfulness and thoughts, observer and observed, undesirable and antidote, and so forth, these are different names for one same meaning, and by understanding it as such, you gain certainty in nonduality. Without wavering from the basic nature, nothing that arises will be uncomfortable. All that naturally arises is recognized in its own place and is self-liberated, so your mind becomes open and carefree.

In this way, if you see mind essence but still haven't attained stability, a brief forgetfulness will occur. In that case, mindfulness is to be emphasized. Unless your meditation is within undistracted mindfulness, you will not be able to connect with a consolidated mindfulness. Meditation will remain like the sun in between clouds. So while not meditating there deliberately, rely on undistracted mindfulness. If you develop the strength of undistracted nonmeditation, then the interstices of mindfulness will join, and it will become consolidated. This is also called "effortless mindfulness."

Even though effortless mindfulness has occurred, it is important to continuously maintain the presence of mind essence. Without it, the stain of concept will not disappear, so postmeditation will lapse into ensuing cognizance, and meditation will not progress. In that case, purposely correct mindfulness and then the realized essence will again be brought out nakedly, without veils or covers, after which sustain bare mind essence itself. Train on the natural expressions of the mind—devotional supplications, development of bodhichitta, compassion, and pure perception—and above all train on objects of perception and situations. If you proceed in that way, the stains of dualistic subject and object in meditation will be purified. Postmeditation will not lapse into ensuing cognizance without your noticing it. As to devotional supplications to the guru, and so forth, these will not be carried out in a mere dualistic way, but the guru will arise as your own mind. Other than that, there will be no need of devotional supplications in order to purify the stains in realization. The cultivation of bodhichitta, pure perception, and other qualities will arise not on a mere relative level but as ultimate bodhichitta of indivisible emptiness and compassion, pure perception, and so on. You will be a genuine great meditator, in whom realization inseparably integrates with perceptions, phenomena, and situations. Since it all turns into perfect mindfulness, knowing how to understand and hear in this way, all of us meditators must put it into practice.

In brief, from the antidote of retentive mindfulness up to nonconceptual presence of mind, the leap of mindfulness pertains to the function of mindfulness itself; understanding it in this way you should constantly apply yourself to undistracted nonmeditation. As said many times in the *Sutra Requested by Mati Sambhava*:

> Through mindfulness maras find no opportunity. Through mindfulness the path will not be mistaken. Though the gate-like mindfulness, all unvirtuous mental events in the mind will find no opportunity. This is perfect mindfulness.

Similarly, as said by Trisna Pandita:

> By recognizing that there is nothing to identify,
> One experiences it as emptiness.
> Knowing how to guard it through the mindfulness-watchman
> Prevents the thief of delusion from finding an opportunity.
> By practicing without interruption,
> You will actualize [emptiness] as inseparable.

In the saying "entrusting meditation activity to compassion," there are two parts: planting the seed of altruism at the beginning, and once realization has dawned, compassion surging from the expression of emptiness. First, planting the seed of altruism at the beginning is precisely the cultivation of bodhichitta that has been discussed earlier. At the initial level, from the time that you begin to accomplish virtue, it is out of the question that you would do it for the purpose of your present life, for to wish for happiness and peace only for yourself would be the view of the shravakas. Also, do not proceed thoughtlessly without contemplating the motivation. Rather, while embraced by the mahayana view, the virtuous actions and Dharma practice you do should be preceded by the precious bodhichitta motivation to attain enlightenment without hesitation for the sake of placing all beings—your old mothers—on the level of buddhahood. Then, during the main practice of virtue, don't forget them, and at the conclusion, dedicate all the merit created by these virtuous actions to their benefit. This is how you should apply yourself.

In addition, practice a compassion in which you never for an instant harbor malicious thoughts for anybody, high or low, and do whatever you can to be of help. In any virtuous Dharma activity that you carry out—such as making offerings, practicing generosity, making representations of sublime beings, or reading the scriptures—precede that with an altruistic attitude to help all beings and conclude it with the dedication of merit for their benefit. Following the same pattern, in brief, all conditioned virtuous thoughts, words, and actions should be carried out with an altruistic attitude and the merit dedicated to all beings. If you do that, it will have immeasurable benefit: Indeed not only for the ordinary benefit of cultivating bodhichitta, but particularly since you are planting the seed of altruism, it will be easy for you to attain fruition and, when this happens, your work for the benefit of beings will be unsurpassable and immense. We should reflect on what Siddha Orgyenpa said:

> Whether merely knowing how to recite the *Heart Sutra* or simply when having water and barley flour, from that very moment one should plant the seed of altruism. If the seed is not planted at that time and beings lose prominence and are neglected by you, you would be ruining the auspicious connection of altruism.

These are in brief the beginner's styles of cultivating bodhichitta motivation.

For those of us who have realized the empty nature of mind, various statements have been made by the masters of the past. It has been said that if we have realized genuine emptiness, through the power of such realization, it is impossible not to have compassion for the situation of all beings who wander in samsara, not recognizing that buddha is within themselves. Once this compassion has arisen, it is impossible not to put into practice the correct cultivation of bodhichitta. Then, because of that, it is impossible not to accomplish vast altruistic activity.

However, it is difficult for this to happen to us in that way: Not only is it hard to realize genuine emptiness, but it is also extremely hard for compassion to arise indivisibly from partial emptiness. The previous statement was meant for the mind level of the past masters. Surely the same will happen to those who have the karma and aspirations to accomplish the two purposes. It will not happen to us, but it is not to be left aside; emptiness having the core of compassion is to be trained step by step, and the seed of vast altruism must be planted.

In this respect, there are many general references as to how to proceed. Lord Tsangpa Gyare mainly considered this point in his "Own Tradition of Interdependence," his distinctive teaching. Similarly, many references are found in such works as the six, three, or eighteen pieces of advice and other sources. How could we cover all of these? The following is an extremely succinct explanation. We may see the essence of mind but fail to cultivate compassion and to continuously practice altruism toward beings, which would create the unequivocal interdependent conditions, and so forth. Instead we somehow remain sustaining mind nature alone, as if it were some money or merchandise. If we do that, even though our spiritual practice is based on our true nature, its strength will not surge forth. Above all, in this life we will not be helpful and benefit beings on a large scale. Shravakas and pratyeka buddhas definitely have the right view of emptiness, but because this is not embraced by the cultivation of bodhichitta, they stray. In the shravaka system, the lack of identity of self and phenomena is undoubtedly realized. Yet because they lack compassion and the cultivation of the mind toward enlightenment, they indeed deviate to the lower path.

Once these defects have been identified, this is what you should do. Your spiritual practice should consist of training in compassion toward all beings while remaining in the continuity of the essence and without wavering from it. If it is hard for compassion to arise, reflect on the many methods for arousing it, like considering all beings as having your parent's kindness. Above all, while you cultivate compassion through devotional supplications to your teacher, make aspirations that you may be blessed with the accomplishment of inseparable emptiness and compassion. Before any physical and verbal practice, arouse compassion. Also, during the main body of the practice, don't forget all beings. For instance, when you are supplicating the teacher, imagine that all beings are also supplicating with devotion alongside you, and that the teacher's blessing enters both yourself and them. In this way, no matter what spiritual, physical, verbal, or mental practice you carry out, think that you are doing it together with all beings without making any distinctions even for a moment. After this, dedicate all the roots of merit to their benefit. At all times, never parting from compassion, help them in any way needed, and no matter what Dharma activity you may be doing, precede it with the generation of bodhichitta and end it with the dedication of merit. When you are having an unpleasant experience such as suffering or sickness, think that it is due to your previous karma, and most of all, feel that all unpleasantness, suffering, and sicknesses of all beings in the three spheres are condensed into yourself. Imagine that they all possess temporal and complete perfect happiness. Then, give away to all beings whatever collection of merit you have generated in the three times, and imagine that it ripens in their mind stream and they become established on the level of buddhahood.

This giving and taking meditation (*tonglen*) is not to be carried out only when you are facing adversity, but on any occasion. Taking it as a commitment, sincerely practice the imagined giving and taking two, three, or many more times every day, as explained. Needless to say, never harbor malicious thoughts or harm any being, big or small. Don't even do that as a joke. Don't participate in something that harms others. Don't rejoice at the harm done by others. Free the lives of animals, down to bugs harming each other or falling into water, as soon as you see their peril. Toward such situations as death, feel compassion and make vast prayers of aspiration. Never separate beings from compassion, however large or small. Help them in concrete ways as much as you can. On seeing bugs and animals, right there recite and count *mani* mantras, dharanis, and so forth with compassion and bodhichitta. Activating the compassion of Avalokiteshvara, visualize that they are being delivered and make open-ended aspirations. In case they are unable to feel this, for instance because they are dead, you should visualize that they are delivered, and properly offer confession and make aspirations. If you are unable to continuously cultivate compassion and bodhichitta, or you lack inspiration and so forth, you should feel ashamed of yourself. Every single being has been your father or mother many times and all they have shown you is kindness. Admonish yourself, telling yourself, "A thoughtless and shameless person like you with a coarse attitude and bad karma doesn't know this, and even if you do act so, you are not taking bodhichitta into account, so you are only thinking about your own benefit. Since you don't even know the key to your own benefit, this is not accomplished; you are making yourself a fake lion."[35] The sutras say:

> Fools acquire their own happiness.
> Since they don't obtain it, this is the constant cause of suffering.
> Because the Buddha always persevered in benefiting others,
> He attained nirvana for the sake of all.

Considering this and other citations, another implication in connection with cultivating compassion and bodhichitta is that you should commit to not even entertaining the term "own peace." Then, as before, train yourself in cultivating bodhichitta and compassion. Supplicate your guru with the aspiration that you may perfect the indivisibility of emptiness and compassion, that you may benefit all beings in all your lives, and especially that—after attaining unsurpassable enlightenment—your altruistic activity may be extremely vast. Once you have merged the essence of spiritual practice with situations involving physical and verbal Dharma actions, don't procrastinate, but with great perseverance, focus your actions and words on benefiting all beings, practicing only the meditation of giving and taking. This is the way to train in cultivating bodhichitta and compassion. Then, from time to time, rest composed in the expanse where your mind and beings are not two. If you exert yourself in this way at all times, then eventually through the strength of your guru's blessing and your own virtues, you might come to realize the inseparability of emptiness and compassion. If you realize this compassionate emptiness, that is quite a good result according to your practice. In this life you would be what is known as a "buddy meditator": a disciple who doesn't benefit themselves alone but who benefits others. In all future lives, you will accomplish boundless altruistic activity.

Here there are also misunderstandings and deviations. You may have just realized compassionate emptiness, but until the fetters of self-interest are exhausted and you reach the expanse of indivisible emptiness and compassion, your work will not be truly altruistic. In other words, the tiny compassion that has arisen through cultivation is of no help. Bearing in mind that you must bring benefit to beings, you should know whether the benefit has been significant or indeed taken place. In case you do not know, this would be what is known as the narrow path of compassion arising as enemy. This is one of the five narrow paths that hinder meditation, so don't proceed in this way. The buddhas of the past said, "Secretly making aspirations is unmatched by ordinary altruistic work." Keeping this statement in mind, as has been taught, still develop the potential of compassion, adhere to the foundation of bodhichitta, sustain the realization, and make aspirations. Be sure about this in your mind. This being so, don't make haste with a small mind, but develop its strength without separating from emptiness and compassion.

What is needed is to arrive at the expanse of compassionate emptiness. Having internally actualized your own purpose, if the time comes to benefit others (saying "Now I must help beings!"), you will not need to go to them. Without any effort on your part, all disciples will gather around you. Then the guru, the Three Jewels, the yidams, and dakinis will make predictions. An otherwise small temporal mind would be a deviation. Furthermore, for vast altruistic work, rather than having a merely one-pointed intention, a farther-reaching scope is needed. If you are concerned with whether your work for the benefit of beings in this life is special compared to that of others, that would amount to just personal interest. Until this personal interest has come to an end, you will not accomplish the genuine benefit of beings. To call your self-centered pursuits altruistic activity is like a hungry person trying to find a job. You go searching here and there doing things that oppose the Dharma. That would be pitiful! Like a king in his kingdom who must first build himself up, start by accomplishing your own purpose. Then the time to benefit others will come.

Regarding these points, there is a danger that the words or language may become distorted here and there. Some enlightened beings of the past set out to work for the benefit of others, and similarly nowadays, masters in the form of buddhas come to help beings. They bring a lot of benefit to all those connected to them, which is excellent. In actual fact, buddhas are without self-interest, but due to the bad karma of beings, it is difficult for the buddhas to attract them. Viewing this situation through their compassionate eyes and disregarding physical hardships, the buddhas come and create great meaningful connections with numberless beings. This is immensely superior to others who, without any sense of urgency, remain bent on their own peace and well-being.

The special activity of the sublime buddhas and great bodhisattvas constitutes the field of praise, the object of homage, and the support of offerings. Otherwise, by prematurely working for others without having accomplished your own purpose, you will go out and perform all kinds of activities motivated by self-centered interest. Not only is that meaningless, it will also result in suffering. That is why it is said that this should be abandoned.

Further, if your own purpose hasn't yet been accomplished and the time to benefit others hasn't yet come, you might set out to help beings, motivated not by selfish reasons but to practice virtue and benefit them. In this case, since there is no significant selfish interest and your intention is altruistic, it would be fine; it is one manner of practicing the Dharma. However, if we want to emulate the lives of the past masters of the practice lineage of true meaning, it is not sufficient because, although your capacity to benefit beings may have become vast, the methods to free them haven't yet come about. So don't proceed in that way, but instead apply yourself to your own ripening. Thereafter you will bring immeasurable benefit to beings. Even if you cannot accomplish that in this life, since samsara is unlikely to become empty, it would be alright to carry out your intention in future lives.

In brief, no matter what purpose you may achieve for yourself or others, the root of whether or not this is in accordance with the Dharma path resides in whether the driving force is personal interest. As long as there is selfish interest it is a samsaric tool, but when there is no such vested interest, whatever you do will be in accordance with the Dharma. Therefore, since it is personal interest that drives anything into being samsara or nirvana, it is of the utmost importance that you should never be driven by this motivation. Thus, in a few words, you begin by entrusting the activity of meditation to compassion. From then on, you also cultivate bodhichitta and compassion, and when the time comes, you benefit beings.

To elaborate on this point, if by properly realizing emptiness you have concluded and mastered that everything is its nondual radiance, you don't need to train as explained. In other cases, it is of the greatest importance that devotion, compassion, bodhichitta, pure perception, and so forth are taken as the path. Beginners may experience an intense overwhelming devotion, with tears rolling uncontrollably from their eyes, with body and mind overflowing with love. Although yearning may be so strong in these and other ways, from then on it is important that your spiritual practice continues to be the prevailing of your own nature. If your realized nature is taken over by fervent devotion, that will partially impair the auspicious connection of blessings. So avoid that, and instead, while experiencing fervent devotion, keep present your realized essence. If you bring fervent devotion into your realized essence, that will bring all the masters and sublime beings under your fold, and it will create the great auspicious connection for the strength of blessings to burst forth. This is the way it should be understood. Nevertheless, if fervent devotion arises, do not block it, deeming that you should apply the mentioned remedy to prevent being taken over by it. As said, "Don't hit the swine's nose with a stone."[36]

Here a misunderstanding may arise. If fervent devotion arises, at first cultivate it to that extent. If you are cultivating it more than that, then do so. Thereafter, devotion itself is placed in the recognition of your own nature. That is the key point to be understood. Taking this as an example, if overwhelming compassion or other similar emotions arise when seeing lower beings afflicted by misery, from the beginning don't block the compassion but allow it to grow as much as it can. Once compassion has reached its limit, you should place it within the recognition of your nature. Similarly, when practicing pure perception, without wandering from your mind essence—the actual point—and while not making any modification, all that radiates from mind essence should be perceived with devotion as the guru, and you should be convinced that it is so. This is what is called "making good thoughts arise as the path." If devotion and compassion don't arise as the path but instead you are carried away by them, you will be slightly spoiling the right conditions for altruistic work. Although you will help beings in that way, you will not have control over your altruistic work. Instead, you will need to go out to pursue helping others. If you bring it to your essence, you will not need to go out to help beings; that will automatically occur. The same will happen with pure perception. In fact, when you are driven outward, you will have some pure perception of all others, but it will be hard for it to be truly effortless. If you bring it under your control, it will become effortless. You should understand these key points.

As said in the earlier citation, the manner of sustaining the meditation is to entrust yourself to decency. In his *Public Teaching on the Cycle of Thinking*, Lord Lhatsewa said that if there is no decency underpinning an experience of intense devotion, there is a danger that eventually you may slip into damaging the samaya. When asked what "indecency" meant, he replied that it referred to shameful actions and lack of embarrassment, so it is important for a practitioner of the Dharma to know what shameful actions are. All teachings that haven't yet been completed should be undertaken free from shamelessness. He was then asked what are the causes and circumstances of shamelessness, to which he quoted glorious Phagmo Drupa:

> The cause is desire. Haven't you heard the saying "desire dims shame"? The circumstances are uncertain, though it is mostly provoked by drunkenness. Not showing gratitude for something you know has been done is shameless. To know what was done and to acknowledge it, and not to underestimate small actions, makes a person someone who remains close to the glorious protector.

In general, this applies to all Dharma practitioners. In other words, one practices the Dharma and keeps all vows and samayas. Normally one must keep decorum in front of Dharma siblings, and in particular it is not all right to consider behavior acceptable just because others are not looking. That would be what is known as the deceit of hypocrisy. So you should place your own mind as the inner witness, reflect on yourself, and avoid acting shamefully. Above all, nowadays some of us are somehow more careless in connection to the guru and the Three Jewels than we are with ordinary people. We will no doubt refrain from a non-dharmic action in front of a layperson, but when it comes to the guru and the Three Jewels, some of us don't perceive them as seeing from the expanse of their wisdom eyes. It is shocking that, without giving it a thought, we can act in that way with such a shameful, confused attitude. More powerful than people, greater than beings, more fearsome and numerous than ordinary people, the guru and the Three Jewels clearly see without any veil. Whatever we do they come to know it precisely.

Therefore, if that situation happens to us, we should reaffirm caution in respect to the guru and the Three Jewels—who have wisdom eyes—and avoid acting improperly. In the case of infrequent minor actions, we should feel very bad about them, thinking that the guru and the Three Jewels see and know, and in that mood we should confess and reaffirm our vows. This being so, we dedicated meditators practice first relying on isolated places and then experience and realizations arise. But then we don't go all the way, and instead our minds are completely taken by the eight worldly preoccupations, interested in accomplishing the aims of this life. From that arise obstacles such as those caused by negative factors or deceitful ones created by maras. If we don't identify these obstacles, there will be no end to them. So to be carried away by such events or, even worse, to be entangled by them, will make us feel ashamed before the deities, the gurus, and people. Therefore, don't act in that way. Until you have perfected experiences and realization, or particularly while you keep the commitment to meditate for as long as you live, reflect on the liberating lives of past masters. Set high aspirations and don't aspire to accomplish this aims of the life even for a moment. Stay on an isolated mountain and, once there, don't be fickle-minded for even an instant because if you are, it would mean that you have a weak understanding of the meaning of solitude. Consider being bashful before the guru and the Three Jewels. In this regard, it is said in the teachings on interdependence that to be what is called a river-like yogin, the outer factor is a secluded place, the inner factor is the meditation hut, the innermost factor is the right body posture, and the real factor is not to waver from the natural state even for a moment. This is the way you should be exerting yourself.

If you proceed in this way, the imprint of your practice—your realization—will gradually be enhanced. If not, at first when practicing, the lowest accomplishment is a meditative experience and the highest is a simple dawning of realization. Then, sustaining your essence simply without distraction, some bliss arises, but from then on your practice becomes less precise and you procrastinate. By continuing with feeble diligence, the experience of mind essence will not be enhanced. Not only that, as defilements have not been purified, the experience itself will later become worse. To carelessly desert the meditation that has been cultivated would be a great loss. Lord Gyare said:

> An unguarded meditation
> Is like wealth blown away by the wind,
> Like a lion losing itself for a dog's bitch,
> Or a precious jewel sunk in mire.

And:

> Therefore, cherish being a commander of your meditation.

Lord Lhatsewa said:

> Our old dedicated yogins don't talk much about progress in meditation, so it is as if we had become an old inanimate thing. Unless meditation progresses, old yogins are devoid of heart.

We should do something to avoid receiving such reprimand. Lord Orgyen said:

> All of us meditators counting the years, particularly during each summer, winter, autumn, and spring, should think, "Persevering in this way on the essence of my practice, today I have made this progress."

Similarly, don't squander years and months only to become ever worse. As outwardly years and months pass, inwardly we are confident and satisfied that our meditation progresses. The imprint of having practiced should not make us be ashamed in front of other people, Dharma siblings, the guru, and the Three Jewels.

# 7. Conclusiveness

- 4. Conclusiveness about Nonorigination and Transparency
  - a. The Meaning of the Term "Conclusiveness"
  - b. The Time for Conclusiveness
  - c. Conclusiveness about the Basic Nature
  - d. The Cause of Conclusiveness, Namely Seeing the Nature of Mind
    - i. Seeing the Realized Essence and the Essence of Phenomena
    - ii. Seeing the Essence of Meditator and Object of Meditation
  - e. The Actual Conclusiveness about Nonorigination and Transparency
  - f. Mingling the Cycle of Day and Night through Conclusiveness
  - g. The Purpose of Conclusiveness

## Conclusiveness about Nonorigination and Transparency

This has seven parts: (1) the meaning of the term "conclusiveness"; (2) the time for conclusiveness; (3) conclusiveness about the basic nature; (4) the cause of conclusiveness, namely seeing the nature of mind; (5) the actual conclusiveness about nonorigination and transparency; (6) mingling the cycle of day and night through conclusiveness; and (7) the purpose of conclusiveness.

## The Meaning of the Term "Conclusiveness"

Conclusiveness stands for not having any more doubts and reaching conviction, or having cut off conceptual elaborations about one's mind such as birth, abiding, and cessation, and the three divisions of time. It has the meaning of deliverance into the expanse of nonorigination and nonconceptual mind. As Tilopa said:

> Drop all mental activity; look at the Dharma of certainty.

The Great Brahmin said:

> Shown by the glorious guru, I today realized
> The never-born natural state.

Shawaripa said:

> Thus, at all times and in every situation,
> The innate state free of extremes is devoid of mental activity.

Maitripa said:

> All phenomena are equal, like space.
> This is what is called "mahamudra."

Many quotations such as these point to this meaning. Also, in this practice lineage, the same understanding is expressed in such texts as the incomparable Takpo Rinpoche's *Revealing the Hidden Characteristic of Mind.* The sequences of conclusiveness were taught later by teachers of the practice lineage through different synonyms.

## The Time for Conclusiveness[37]

Once practitioners have purified dense experiences of bliss, clarity, and nonthought, and brought out the bright lucidity of awareness, they reach final conclusion when the sky-like meditation of empty lucidity has become an uninterrupted cycle, or when they predominantly go into that experience while being awake. In this case, whenever thought is caught on movement, eventually movement will arise as lucid emptiness and emptiness as movement. When mindfulness catches any phenomenon, it will eventually arise vividly as manifested emptiness. In short, realization and all phenomena—being empty lucidity and empty phenomena—are experienced like an illusion. When conviction and certainty about this are born, there is final conclusion.

If this conclusion is premature, without having a firm footing on the experience of your own awareness coupled with conviction, but depending simply on theoretical understanding, the Dharma will make you impervious, and this will lead to empty babbling about high states. Your mind confused by it, you will also fall prey to delusion and self-importance, even though others may perceive you as having realization. That would be the case of a stubborn practitioner who knows about the Dharma but, as has been said, is outwardly inflated but inwardly empty, similar to an empty locked house. Unable to be constantly in the actual truth, one would be deluding oneself. If conclusiveness is not known, much later on, in those fortunate ones with the right karmic fruition, their mind and perceptions will eventually arise as the master, and once attachment to experiences is purified by itself, they will gain liberation. However, perhaps there is an increase in clinging to one's experiences due to good thoughts and conviction. In this case, it would be as the saying goes, "The meditator is stuck to the glue of experiences," which would be falling into a deviation. As Lord [Tsangpa] Gyare said:

> Many know how to meditate, few how to destroy it.

Although this pith instruction on conclusiveness is a method for those who have the karmic destiny of sudden liberation, it will also enhance the practice of the rest throughout the four yogas, from lower to higher. As it is a special instruction to make spiritual practice progress, it is said that even those who have a hazy realization of the genuine state and who need to practice meditation for many years to attain the actual truth will increase their sublime qualities remarkably in just a few days.

## Conclusiveness about the Basic Nature

As discussed earlier, when we determined the essence of the nature of mind, we saw that the fundamental natural state of all phenomena is nonorigination itself. Yet, if we are to further discuss this concisely, all phenomena of samsara and quiescence are nothing but perceptions of one's own mind. The essence, nature, or way of being of one's mind is unoriginated; in its very essence, mind is neither substantial nor insubstantial, existent nor nonexistent, manifesting nor empty, and so forth. It is free from every characteristic such as subject and object. It is unmoved by change or transition, coming or going, and the like. Since it never changes within the three times, it is an unbroken flow. Like space, nothing whatsoever taints or changes it. The Archer [Saraha] said:

> The innate nature itself
> Is said to be neither substantial nor insubstantial.
> This archer is always crying this aloud!

Virupa said:

> Mind essence is the mahamudra, nameless, and free from elaborations.
> It is like the nature of space, primordially empty.
> It is inherently unborn and free from characteristics.
> Like space, it pervades everything and is without transition or change.
> Ever empty, it has never had an intrinsic identity.

Furthermore, it is not that the basic nature of mind has adventitiously become like this; it has been this way since primordial time and does not change. For instance, conventionally it may be said about space that it is or is not empty, and so forth, but nobody can say that the nature of space is this or that. As Tilopa said:

> Even if we conventionally refer to space as being empty,
> We cannot say that space is like this.
> Likewise, even though we say the mind is luminous,
> There is no basis for labeling it as something that exists.
> Thus, the nature of mind has been like space from the very beginning.

Therefore, since mind and all phenomena arising from it have been devoid of true nature from the timeless beginning, they are unoriginated, unabiding, and unceasing. Mindfulness, distraction, or anything else is incapable of bringing about attainment or loss, transition or change. They are the great transparency of nonorigination. Shawaripa said:

> If mind is existent, all phenomena are perceived as existent.
> When there is no mind, who is there to know a phenomenon?
> When searching for mind and perceptions appear as phenomena,
> They are not found; even the seeker exists nowhere.
> Since it does not exist, it is neither born nor ceases in any of the three times.
> It does not change into anything else.
> Its nature is the way of abiding of great bliss.

## The Cause of Conclusiveness: Seeing the Nature of Mind

This has two parts: (1) seeing the realized essence and the essence of phenomena, and (2) seeing the essence of meditator and object of meditation.

## Seeing the Realized Essence and the Essence of Phenomena

In general, this is a path of blessings so it is necessary to cultivate the strength of devotion to the guru. In particular, it is the tradition of the precious lineage of true meaning to deem devotion as the source of progress in meditation. In the *Two Segments* it is said:

> Because this is through the phase of blessing,
> Omniscient wisdom is somewhat like this.[38]

And:

> It isn't something described by someone else; it is innate.
> It is nowhere to be found.
> It is something known from the timely method shown by the guru
> And one's own merit.

Maitreya said:

> The absolute level of all that self-arises
> Is only realized through faith.

As taught in the various sutras, tantras, and shastras so numerously that it cannot be expressed in words, it depends only on the function of devotion and blessings. At this point, once you have cultivated devotion toward the guru dharmakaya by exerting yourself in whatever practice and especially in guru yoga, you should start with a fervent supplication to realize the world and beings as dharmakaya. Through this, sustaining one-pointedly the technique for resting composed in the essence as explained before, awareness will be separated from the impurities dross. Then, without wavering from awareness, and not placing this as the target of your meditation, rest in the continuity of immaculate carefree mind. Subtle, joyful, or anxious thoughts will not arise excessively; in that case deliberately produce them. While they clearly continue to appear, look at the essence directly without fixation or distraction. Similarly, when subtle or coarse thoughts that give rise to pleasure or pain appear, whether completely evident or else induced deliberately, look over and over again at the essence of these subtle and coarse thoughts to see what the difference is. If doubts are resolved, then look to see if there is a difference between the essence of those thoughts and that of the mind resting still. Likewise, look at happiness, suffering, or the rest of the eight worldly preoccupations, as well as thoughts about the many kinds of afflictions such as desire. Sometimes block thoughts and sometimes increase them. At other times, extend and steer the flow of the realization; having looked at the essence of each of these, resolve all doubts and misunderstandings. Analyze external objects of perception in the same manner: beautiful or ugly forms of various sizes, colors, shapes, and so forth; many different sounds—pleasant or irritating, loud or low, modulating sweet sound waves; a range of body postures; open or closed eyes, looking right or left. Allow these perceptions appearing in different ways to happen, and see whether there is any difference between their essence and mind essence. For a few days, clear doubts and misunderstandings by distinguishing the objects focused upon. As to what is being attained by acting this way, no matter what thoughts and phenomena may arise, there is no need to block them. What is required is that, while the form is clearly manifest, you are definite that, within the single sphere of self-awareness, that form is empty lucidity or empty phenomena, lacking any identifiable essence. The meaning of this point has already been explained before, when introducing the coemergence of thoughts and phenomena. Here, the Great Brahmin said:

> All phenomena appearing before you,
> Coemerge them with the root, emptiness.

Virupa said:

> Thoughts and concepts are devoid of concrete characteristics, like water in a mirage.
> Without binding or releasing, don't move from the continuous genuine nature.

Maitripa said:

> In nonorigination, thoughts are adventitious.
> The thought itself rests in the essence of space.

And also:

> All kinds of phenomena and the essence of mind
> Are a mere coincidence, so they don't exist. This is mahamudra.

## Seeing the Essence of Meditator and Object of Meditation

What is to be meditated upon here is the essence of one's mind. It is not sufficient to reach the conviction that it is unoriginated, unabiding, and unceasing, as well as unidentifiable and beyond concept, from a mere intellectual understanding through thinking. Yogins actualize this mind essence itself on the spot based on direct experience, whereby all doubts and misunderstandings are resolved. As before, for this you will need to meditate on the actual essence while awareness is undistracted, carefree, and vividly clear. Looking at that directly and alert, without wandering or fixating, look again and again at how it is. Likewise, by staring at the essence of the meditator's cognizance, if these two are on either side, inner and outer, appearing as dual, you have not resolved doubts, so check again.

In brief, the meditator and object of meditation are not distinct from one another. They appear as illusory, inseparable from mindful presence. Also, mindful presence is but a name assigned to it because, in actual fact, there is not even a hair's tip of anything identifiable or a basis to reference. You need to be definite about it being originally empty and vastly open. Once you resolve your doubts in that way, look at the cognizance of the three times in the same way to see what is the difference between them. In other words, look at where past mind has gone, whence future mind arises, and how present mind is abiding. If you see that the minds of the three times somehow originate, abide, and cease, at this point you have not fully ascertained the true meaning, so continue checking. Since the nature is unidentifiable and has never been interrupted, it is not split into the three times. You should be convinced that, like space, it is always transparent and uniform.

Likewise, the cognizance that fixates thinking "I" and "myself" and the cognizance that clings to "others" and "outsiders" should also be investigated. That is to say, if these appear to be dual, in the manner of outer and inner, here and there, doubts haven't yet been resolved, so check it out again properly. After doing so, you should be convinced that everything is mind essence, primordially groundless and rootless, unique and unparalleled, self-existing and naturally free, insubstantial and vastly open.

Thus, meditation object, meditator, cognizance of the three times, cognizance of self and others perceived as dual, all have different names and mere mentally distinct designations, yet there is no mind continuum apart from them. Although the essence is not existent, through conditions, mind essence arises like an illusion as all kinds of things. Decide that the essence is neither deluded nor free, is untouched by virtue or vice, has nothing to attain or be rid of, and is beyond union and separation. For a few days, avoid purposely fixating, blocking, or acquiring. Let whatever arises flow naturally and sustain it loosely, without modifying or fabricating, and cultivate a decisive conviction. The Great Brahmin said:

> *Kyema!* Being without true nature, nobody says that it is
> something to be meditated upon.
> When meditation object and meditator are conceptualized as
> two,
> That mind fixating on duality is relinquishing enlightened mind,
> And one is thus inflicting harm on oneself.

And:

> The mind devoid of meditation object and meditator has no true nature.
> Vajra mind is the culmination of freedom from hope and fear.

Virupa said:

> In the expanse of the absolute reality of the mind, nothing "is."
> So the meditation and meditation object are not two.

And:

> By being free from meditation object and meditator, this distinction vanishes in itself.
> The practitioner collapses, so there is no striving.
> The fruit to be attained is destroyed, so all hope and fear has ceased.
> I and myself have been removed, so the battle against Mara has been won.
> Reification is destroyed in itself, so you are freed from the whole of samsara and nirvana.

The meaning is reflected in many such quotations.

## The Actual Conclusiveness about Nonorigination and Transparency

If a definite conviction regarding what was explained before is born, then the manner of meditating is to dismantle the grasping of being convinced and relax the meditator, mindfulness. Similarly, the desire for an experience is let go, the effort to bring about the experience is discarded, the purpose of reaching realization is relinquished, and the mind that brings about the realization subsides. In brief, abandon holding the idea "it's this," and all mental activity that thinks "it's like this." Cast away all ambitions such as desiring to meditate, to be mindful, to have an experience, and to be aware. Without any mental activity whatsoever and having no thoughtful intention, remain comfortably in ordinary mind as it is, letting it be without modifying, fabricating, or managing it. Don't modify through the mind that blocks or acquires, or manipulate in any way whatsoever any thoughts or perceptions arising of their own accord; but just let them be of themselves. Don't pursue a mental event. When occasionally the mind is distracted, don't worry about it, regard it as a fault, or analyze it. When mindful, let go right into the unfabricated ordinary state, avoiding any such things as meditating, experiencing, or acting upon.

Also at the time of eating, moving about, or lying down, don't get involved with coarse impulses and ideas about what you are doing or will do, but try as much as you can to carry out these activities while in a nonconceptual state. Apart from this, don't perform any physical activity or work. Besides offering *torma* and very few supplications, give up any other prayers or verbal spiritual practices and keep silent. When going to sleep, be free of any ambition, and rest openly in the ordinary[39] state without modifying. Thus, after abandoning all mental activity and remaining casually for some days, attachment to good experience and liking is freed, and clinging to ill feeling toward negative thoughts and delusion, holding them as faults, subsides. No matter how ordinary mind is or what arises or appears, that itself is the nature of the meditation: it is the expression of emptiness, ultimately unborn and unceasing, where there is nothing to eliminate or attain, adopt or reject. When the world and beings arise in the mind, they do so of their own accord, regardless of whether or not the mind is distracted, held by mindfulness, experiencing, or realizing the nature. When they subside, they are freed by themselves. It is an unmatched transparent oneness. Everything is the nature of meditation and within the meditation environment, and never goes beyond meditation. You should arouse such definite conviction.

At this point, some people, finding it difficult to stop mental activity, spin around in blank shamatha, and for some this results in mind energy being sucked within; they feel uneasy and suffer as their minds become uptight. They should do something to cheer themselves up and rest for a while in an uplifted mood. If the experience arises faultlessly, be at ease for a few days, and at times observe whether what is happening is a nonmeditating mind. As to this, if you consider distraction, sleep, and so forth as not being meditation, then investigate the essence and nature of those states and be aware of their natural state. The Great Brahmin said in relation to these points:

> When the active mind is not searched for at all,
> There is no need to look for sublime qualities, and anything incompatible with these vanishes.
> This is not found in any of the tantras and commentaries,
> So the passionless mind is free from the stain of causality.

And Shawaripa said:

> All phenomena of samsara and nirvana,
> When seen, are found to have no true nature.
> Therefore, since all hopeful and fearful thinking comes to an end,
> What is the use of applying effort to adopt and reject?

Virupa said:

> Since there is neither anything realized nor anyone realizing, the limitation of bias vanishes.
> Since there is neither with nor without, it is equality, the continuous flow of the genuine nature.
> If you have decidedly realized it this way, there is nothing to ask from anyone.
> Since the myriad things are clearly perceived as dharmakaya, the mind that adopts and rejects doesn't arise.
> Since there is neither meditation nor nonmeditation, characteristics do not stain.

> Since there is neither phenomena nor nonphenomena, taking support on an object doesn't happen.
> There is no mind of action-and-actor; mind is free from all reference points.
> There is no mind of hope and fear; mind is free from all attachment.

Tilopa said:

> When ambition arises, luminosity is veiled and you don't see it.
> If the vows are guarded conceptually, the samaya declines from the absolute.
> Without mental activity, free from all ambition,
> Like the waves of water, arising and subsiding by themselves,
> If you don't dwell, focus, or waver from the truth,
> You will not stray from the samaya, and this will be the torch in the darkness.
> If you are free from all passion, and don't dwell in extremes,
> You will see every single teaching of the Three Baskets.

There are a great number of quotations such as these from the mahasiddhas.

Also Gampopa said:

> Not adopting or rejecting anything at all, you don't look for the path.
> Without any fruition whatsoever to see, hope and fear subsides.
> When you are aware of reification, deception collapses.

And:

> Since from the beginning, mind essence is not existent,
> Who is aware of the wisdom of stillness and movement?
> So all that was or is done
> Is nothing more than the hardships of harvesting space.

And:

> With no reference point, it is omnipresent.
> Without anything to grasp on to, mindfulness that fixates is abandoned.
> The continuity of nonmeditation is to remain in simplicity.
> Since there is no master, no matter what happens, it's alright.

And:

> Since there is no nurturing of mindfulness, there is no fear of distraction.
> Since there is no alternation between meditation and postmeditation, there are no in-between periods.
> No matter what arises, in the dharmadhatu there is neither acceptance nor rejection.
> Know that everything is the false structure of reification.

And:

> If non-mind is realized, the whole phenomenal world is carefree.
> If there is no evaluation, the birth and liberation of thought is simultaneous.
> If there is no desire, everything is equal.
> If this is realized, there is no interruption to meditation.

There are many pronouncements such as these made by the masters of the past.

## Mingling the Cycle of Day and Night through Conclusiveness

The meditation explained earlier should be continuous so that meditation and postmeditation mingle during the day and at night. The manner of sustaining meditation and postmeditation has mostly been explained before. However, at this point of conclusiveness, if a retentive mindfulness is excessive, it will induce an experience to which there is a danger of becoming attached. Therefore, while you are mindful, let go of all ambition and don't make efforts to be determined to be equanimous. Sustain the inseparability of meditation and postmeditation casually, being carefree, very relaxed, and in the best meditative state. It is as Lord Zhang said:

> In mahamudra meditation,
> Don't be too meticulous about doing this or that
> At the beginning, middle, and end.
> While being mindful, rest loose.

You might think, "If I did that, wouldn't it turn into a meditation that has slipped into apathetic absentmindedness?" There is no fault in that. In general, while you are present, looseness itself is the awareness that destroys attachment; you remain in the state free from mental activity. Since this is the perfect presence of the natural state as it is, this presence is much more special than vigorous or retentive mindfulness. As Shawaripa said:

> In concept-free mahamudra,
> There is not even an atom of meditation, so it is nonmeditation.
> The nonmeditation that never leaves the actual truth is the supreme meditation.

However, even if it occasionally slips into ensuing cognizance, the ensuing aspect ceases the moment you know its natural state through postmeditation mindfulness. If this happens, you will have come into the fold of inseparable meditation and postmeditation. This is what is normally accepted as continuous meditation. Likewise, in order to mingle daytime continuity with nighttime, when you are about to sleep, start by going to sleep while in the state of the daytime practice free from all effortful mental activity. If as a result you take sleep and dream as the path, that would be the best. Nevertheless, this is merely a possibility because in most cases it will not happen like that. Even if you are not conscious of your sleep and dreams arise as delusion, it would be sufficient to become aware of their natural state as soon as you wake up. What is accepted commonly as being the cycle of day and night is, as Lord Gampopa mentions in the texts on questions and answers:

> Question: Well then, when not recognized by mindfulness, the essence doesn't arrive and thoughts happen at their will. By becoming aware of these, do past thoughts have any effect or not? Is it necessary or not to persist at all costs to catch thoughts through mindfulness?
> Gampopa: As soon as unrecognized unbridled thoughts are captured by mindfulness, they are cleared and purified. There is no need to catch them at any rate. Nonetheless, if you practice nondistraction through mindfulness, this will accelerate the mingling of meditation and postmeditation. Even if mindfulness is not capturing thoughts, they would be totally harmless, without veiling or interrupting at all.

And:

> At the time of sleep and dreams, the innate luminosity is sufficient, despite these states not being recognized by mindfulness. Upon waking up, looking back, there will be nothing apart from luminosity. Trusting that this is so will result in the river flow.

Lord Gampopa severed doubts such as these in many texts of questions and answers.

If you are very concerned about gain and loss in regard to being mindful or distracted, you have not yet realized the nature or genuine state of mind, so conclusiveness is a bit premature. As Lord Gampopa said:

> While distracted, that is delusion as such.
> But if during mindfulness I feel that I attained the essence[40]

> That would be dualistic. It's not at all like that.
> In meditation, I don't know whether there is something to gain or lose.
> If there were duality, it would be a matter of adopting and rejecting.
> To say that there is nothing to adopt or reject is also a fault.

And:

> Attainment through mindfulness and delusion through distraction
> Are indeed conceptual grasping; in truth there is neither gain nor loss.[41]

When conviction about conclusiveness in these is born, avoid doing anything else that involves attributes or mental activity. Every five days or so be suspended in the state of conclusiveness. Then take a rest for about a day. Then for seven or ten days' practice, conclusiveness is alternated with rest until the realization of the natural state is continuous during the day. When it has become continuous, familiarize yourself with that so that during the night it arises little by little. It is said that when you are extremely habituated, day and night finally become integrated.

## The Purpose of Conclusiveness

Once having dismantled all attachments—such as fixation on emptiness, or dualistic fixations on meditator and object of meditation, experiencer and experience, realizer and realization—the practitioner continues serenely in the nature of the ground. The realization of the natural state free from duality will arise for a number of days depending on the practitioner's superior or middling level. The manner of arising will vary based on the amount of training, so it cannot be specified. If such a realization does not arise in some people, no matter how hard they try, for some time they should sustain the practice of integrated meditation and postmeditation as explained before. Later, after gradually shedding over and over again fixations on duality, emptiness, and so forth, it is considered that realization will progressively arise. If the realization of the genuine natural state is born—since this is exactly the heart meaning of the Conqueror's words, sutras, and tantras, along with the pith instructions—this path is far superior to other paths and lineages.

# 8. The Realized Essence and the Potential of Unceasing Appearances

5. Enhancement of the Realized Essence in Meditation
6. Development of the Potential of Unceasing Appearances
   a. Transforming Nonvirtue into Virtue
   b. Transforming All Neutral States into Virtuous States
   c. Increasing the Accumulation of Merit through All Virtues

## Enhancement of the Realized Essence in Meditation

It has been said that we should sustain the essence while being in a meditation that is devoid of true nature. We have seen the essence of the mind, and it is sufficient to simply recognize whatever arises on its own in its original condition, without needing to deliberately grasp at it, based on the flow of totally knowing the nature. Nonetheless, high and low experiences of all kinds happen. Lord Milarepa said:

> In the experience of yoga anything arises.
> In summer all kinds of things are born in the plains.

Therefore, all kinds of somewhat high or low experiences are surely bound to occur to some meditators. Lord Milarepa seems to refer to the early experiences such as those of stillness. On the other hand, regarding the term *yoga* (*naljor*), its meaning is to master the genuine state, mind essence. So it is fine also to apply it to realization. Thus, concerning the emergence of the realization in a yogin, due to temporary objective events and aspects such as the person's constitution and capacity, a variety of highs and lows will definitely occur. During these occasions, the main practice is to be aware of the state of lack of true nature.

In other words, external phenomena, the experience of internal mind, oneself the meditator, the object meditated upon, and the meditation, none of these have any existent essence at all. Their nature is emptiness, and while in that continuity, we should sustain the realization without distraction. When the mind temporarily feels happy or sad, or when the realization is stably sustained or not—no matter what occurs—everything without exception is at once nothing but the manifestation of the natural radiance. All this is the magical display of the luminosity of mind essence. Once you understand it as such, present happiness or sadness is not even for a moment held as positive or negative. After having recognized dualistic fixation, you will see that the root of all unfavorable circumstances and the basis of all that is ruinous are precisely that dualistic fixation, so cast it off. You should sustain the original face of nondual wisdom deliberately without distraction, whatever appears or arises in your mind being just that.

Otherwise, at first you may somehow comfortably sustain the realization but then, whether caused by circumstances or your own constitution, you start to perceive that there are fluctuations in the level of your experience. Then you think, "How come this happens?" Dualistic mind makes you nervous, and you divert from the essence of the practice. If so, the meditation is making the vital point of using as the path ineffective. Dualistic mind prevents one from overcoming the fluctuations and making progress, and the practice is mediocre. Therefore, don't proceed like that. Instead, as explained before, be convinced that everything is your mind and its radiance, and that the mind in turn is devoid of true nature; and point to the expanse of emptiness. Let be whatever arises, be casual, and don't evaluate; rather consciously emphasize the natural mind in all that appears or arises. You must sustain through the key point of undistracted nonmeditation. In actual fact, there is no deliberate meditation on the essence of mind, and there is nothing to be intentionally done to the variety of your own projections that may arise. Within self-occurring expression, you should look at its natural face without fixation and let it go in self-liberation. The masters of the past have named this "the path where the self-existing essence is sustained of its own accord." When you know this style of using as the path whatever appears, as ornaments as the path, that would be said to be "whatever appears arises as ornament."

## Development of the Potential of Unceasing Appearances

If we see the genuine essence of mind, there is no better way to develop its potential than that. In case we haven't perfectly realized the essence, if we were to sustain familiarity with a realization we had according to our possibilities, for sure conviction will gradually be born and the qualities of having purified stains will arise. However, as Lord Mila said:

> The many joints in a bamboo cane
> Represent the subtle thoughts
> That this Tibetan yogin has.

He thus acknowledged having dormant subtle delusion. Similarly, simulating being distracted, the masters of the past would pretend to be harmed by it and rely only on solitude. Furthermore, Lord Chodrup Palzang said:

> When I was staying in Namtso Semodo (Sky Necklace Lake), I thought ensuing cognizance was not born, but later when seeing bad conduct in someone else, ensuing cognizance occurred.

When Lord Lhatsewa was asked in relation to that how practice was to be done, he replied three times, "You need to examine it." This is so, so true. When we have uninterrupted mindfulness—an effortless perfect mindfulness that somehow adjusts to situations—if without forgetting the essence we remain properly examining how doubts are, the expression of awareness is brought forth, and we carefully see how its radiance is. Always in undistracted nonmeditation, these are the trainings in using the equality of phenomena as the path. Particularly, Lord Gyare said:

> Sustaining the realization of nonconceptual mind
> And arranging the conceptual auspicious circumstances,
> I feel they are like the base and top of sand mounds.[42]

Ultimately, in order to attain perfect buddhahood we need to plant the seed of rupakaya while being in indivisible emptiness and compassion. How is that? While knowing the essence of mind, there is compassion toward all beings, and through the great development of bodhichitta, all unceasing phenomena are transformed into virtue. In short, there are three conditions: transforming unvirtuous action into virtuous actions, transforming all neutral states into virtuous states, and increasing the accumulation of merit through all virtues.

## Transforming Nonvirtue into Virtue

First, apply the fivefold practice, or else proceed as follows. When anger suddenly arises, without adopting or rejecting or being carried away by it, after looking at its identity, make the following aspirations one-pointedly. "May the anger of all beings ripen in me. May I be able to take upon myself the anger of all beings. From today onward, may the thought of anger not even arise for a moment in any being. May the sound of the word 'anger' not be heard in my buddha field." Apply the same to all other afflictions.

## Transforming All Neutral States into Virtuous States

This happens when the four types of daily activity are carried out in a neutral way, without any good or bad intention, such as according to the instructions, when one perceives eating and drinking as a tantric feast, or sitting and moving as circumambulations. When eating and drinking, partake of that in accordance with deity yoga, guru yoga, and so forth. When moving, visualize the refuge field as being to your right and have the intention of circumambulating it, and so forth. Of course, this is to be extended to many other activities. At the very least, when putting on a hat, think that for the benefit of all beings you are carrying on your head the refuge of the Three Jewels, without parting from it. When putting on clothes, think that you are wearing the garment of perfect conscientiousness. When tying your belt, feel that you will not depart from fierce diligence. These and other purposes are clearly found in the biographies of the masters of the past. Above all, you should wrap yourself in the understanding that comes from the scriptures and your realization. Gyalwa Gotsangpa said:

> When seeing a beautiful object, the intention of offering it to the Three Jewels did not take place. Attachment and self-interest were what arose, and the offering was wasted. Saying (to myself), "Offer it to the Dharma Lord," I understood the key point of nonattachment.

## Increasing the Accumulation of Merit through All Virtues

When the thought of attending your guru or practicing the various levels of the ten Dharma activities[43] arises, don't be discouraged by thinking that you cannot accomplish that. Instead think, "I will do it!" and make the wish to be able to achieve it. Whatever the endeavor may be, carry it out focusing on the benefit of all beings. In the case of generosity, if you give even a single grain of food to a bird and you do it for the sake of all beings, it is said in many sutras and tantras that the fruition will be as great as the number of beings. So whatever the degree of virtuous intention and action, it should have a motivation that is congenial with the Buddhist path and be sealed by bodhichitta, dedication, and aspiration. If you keep in mind the meaning of such topics, since it is said in the scriptures that all things are embodied in the intention, the fruition will increase enormously. You will take up the enlightened intent that knows this to be the instruction to turn the extent of whatever you do into something dharmic. You will also understand the essential points of all teachings, such as interdependence. You will also be creating the conditions for the spontaneous accomplishment of the two purposes to swiftly take place. The Dharma Lord Gyare said:

> If you are skillful in modifying a thought,
> You will be able to carry out all sublime qualities.

There are innumerable references such as this by the saints of the past. The mahasiddha Lord Mipham said that a gilded object[44] illustrates the meaning of these points. Key points of the Dharma such as this have been explained both directly and indirectly in a hundred instances in sutras, tantras, and shastras, but the philosophers haven't brought it into their sphere of experience.

As for us followers of the lineage of practice, in general, those who have concluded that everything is a projection of the perceiver of this present experience are as stars in the daytime. However, there may be one or two fortunate ones practicing to attain enlightenment who don't even know about this, and certainly some others regard it as being a moot point. Thus, although they have realization, they don't have an occasion to develop the potential. They may slightly develop the potential, but the time never comes for sublime qualities to arise. Even if qualities arise, there is no occasion for benefiting others, so the teaching deteriorates. Since they don't know these means to prevent that deterioration, they should put the instructions into practice no matter what. Furthermore, once we practitioners of mahamudra have decided that thoughts are our own family, no matter how good or bad intense thoughts may be, it would not result at all in maliciousness or any intention toward worldly affairs. As soon as something arises, use it as the path. In addition, the moment you wake up from sleep, at dawn, at mealtime, when perceiving phenomena during postmeditation, and so forth are when the risk is greatest. Since these are critical moments, it is important to keep to the key point through practice. This is also a good time to enhance the practice and remove obstacles.

# 9. The Layout of the Four Yogas

E. Making Fine Distinctions between Experience and Realization
  1. An Explanation of the Layout of the Four Yogas
    a. The Capacity Levels of Individuals, the Field Where Experience and Realization Is Born
    b. What Is Born: The Experience and Realization in the Manner of the Main Practice of the Four Yogas as Taught in the Sutras and Tantras
      i. Treatises of the Sutras and Tantras of the New Traditions (*Sarma*)
      ii. The Dzogchen Teachings in the Main Texts of the Old Tradition (*Nyingma*)
    c. The Common Coarse Meaning of the Four Yogas
      i. Their Individual Specifics
        A) Four Divisions of Mindfulness
        B) Four Identifications of Samadhi
        C) Four Realizations of Resting in Composure
        D) Four Confusion Spots for Realization
        E) Four Ways in Which Ensuing Cognizance Arises
        F) Four Stains of Ensuing Cognizance
        G) Four Ways of Purifying Postmeditation
        H) Four Borderlines between Meditation and Postmeditation
        I) Four Meditation Times
        J) Four Ways of Purifying Obscurations through Realizations Corresponding to Resting in Composure
        K) Four Borderlines between Experience and Realization

L) Four Ways of Knowing Relative Cause and Effect
ii. Other Distinctions
A) The Essence
B) Meditation and Postmeditation
C) The Antidote
D) The Undesirable
E) The Realization of the Natural State

---

## Making Fine Distinctions between Experience and Realization

This consists of: (1) an explanation of the layout of the four yogas, and (2) a special explanation of each of the four yogas.

## An Explanation of the Layout of the Four Yogas

This includes explanations on: (1) the capacity levels of individuals, the field where experience and realization is born; (2) what is born—the experience and realization in the manner of the main practice of the four yogas as taught in the sutras and tantras; and (3) the common coarse meaning of the four yogas.

## The Capacity Levels of Individuals

An extensive account in the *Guhyasamaja* mentions five types of individuals. In dzogchen, three types of individuals are discussed, each of which has three types, resulting in nine capacity levels. Although there are many accounts such as these, here we will briefly discuss three classifications: those individuals of higher, middling, and lower capacities.

The manner of occurrence of the highest, the sudden type, is where intellectual understanding, experience, and realization occur simultaneously at the outset in shamatha, during the guiding instructions in simplicity, or when receiving pointing-out instructions. There also may be a sudden dawn in just one-pointedness, lesser simplicity, lesser one taste, or lesser nonmeditation, with the realization remaining stable. For example, when the sun rises on a valley in a deep gorge, darkness is cleared at the same time as the earth and stones warm up. The mastery of this type of individual is enormous.

The middling one is the type that bypasses stages: understanding, experience, and realization, as well as the four yogas. Each of these takes place suddenly, not depending on the previous one. However, what arises is not stable; there is huge variation between increase and decrease. For instance, this is like the sun appearing and disappearing between the clouds. This individual has middling mastery. Nonetheless, once the person stays a long time in solitary retreat, has devotion to the guru, and supplicates fervently, if they meditate, it is said that realization will become stable. If the time for meditation is short and realization is not stabilized in this life, it is believed that genuine realization will arise during the bardo.

Last, the manner of the gradual type is that understanding, experience, and realization, as well as the four yogas, arise step by step, each one arising in dependence on the previous one. Besides, these stages take time to arise; one may have slightly seen the essence but neither immediately abandons what is to be abandoned, nor has mastery of the remedies. For example, if the sun is blocked by hills[45] while it is rising in the sky, it cannot warm up the earth and stones or melt ice as soon as it rises, but needs to warm up everything gradually. This individual's mastery of the practice is feeble. It is said that if both these last two types develop devotion and exertion, through the key point of blessings they will turn into the sudden type without hardship. Furthermore, it is said that if realization arises at an unpredictable time, there may be a variety of situations. One may indeed gain conviction. Otherwise, even though realization has arisen, one may not recognize it, be unsure, and disregard it. So, it is important to rely on the guru or on experienced Dharma siblings and spiritual friends.

As to the distinction between understanding, experience, and realization, through study and reflection one understands the instructions, whereby one comes to assume that the nature of mind is "like this." This is intellectual understanding. When the meanings are brought correctly to the fold of experience, and there is an experience on the basis of awareness, this is experience. Due to the strength of one's merit and the blessings of the guru entering one's being, to see mind essence is called realization. As Lord Gyare said:

> To analyze is understanding.
> The highs or lows of bliss and clarity are experience.
> To recognize the natural state is realization.

In our case, understanding is not satisfactory and it is not enough to have experiences. What we need is realization dawning by itself. As Lord Yangonpa said:

> What is written on paper is called letters. What has been taught by the master and the knowledge you express verbally are called words. What arises in the conceptual mind as an assumption that "It is thus" is intellectual understanding. This neither subdues afflictions, nor cuts the thread of thoughts, nor equalizes the taste of good and bad circumstances. Finally, you fall sick and you die. At that time, even if you have five hundred yak loads of books, they will all be left behind. To carry even a single sheet of paper doesn't help. You may look for ten sealed profound instructions each annotated at the beginning with red ink, but you are still in danger of dying like a rough person.[46] This is not the place to examine minutely the meaning of all these points. You may be able to put into words the Three Baskets and the four orders of tantra, but it is possible that nothing stays in your mind at the time of death. When the great translator Ngog went to the Sand Mountain Root in Samye, he thought, "Relying on these books, we will be freed from the ocean of samsara." Later he said, "For one who enters the ocean, the piled-up froth that springs forth, similar to a supreme mountain, is

> totally deceptive." His words reflect his disappointment with engaging solely in hearing and reflection. He was considering the great teaching on Liberation Upon Hearing. What he said is of great import for future generations who subscribe to only hearing and reflection. In the *Avatamsaka Sutra* it is said, "Just as the sweet taste of molasses cannot be savored by hearing about it, it is through meditation that the taste [of this teaching] will be relished."

And:

> For example, a hungry person may exclaim "Food! Food!" but that doesn't help fill up the stomach. What will satiate it is to roast barley, grind it, mix it with water to form a dough, cut a piece with the hand, and eat it. Similarly, this teaching must be born in one's being, and whatever is born must be meditated upon. In meditation we should abandon interest for the mundane and cut off attachment to this life. We should reduce food and clothing to bare necessity, have little concern for body and life, reflect on the liberating lifestyles of the Kagyus, develop armor and endurance, and wander in mountain hermitages genuinely extending our practice. When renunciation takes place, a certain way of arising will occur from within.

Regarding the distinction between experience and realization, according to the teachings of the Kagyu masters of the past, watch out because experience can be mistaken for realization, so there is a strong basis for error. You must not make that mistake. At first you might not be very sure about aspects such as the way each experience manifests, or how habituated or stable you are. Nonetheless, broadly speaking, at the time of an experience, while your mind is quite still in thought-free empty lucidity, the perceptions of the six senses that arise from it are vividly recognized in their nakedness, and the experience grows fainter, floats, and vanishes right there. When there is realization, once the previous obscuring stains happening at the time of experience have become purified, you recognize your mind as ordinary cognizance, the original face of basic nature. Since you have realized its myriad expressions as unborn, unabiding, and unceasing, nothing is an object of conceptual reification, so anything that appears occurs in the vast boundless expanse of thoroughly knowing its nature.

In brief, the borderline between an ephemeral experience and the realized essence is that when there is an experience—no matter how stably bliss and clarity may occur in the mind—its essence is not realized and its nature is not known. Experiences are stained by such conceptual mental stances as doubt, fixation on attributes, and clinging to superiority, as well as pride, self-importance, and verbally spouting one's conviction. In addition, devotion, compassion, and other positive emotions do take place but in a concrete manner. As to genuine realization, there is a conviction right on the fundamental nature, the immaculate unfabricated mind essence, free of doubts, fixations, and pride. The realization of the essence of your own mind will bring about great compassion to all beings who haven't reached that realization and steady devotion to your root guru, the lord of blessings who introduced you to the nature of your mind, perceived as a buddha in person. As the incomparable Takpo clearly explained when asked what was the difference between experience and realization:

> Since experience hasn't gone beyond the field of conceptual mind, it would be like, for example, the sun covered by clouds. Bliss, clarity, and nonthought, these three sometimes will be high, sometimes low, and yet sometimes stable. By sustaining these without attachment, once mind stains are purified, realization will swiftly take place. Realization is when phenomena and mind are indivisible and arise incessantly in the state of luminosity from the depths of the mind. When meditator and object of meditation are inseparable, it is said that realization and attainment arise simultaneously.

In one-pointedness, which is one of the four yogas, there are only meditative experiences. In the other three—simplicity, one taste, and nonmeditation—experience and realization must be differentiated. Let us start with the experiences in one-pointedness. The identity of the experience is a brightly clear cognizance. If it happens in varying degrees, it is still an experience and unstable. If the fluctuations diminish, that means there is progress. Generally speaking, one-pointedness is an experience, not a realization. In simplicity, there is slim knowledge of nonorigination. You think, "I wonder if this is what the guru has taught," but this recognition of the mind is an experience. The cognizance that vividly realizes that it lacks true nature is realization. In one taste, to think "It seems my body, outer phenomena, and my mind are without true nature" is an experience. To realize clearly that outer phenomena are like reflections in a mirror, and that although they appear as diverse they are one, is realization. In nonmeditation, no matter how much you exert yourself, to feel that there is neither meditator nor object of meditation is an experience. Cognizance realizing clearly that within itself there is no meditator is realization. Thus, it is important to distinguish experience from realization without making mistakes.

## What Is Born: The Experience and Realization in the Manner of the Main Practice of the Four Yogas as Taught in the Sutras and Tantras

This includes explanations on: (1) treatises of the sutras and tantras of the New Traditions (*Sarma*), and (2) the dzogchen teachings in the main texts of the Old Tradition (*Nyingma*).

### Treatises of the Sutras and Tantras of the New Traditions (*Sarma*)

In the *Descent into Langka Sutra* it is said:

> The Bhagavan said, "Mahamati, the bodhisattva mahasattvas endowed with the four dharmas will possess the four great yogas. What are these four? To meditate on one's mind

> and phenomena; to completely get rid of the views of origination, abiding, and destruction; to realize that external things are not real; and to aspire to fully comprehend their sublime intrinsic primordial wisdom. Mahamati, the bodhisattvas mahasattvas endowed with these four dharmas will possess the four great yogas."

These statements are taken to be the teaching on the four yogas. Let us distinguish and discuss them one by one. That phenomena are fully meditated as mind is the teaching of one-pointedness. The same text continues:

> Mahamati, if you ask how does a bodhisattva mahasattva know to meditate on one's mind and phenomena, it is like this. These three worlds are merely mind. They are free from I and mine; they are immobile, with nothing to adopt nor reject. They are divided because of the attachment to distorted tendencies elaborated through beginningless time. One is connected by fully engaging with the myriad forms of the three worlds. One experiences subsequent thoughts about body, wealth, staying, and going. This is how you should fully understand it.

The meaning of these words is similar to what is said in the yoga of one-pointedness.

The yoga of simplicity is taught through a complete abandonment of the view of origination, dwelling, and destruction. Continuing with the quotation:

> Mahamati, if you ask in which way the bodhisattva mahasattva completely abandons the view of origination, dwelling, and destruction, it is like this. All things are forms like those appearing in an illusion or a dream; since oneself, others, and both do not exist, they are not born. One's mind will follow after things as being mere appearances, and will see

> external things as unreal. Since they are seen as unreal, the consciousnesses do not get involved with them. Seeing that all conditions are neither aggregates nor heaped up, one sees that the three worlds arise from conceptual conditions. So external and internal phenomena are not conceptualized and are seen as devoid of true nature. Because of this, one reverts completely from the view of origination, realizes that they are phenomena that are illusory by nature, and so forth, and thus one patiently accepts that phenomena are not originated.

The meaning of these words is in accordance with the yoga of simplicity.

When one has mastered the realization that outer things are insubstantial, the yoga of one taste is taught. In the same text it is said:

> Mahamati, if you ask in which way the bodhisattva mahasattva masters the realization that external things are insubstantial, it is like this. All things are similar to a mirage, a dream, a mesh of optical hair strands. They are caused by the attachment to the myriad distorted conceptual tendencies elaborated through beginningless time. Thus, they do not have true existence.

So when one sees perfectly, one is called bodhisattva because it is in accordance with the yoga of one taste.

Since they aspire to fully comprehend their sublime intrinsic primordial wisdom, the yoga of nonmeditation is taught. In the same text it is said:

> Mahamati, if you ask in which way the bodhisattva mahasattva aspires to fully comprehend their sublime intrinsic primordial wisdom, it is like this. Once they have perfectly attained the patient acceptance that phenomena are unoriginated, they abide in the eighth bhumi. Since they fully comprehended the perfect realization of mind, intellect, and conceptual consciousness, as well as the five objects of

> perception, the true nature, and the twofold selflessness, they also obtained a mental body.

Thus, this is in accordance with the meaning of the yoga on nonmeditation. Similarly, in the *Descent into Langka Sutra* it is said:

> Based on mere mind
> The external are not designated as true.
> Focused on absolute reality,
> One also transcends mere mind.
> Having gone beyond mere mind,
> One goes beyond phenomena.
> The yogin who abides in nonphenomena
> Sees the mahayana.

The meaning of this is explained in the stages of the path and in the prajñaparamita instructions, all these explanations being in accordance with the four yogas. Also, in the *Great Ali Kali River Tantra,* we find this renowned quotation:

> Through the samadhi of the lion's graceful stance,
> Lucid unmoving one-pointedness clarifies cognizance.
> Self-existing wisdom is awakened from within.
> Since patience is enduring, the three lower realms are abandoned.
>
> Second, through the samadhi similar to illusion,
> There is the great composure of simplicity.
> An inconceivable strength of samadhi arises.
> Once the warmth of spiritual attainment is gained, one masters rebirth.
>
> Third, through the samadhi of courage,
> It is said that one realizes the tenth bhumi of multiplicity in one taste.

As the heir of the buddhas of the three times, one benefits beings.
Having attained the peak, progress is without break.

Fourth, through the diamond-like samadhi,
Those who have applied themselves to the practice of nonmeditation
See countless buddha fields of omniscience.
This is the great, spontaneously present, supreme Dharma, seen without searching for it.

In brief, the coemergent mind essence being the dharmakaya explained earlier is like the great ocean, the basis of all. You rest one-pointedly on the realization of that natural state. Coemergent thoughts being the expression of dharmakaya, they are like the waves of the ocean. You rest in simplicity on the realization of that natural state. Coemergent phenomena are the light of dharmakaya; they are like the myriad images reflected on the ocean, the natural forms of thinking. You rest in one taste on the realization of that natural state. Having reached the culmination of these three realizations, there is no meditation with effort and that is perfect buddhahood; this is said to be resting in nonmeditation. Therefore, sutras and shastras, tantras and the many profound pith instructions, all rely on the four yogas; they all consider them essential. There are no buddhas, bodhisattvas, or sublime practitioners who haven't tied their practice to the four yogas. As said in a sutra, just as all rivers acquire the same salty taste when reaching the ocean, all teachings are of one taste in mahayana. Particularly, the Great Brahmin said in the *Immortal Vajra Song*:

While entering the nonconceptual state without stopping thoughts,
If you leave cognizance of its own accord, it will rest still.

And:

If it rests there, the experience of great bliss will dawn.
First, the mind experiences phenomena as empty;

> Although they appear to be ice, they are recognized as being water.
> Second, without blocking mental phenomena
> Their emptiness and bliss arise as inseparable.
> This is similar to when ice melts into water.
> Third, the nonconceptual state dissolves into nonorigination.
> Everything is inseparable and at one with great bliss.
> This is similar to all the ice and water becoming inseparable.
> Attainment of the nonconceptual fruition, desirelessness, is like the *seta*, one of the best medicines.

Nagarjuna taught this in five steps. Isolated mind and one-pointedness mean the same. Luminosity and simplicity mean the same. Indivisibility in the path of training and one taste mean the same. Indivisibility in the path of no more training and nonmeditation mean the same. Mahasiddha Lawapa said:

> Spontaneously present, inconceivable, indivisible, and perfect is what was taught as the four yogas.

Shawaripa said:

> The names samadhi experience, yoga, utter yoga, and great yoga are each of the four yogas respectively.

Maitripa said:

> The time of resolving doubts. The time of acquiring strength. The time of gaining confidence. The time of liberation within awareness itself. In each of these four times, there are nine subdivisions.

In the *Secret Wisdom Tantra* it is said:

> First is the samadhi of stillness.
> Second is immobility.

> Third is the unification in equality.
> Fourth is the naturally present wisdom.

As explained in the glorious *Kalachakra*:

> Coarse one-pointedness shapes the form. Simplicity is subtle energy. One taste is utterly subtle mind training. Since nonmeditation is wisdom training, it is considered to be the fruition. So it is in this order: body mahamudra, voice mahamudra, mind mahamudra, and wisdom mahamudra.

Furthermore, considering the four yogas one by one, the three experiences of bliss, clarity, and nonthought arise, and each has the following four stages. The distinctiveness of bliss is the upward-supporting four joys from below: joy, supreme joy, joyless joy, and coemergent joy. The distinctiveness of clarity is the four stages of vivid presence: the luminosity of appearance, increase, attainment, and full attainment. The distinctiveness of nonthought is the four voids: void, utter void, great void, and everything void. In the six practices of Naropa, we find these four: "capture, stabilize, empower, and master." In path and result, we find such statements as "combining with the progression along the paths of the four empowerments," which closely relates with the progression along the four empowerments according to Lord Naropa. He said to Sanghapa Rolpe Dorje:

> In the realization of mahamudra,
> At first, thoughts are adventitious.
> When you revert from ignorantly looking at them
> And realize luminous awareness free of fixation,
> This is called the empowerment of awareness.
>
> If the five poisons abide as the five wisdoms,
> This is regarded as the vase empowerment.
> When the unobstructed radiance in it
> Manifests without any bias,

Bliss arises from the state of emptiness.
This is regarded as the lucidity of the second empowerment.

Coemergent wisdom
Is inseparable bliss and emptiness in continuous space.
This indivisibility is greater one taste,
In which inseparable phenomena and mind are savored as great bliss.
This is explained as being the knowledge wisdom empowerment.

The three empowerments are inseparably integrated within the mind.
In the space-like pure mind essence,
Without meditation and postmeditation,
The two truths are united, the fourth empowerment.

The Great Brahmin Saraha replied to Queen Kapar Bhudza's question:

One-pointed awareness is the vase empowerment.
Bliss free from elaborations is the secret empowerment.
The third one is union in equality.
Nonmeditation is the fourth.

In brief, it has been taught that those who practice the path of methods open the knots of the four chakras, and through the stage of binding bindu and energy, they move from one yoga to the next. In Lord Milarepa's biography, we find that Bharampa and others said that the signs of the path in terms of experiences are fourfold, and from the perspective of the four empowerments, it must be understood that this certainly coincides with progression in the path of mantra.[47]

## The Dzogchen Teachings in the Main Texts of the Old Tradition

In the *Key Notes on Dzogpa Chenpo* it is said:

> Since these have been purified within the mind,
> Negative actions are automatically abandoned.

This is one-pointedness.

> In mind essence free from conceptual elaborations,
> All subject and object is abandoned.

This is simplicity.

> Since phenomena arise as dharmakaya,
> Conceptual thoughts are automatically abandoned.

This is one taste.

> By knowing that samsara and nirvana have no true nature,
> All dualistic clinging is abandoned.

This is nonmeditation. These have been taught in combination with the four perfect abandonments. Also, the text says:

> Warmth is seeing mind essence.
> Peak is nonorigination in dharmakaya.
> Patient acceptance is samsara and nirvana free of adoption or rejection.
> Supreme Dharma is samsara and nirvana dissolving in the mind.

Among others, this is a teaching that combines the four distinctive certainties of the path of connection with the four yogas. Both New and Old Traditions agree on this viewpoint. In a similar fashion, sutras, tantras, New and Old Traditions, as well as pith instructions, intend to teach that resting composed one-pointedly indicates one-pointedness; nonorigination and freedom from extremes indicate simplicity; great bliss and equality indicate one taste; and the absence of adopting or rejecting, removing or adding, indicates nonmeditation.

## The Common Coarse Meaning of the Four Yogas

This includes explanations on: (1) their individual specifics, and (2) other distinctions.

## Their Individual Specifics

This includes the following twelve points: (1) four divisions of mindfulness, (2) four identifications of samadhi, (3) four realizations of resting in composure, (4) four confusion spots for realization, (5) four ways in which ensuing cognizance arises, (6) four stains of ensuing cognizance, (7) four ways of purifying postmeditation, (8) four borderlines between meditation and postmeditation, (9) four meditation times, (10) four ways of purifying obscurations through realizations corresponding to resting in composure, (11) four borderlines between experience and realization, and (12) four ways of knowing relative cause and effect.

## Four Divisions of Mindfulness

In general, regarding mindfulness there are: retentive mindfulness as antidote and retentive mindfulness of emptiness, effortless mindfulness, perfect mindfulness, and nonconceptual mindfulness.

What is called "retentive mindfulness as antidote" takes place at the time of the first one-pointedness. It is the mindfulness that identifies thoughts and operates as an antidote, nothing more than the undesirable and antidote being separate.

Then, once mind essence has been seen and until stability has been reached, it is "retentive mindfulness of emptiness." This means that through seeing mind essence, the undesirable and mindfulness are cognized as indivisible and emptiness is realized. However, since stability hasn't yet been attained, one often forgets the essence, at which time mindfulness is required.

Once stability has been attained, then comes "effortless mindfulness." Many names have been given to it such as: samadhi of single mindfulness, purified retentive mindfulness, uninterrupted mindfulness, and continuous meditation. However, on close inspection, what is called samadhi of single mindfulness does not merely refer to undistracted samadhi but to the aspect of conviction. For continuous meditation to be such, it must be merged with oneself day and night. In other words, what is called effortless mindfulness happens when one is not distracted from the realized essence even for a moment, so no circumstance whatsoever will be able to harm it.

This is not the case of an alternating meditation that takes place during the daytime but is absent during the night. If through this effortless mindfulness day and night merge, then that is continuous meditation. In addition, if from the flow of this effortlessness itself, you can go to sleep at nighttime while in the continuity of the essence and wake up with the essence effortlessly present without needing to be stabilized, that is called day and night uninterrupted. When that does not happen, but on waking from sleep, and so on, you again need to deliberately stabilize the essence, that would be called day and night interrupted.

Some pith instructions indicate that if day and night are connected, it is also alright to call this the merging of day and night. Furthermore, there are teachings that call it "effortless perfect mindfulness." Some say that once effortlessness has taken place, it is implied that it is perfect, but this is not so. While in the samadhi mentioned earlier and this one, in general, what matters is not to be distracted from the essence. In carrying out both perfect and samadhi types of mindfulness, there are still subject and object stains—such as desiring to have the experience—that need to be purified, as well as a decisive strong conviction that is yet to take place.

When classifying mindfulness at the time of the four yogas, some teachings say that in one-pointedness there is retentive mindfulness of thoughts, in simplicity mindfulness of emptiness, in one taste mindfulness of nonorigination, and in nonmeditation mindfulness of the nonconceptual state. Some others coincide in the case of one-pointedness, but indicate mindfulness of nonorigination for simplicity, mindfulness of the nonconceptual state for one taste, and dissolution into space for nonmeditation. These have been taught thus, so that their distinctive features are in accordance with the individual karmic destiny of the disciples.

In my case, I am familiar with the following classification. One-pointedness coincides with the ones mentioned above. Regarding simplicity, generally those who lack sharp capacity barely see the essence of a thought, but since they haven't gained stability, they will surely forget. When forgetfulness happens, it would be similar to the retentive mindfulness of emptiness, but one hasn't given much value to the genuine nature of freedom from conceptual constructs—to that authentic simplicity. When encountering an event [that causes the forgetfulness] the essence must really emerge, so for simplicity mindfulness must be effortless. This is also known as "pure retentive mindfulness" and is the mindfulness connected to the phase between waking and sleep.

The difference between simplicity and one taste resides in such points as whether or not clinging to the experience of the essence, and so forth, are purified, and especially whether one has trained in the skill of these stages in connection with phenomena or not. Because in perfect mindfulness such points are needed, it is perfect mindfulness which corresponds to one taste and the samadhi of single mindfulness. This being the case, the difference between one taste and nonmeditation resides in whether or not the concept of effortless perfect mindfulness has been purified, or whether mindfulness is conceptual or not. So nonconceptual mindfulness corresponds to nonmeditation.

The term "nonconceptual" also has many classifications. To simply transcend the concept of meditator and object of meditation is called nonconceptual. Since this occurs at the time of simplicity, concepts are transcended from then onward. "Nonconceptual" is merely a verbal expression; it is not the genuine transcendence of concepts. At this point, in nonmeditation what is called "nonconceptual mindfulness" is the "great nonconceptuality" itself, the reason being that all undesirables and antidotes have come to an end, and that even the notion of perfect mindfulness has transcended concept, so it is "nonconceptuality." And since there is nothing higher than this, it is "great." In what is called "nonconceptual mindfulness in the yoga of nonmeditation," the meaning of nonconceptual is similar to what was discussed earlier. Here nonconceptual mindfulness in general is that all thoughts and awareness have dissolved into space, where both the object of mindfulness and that which is mindful have been totally annihilated from their root. However, although there is no longer mindfulness, the word is used in the context of the previous classifications of mindfulness so that one can refer to it as coming to an end.

## Four Identifications of Samadhi

Lord Gomchung said:

> To rest still in the state of lucidity is one-pointedness.

The awareness in which stillness and movement have merged is empty lucidity, similar to space, without center or fringe. To rest still in that state, lucidly, serenely, and wakeful, is one-pointedness.

> To have cleared misconceptions is simplicity.

Once you are free from subject and object duality or the defining characteristics of origination, abiding, and cessation of all external and internal phenomena, misconceptions are resolved within the fact that everything is unborn and empty.

> Without acceptance or rejection is one taste.

In the absence of acceptance or rejection, stopping or acquiring, such stances as whether all phenomena in the world and beings, or samsara and nirvana, are beyond conceptualizations of their being originated or destroyed, empty or not empty, are all equal in the state of the genuine nature.

> Purified experience is nonmeditation.

Once all the stains of earlier meditative and personal experiences have been purified, and the realization of the path has merged with the natural state of the essence, there is no longer distinction between meditation and postmeditation, mindfulness and distraction.

## Four Realizations of Resting in Composure

Lord Gomchung said:

> At the time of one-pointedness, the essence is realized.

In concept-free lucidity, mind is unidentifiable. In one's experience, conviction is born and mind essence is seen.

> At the time of simplicity, the nature is realized.

The mind, unoriginated, unabiding, and unceasing, is unconditioned. To know it as devoid of true nature is to realize the nature of mind.

> At the time of one taste, the defining characteristic is realized.

The images of the habitual patterns of the mind manifesting as the myriad phenomena are realized in the state of nonorigination as having the same taste, as an unobstructed expression of emptiness, and also as the interdependence of the myriad phenomena. To know this is to realize the characteristic of the mind.

> Nonmeditation is all-encompassing realization.

Without division between experiencer and experience, realizer and realization, everything is realized as the great equality of the genuine state. This realization is all-encompassing.

## Four Confusion Spots for Realization

Lord Gomchung said:

> One-pointedness is lost in the midst of darkness.

Some bright and serene stillness arises while the mind is in empty lucidity. Nonetheless, once it becomes veiled by any of its experiences, decisiveness and conviction about the unimpeded cognizance within the lucidity of awareness cease to arise, so it is like being lost in darkness, and what is to be seen is not seen.

> Simplicity takes nothingness to be what is important.

Concerning any issue, there is a fixation on the void aspect of outer and inner phenomena. Overtaken by the experience of being convinced about that, one does not master the interdependence of the cause and effect of phenomena, thus neglecting or underestimating it, and one proceeds with a nihilistic view that attaches importance to nothingness.

> One taste wanders off in the waves of integration.

When experiencing and realizing phenomena and mind to be the same, one doesn't find the objects of such emotions as devotion and compassion; one becomes obtuse regarding the aspect of skillful means, including pure perception, compassion, and so forth; and it is considered that one falls into the hinayana. It is like being tossed by waves of water. It is a deep abyss.

> Nonmeditation is the sun obscured by clouds.

Even though one is only resting composed in the realization that there is neither meditator nor object of meditation, if one doesn't recognize the illusory dualistic perception and absence of concepts, it would be like the sun covered by clouds, and obscuring thoughts are considered not yet to have been eliminated.

## Four Ways in Which Ensuing Cognizance Arises

Lord Gomchung said:

> The ensuing cognizance of one-pointedness reifies.

Since within oneself the attachment to experiences hasn't been purified, during ensuing cognizance, the reification of subject and object entities also remains undestroyed, so reified perception clinging to substantiality arises.

> The ensuing cognizance of simplicity is illusion.

Since all phenomena have been realized as unoriginated and empty, even though during ensuing cognizance there is an appearance of perceiver and perceived, these are not reified, so they arise as illusory.

> The ensuing cognizance of one taste is the void.

In the ensuing cognizance, some do not cognize all phenomena and emptiness as being nondual and indivisible. Due to the strength of a previous fixation on emptiness, what arises is only the empty aspect, so the ensuing cognizance arises as the void.

> The ensuing cognizance of nonmeditation is compassion.

Since at this time meditation and postmeditation have merged, there is no ensuing cognizance as such. Nonetheless, since in a bare sense of postmeditation there is an occurrence of nonreferential compassion, this is conventionally known as "ensuing cognizance arising as compassion."

## Four Stains of Ensuing Cognizance

Lord Gomchung said:

> In one-pointedness, the stain of reification.

Since attachment to experiences, as well as conviction, hasn't been purified, there is the stain of reification.

> In simplicity, the stain of recognizing or not.

Since, in whatever it may be, there is the aspect of the conviction clinging to emptiness, one feels good about spiritual practice in terms of the empty aspect but uncomfortable about the aspect of phenomenal appearances, so one fails to recognize their indivisibility, and this is a stain.

> In one taste, the stain of experiences.

Since here again one hasn't penetrated indivisibility, there is a subtle fixation on the aspect of emptiness. Even if one has managed to penetrate indivisibility, there is the experience of perceiving that as being similar to an illusion, and this is a stain.

> In nonmeditation, the stain of what is known.

He is explaining that in ensuing phenomena one rests apathetically in the thought-free ground consciousness that lacks the recognition of nonthought. Since this means that the dharmata hasn't dawned within natural lucidity, it is the stain of the object of cognition.

## Four Ways of Purifying Postmeditation

Lord Gomchung said:

> In one-pointedness there is separation and not attainment.

If there is distraction during thought movement, the meditative state can be lost; this is separation. Although mindfulness may have taken hold, all that has happened is that one has simply found the flow of this practice itself; meditation as such hasn't been attained.

> In simplicity there is both separation and attainment.

If emptiness slips away due to retentive mindfulness, once that meditation happens, there is separation from emptiness. When it is held by mindfulness, one achieves the right meditation, which sees the essence of nonorigination, so there is attainment.

> In one taste there is attainment and not separation.

Although mindfulness may not hold in ensuing phenomena, the continuity of the realization is not interrupted, so there is no separation. Besides, since phenomena arise as indivisible from emptiness as soon as the practice is held by perfect mindfulness, that is the attainment.

> In nonmeditation there is neither separation nor attainment.

Since mindfulness arises in the sphere of wisdom, there is no separation from meditation. Because that itself is sufficient no matter what phenomenon arises, there is no new meditation that is to be attained.

## Four Borderlines between Meditation and Postmeditation

Lord Gomchung said:

> One-pointedness has a normal division between meditation and postmeditation.

Nonconceptual wisdom as it is hasn't dawned, so the meditation of resting in composure is not authentic. Without having realized phenomena as unoriginated, ensuing phenomena do not arise as illusory, so postmeditation is not authentic. However, in the specific practice of one-pointedness there is a meditative composure to be settled and, when distracted, a subsequent mindfulness to be attained.

> Simplicity has a divided meditation and postmeditation.

In all outer and inner phenomena there is freedom from the dualistic fixation of subject and object, and nondual wisdom arises unimpededly. Since this is nonconceptual wisdom, meditation is authentic. In the ensuing cognizance, subject and object arise as barely dualistic, and they appear as unreal and illusory. Since this is authentic postmeditation, meditation and postmeditation are separated individually.

> At the time of one taste, meditation and postmeditation merge.

At the time of meditative composure, phenomena and emptiness, as well as all other dualistic phenomena, abide as nondual. Also in the ensuing experience, by being mindful of indivisibility, eventually nondual phenomena and emptiness appear as an illusion. Therefore, meditation and postmeditation are commonly considered to have merged.

> In nonmeditation, there is only meditative composure.

Although there are phenomenal occurrences, these arise from the state of composure, so they do not go anywhere else; therefore meditative composure is considered to be all there is.

## Four Meditation Times

Lord Gomchung said:

> The time of reified meditation is one-pointedness.

At the time of meditative composure as such, one continuously fixates mindfulness and sustains tangible experiences. In the ensuing cognizance, thought movement is brought back to meditation by mindfulness. Since this is what prevails, it is a reified meditation.

> The time of [separate] meditation and postmeditation is simplicity.

Developing the strength of a retentive mindfulness, one sustains a meditative composure like the sky and a postmeditation that resembles an illusion. Therefore, meditation and postmeditation are two separate practices.

> The time of meditation on indivisibility is one taste.

Through perfect mindfulness that knows phenomena and emptiness as being inseparable, meditation and postmeditation are all practiced indivisibly.

> The time of actualization is nonmeditation.

After reaching the culmination of the realization, indivisibility is actualized, and the genuine state is realized as the "continuously flowing river yoga."

## Four Ways of Purifying Obscurations through Realizations Corresponding to Resting in Composure

Lord Yangonpa said:

> At the time of one-pointedness, there is freedom from the skandha of form, and the five sensory consciousnesses are purified.

Since the essence of apparent forms has no true existence, the five sensory doors arise as empty of identity.

> At the time of simplicity, the skandhas of sensation and evaluation and the mind consciousness are purified.

Since grasping at sensations, experiences, and cognitions of happiness and suffering are purified into lucid emptiness, they are not conventionally considered as existing things.

> At the time of one taste, the skandha of karmic formations and the afflictive consciousness are purified.

The indulging, grasping mind ceases, and all fixations on "I" and "mine" are realized as rootless and groundless.

> At the time of nonmeditation, the skandha of consciousness and the all-ground consciousness are purified.

There is no fixation on the experience of conviction as a tangible object, and by having purified the thought-free neutral state, nonthought arises as natural luminosity.

## Four Borderlines between Experience and Realization

As said:

> In one-pointedness, experience and realization are defiled.

There is simply the bondage of grasping.

> In simplicity, experience and realization are separated.

Stable realization arises as objectless, so experience and realization are cognized as distinct from one another.

> In one taste, experience and realization are indivisible.

Since experience itself arises as realization, they are inseparable in one taste.

> In nonmeditation, realization is continuous.

In nonduality, the uninterrupted primordial wisdom is actualized.

## Four Ways of Knowing Relative Cause and Effect

As said:

> At the time of one-pointedness, cause and effect is reified.

In the perception of an extremely vivid clear awareness, subtle and coarse cause and effect are resolved, but there is reification toward all things.

> At the time of simplicity, cause and effect is illusory.

The basic nature of mind is emptiness, devoid of birth, cessation, and change. Its unimpeded radiance is understood to be interdependent illusory cause and effect.

> At the time of one taste, cause and effect is like space.

From the primordially pure dharmadhatu—emptiness being the supreme emptiness—arises its unceasing expression of interdependence.

> At the time of nonmeditation, there is groundless dependent origination.

From inner space, the naturally perfect wisdom as it is, its unimpeded radiance as all that exists, arises dependently. On actualizing that, dualistic phenomena are cognized as inseparable.

## Other Distinctions

This includes the distinctions regarding: (1) the essence, (2) meditation and postmeditation, (3) the antidote, (4) the undesirable, and (5) the realization of the natural state.

## Distinctions Regarding the Essence

In one-pointedness, there is no realization of the basic state of one's mind as dharmakaya, whereas in simplicity there is. While the basic nature of one's dharmakaya mind and its radiance are inseparable, in simplicity perceived objects do not arise within that inseparability. However, in one taste they do arise within the essence, indivisibly with original dharmakaya, vividly, and without losing freshness or becoming faded. In one taste, there is a subtly fixated conviction, whereas in nonmeditation this is purified, and everything is the same in the sphere of wisdom.

## Distinctions between Meditation and Postmeditation

Meditation and postmeditation in one-pointedness differ in whether there is resting or not: to rest in bliss, clarity, and nonthought is meditation; not resting is postmeditation; if there is distraction, it is ensuing cognizance. The meditation and postmeditation in simplicity differ in whether there is mindfulness or not. To rest in the lucidity of one's original face is meditation; the manifestation of its radiance as alertness is postmeditation; to be carried away by thoughts is ensuing cognizance. The meditation and postmeditation of one taste differ in whether there is fixation or not. To rest nakedly and without fixation in the triad of phenomena, awareness, and mind is meditation. Without wavering from nonfixation, the natural radiance arising as the myriad things is postmeditation. To enter into a subtle fixation during daytime or particularly to be fixated at the time of sleep is ensuing cognizance. In nonmeditation, meditation and postmeditation are inseparable, yet it is said that there may or may not be an extremely subtle fixation.

## Distinctions Regarding the Antidote

At the time of one-pointedness, by resting composed in the continuity of one's unfabricated mind of its own accord, the experiences of bliss, clarity, and nonthought arise. This cuts the strength of what is to be abandoned—thoughts and emotions—so that their being released by themselves becomes the antidote. During simplicity, thoughts captured by mindfulness arise as dharmakaya, but while one forgets they arise as ensuing cognizance. At that point sustaining the practice through identifying them, the undesirable thoughts themselves function as an antidote. At the time of one taste, without wavering from the state of sky-like mind essence, all kinds of thoughts and phenomena arise. Upon their very arising, they are realized as dharmakaya mind, so indivisibility is practiced as the antidote. During nonmeditation, one is free from the fixation of conceptual constructs. Since dharmata has reached exhaustion, there is no meditation whatsoever.

## Distinctions Regarding the Elimination of the Undesirable

At the time of one-pointedness, because good experiences arise, one turns away from attachment to sensual objects. During simplicity, the natural state is understood, so one renounces interest in this life. At the time of one taste, phenomena are cognized as mind, so the eight worldly preoccupations are subdued. During nonmeditation, concepts and phenomena come to an end, so even all the subtle defilements are purified.

## Distinctions Regarding the Realization of the Natural State

At the time of one-pointedness, phenomena are realized as mind. During simplicity, all dependently arising external and internal phenomena are realized as emptiness. At the time of one taste, emptiness being the essence, all phenomena—outer and inner, samsara and nirvana—are realized as the myriad interdependencies. During nonmeditation, emptiness and interdependence are realized as perfect equality.

Furthermore, Lord Takpo said:

> The yoga of one-pointedness is the instantaneous cognizance in unimpeded clarity. The yoga of simplicity is such that, once the essence of awareness has been seen as unoriginated, there is no hope for high buddhahood, no fear of low samsara, in between no grasping at phenomena, and no other factor is able to make alterations. The yoga of one taste is when the indivisibility of phenomena and emptiness is realized. The yoga of nonmeditation is when whatever appears or is born arises as having the same essence; all thoughts and thinking become meditation.

And Lord Gyare said:

> One-pointedness is when experiences have highs and lows.
> It is a worldly path and accumulates karma.
> Simplicity is when the native place is seen.
> Meditation is mostly intermittent.
> One taste is when phenomena arise as meditation,
> Which has become continuous.
> Nonmeditation is the seat of dharmakaya,
> Which typically receives the name "nonmeditation."

One-pointedness is a worldly path; simplicity is when the natural state is seen; one taste is when phenomena arise as meditation; and nonmeditation is actual dharmakaya—nowadays it is largely accepted that it can be called nonmeditation. Lord Gyare added:

> When one-pointedness is sustained for a long time,
> You turn away from uncontrollable attachment to sensual objects,
> And acquire supernatural perception, miracles, and so forth,
> As well as just a fraction of an arhat's qualities.
>
> By sustaining the realization of simplicity,
> Deceptive phenomena are an unpredictable great spectacle.
> Through the strength of training and acumen,
> A fraction of a bodhisattva's qualities appear:
> Compassion free of attachment is ready to dawn.
>
> When one taste is sustained for a long time,
> There is the great spectacle of buddha fields.
> No matter whether you roll back and forth, or stand on your head,
> You never waver from the royal seat.
> When interdependence of cause and effect arises,

> It is like golden brocade spread out in the sun.
> You have some of the buddha qualities,
> And you benefit beings without bounds.
>
> When you have utterly reached nonmeditation,
> Your activity emerges to perfection, and sublime qualities arise.

Thus, he indicates the signs and qualities that arise for each of the four yogas by practicing them. Also, Lord Gotsangpa said:

> This self-luminous nonreferential awareness,
> As you become more familiar with it,
> Its realizations will be labeled as the four yogas.
> Ultimately, it is the transparent wisdom.

As Siddha Tsang Nyon advises:

> All phenomena of sights and sounds are perfect and included in an instant of sudden awareness. In other words, resting in the identity of ground, path, and fruition, or the four yogas, right when a phenomenon of the six senses appears and not moving from the continuous state is one-pointedness. While in one-pointedness, simplicity is when one no longer fixates on conceptual attributes. When conceptual elaborations are no more, since samsara and nirvana are equal and of the same taste, that is one taste. While in one taste, since one is beyond conceptual mind, that is nonmeditation.
>
> Furthermore, an abruptly arising thought, fresh, unfaded, and complete, is one-pointedness. Recognition of its essence is simplicity. To experience it within indivisible clarity and emptiness is one taste. Its liberation into the great transcendence of concepts is nonmeditation. Alternatively, its undamaged freshness is one-pointedness, its looseness is simplicity, its self-luminosity is one taste, and its ineffability is

> nonmeditation. Then again, transcending nonorigination is one-pointedness, arising unimpededly is simplicity, experiencing without duality is one taste, and the purified experience is nonmeditation.

In brief, to be able to rest in composure for as long as you wish is one-pointedness. To recognize ordinary mind and realize that it is groundless and rootless is simplicity. Being free within awareness of the fixation of perceiving samsara and nirvana dualistically is one taste. The purification of conviction and all stains of habitual patterns is nonmeditation.

The identities of the four yogas are here subsumed and discussed as the three yogas in the pieces of advice by Lord Phagmo Drupa, the considerations by glorious Taklung Thangpa, and the oral tradition by Siddha Tsang Nyon. This includes nine topics.

First, the three styles of realization: Through simplicity the nature is realized as unoriginated, through one taste the essence is realized as indivisible, and through nonmeditation the characteristics are realized as nondual.

Second, the three styles of freedom: Through simplicity there is freedom from the conceptual boundary of samsara, through one taste there is freedom from the seal of the karmic body, and through nonmeditation there is freedom from the seal of habitual perception.

Third, the three actualizations: In simplicity coarse cause and effect is actualized, in one taste subtle cause and effect is actualized, and in nonmeditation purified cause and effect is actualized.

Fourth, the three manners of purification: During simplicity the afflictive obscuration is purified, during one taste the karmic obscuration is purified, and during nonmeditation the cognitive obscuration is purified.

Fifth, the three manners of realization: During simplicity dharmakaya is realized, during one taste rainbow body is realized, and during nonmeditation the three kayas are realized.

Sixth, the three bodies: Simplicity is the body of aspiration, one taste is the body of samadhi, and nonmeditation is the body of enlightened activity.

Seventh, the three manners of arising: In simplicity first prajña beyond form arises, in one taste the intermediate prajña arises, and in nonmeditation the third prajña arises.

Eighth, the three possessions: In simplicity compassion with effort is possessed, in one taste effortless compassion is possessed, and in nonmeditation nonreferential compassion is possessed.

Ninth, the three times: During simplicity thoughts arise as dharmakaya, during one taste thoughts arise as meditation, and during nonmeditation all effort vanishes into space and primordial wisdom is attained within oneself.

# 10. An Explanation of Each of the Four Yogas

2. A Special Explanation of Each of the Four Yogas
   a. The Origin of the Classification as the Four Yogas
   b. Explanation of This Classification
      i. The Yoga of One-Pointedness
         A) Identity
         B) Experience
         C) Strayings
         D) Classification
            1) The Three Types of One-Pointedness
            2) The Four Types of One-Pointedness
            3) The Six Types of One-Pointedness
         E) Sustaining and Enhancing Techniques
         F) Borderlines
      ii. The Yoga of Simplicity
         A) Identity
         B) Experience
         C) Strayings
         D) Classification
            1) The Three Types of Simplicity
            2) The Four Types of Simplicity
            3) The Six Types of Simplicity
         E) Sustaining and Enhancing Techniques
         F) Borderlines
      iii. The Yoga of One Taste
         A) Identity

B) Experience
C) Strayings
D) Classification
1) The Three Types of One Taste
2) The Four Types of One Taste
3) The Six Types of One Taste
E) Sustaining and Enhancing Techniques
F) Borderlines
iv. The Yoga of Nonmeditation
A) Identity
B) Experience
C) Strayings
D) Classification
1) The Three Types of Nonmeditation
2) The Four Types of Nonmeditation
3) The Six Types of Nonmeditation
E) Sustaining and Enhancing Techniques
F) Borderlines

## A Special Explanation of Each of the Four Yogas

This includes: (1) the origin of the classification as the four yogas, and (2) explanation of this classification.

## The Origin of the Classification as the Four Yogas

As mentioned earlier, the source has been clearly taught in the sutras, tantras, and shastras. Nonetheless, the Indian and Tibetan masters haven't specifically taught anything apart from resting in the natural flow. Their great kindness is reflected in adaptations which make it easy for practitioners of current times to understand. In the works of Lord Gampopa, among the pieces of advice given to Lord Gomtsul, we find classifications in terms of higher, middling, and lower in each of the four yogas. Also, Phagmo Drupa taught these in his questions and answers. Gomtsul taught them concisely in verse. Lord Phagmo Drupa differentiated them. Master Zhang Rinpoche also taught them in an abridged form. In addition, the disciples of Takpo Rinpoche taught them to their own disciples, and the disciples of Phagmo Drupa, such as Drikungpa and Taklungpa, taught them as well. Indeed, there have been innumerable teachings on these four yogas.

The distinctive feature of our lineage is that the protector of beings Tsangpa Gyare taught the four yogas as having three aspects each, adding up to twelve, plus thirteen differentiations, and he explained their connection to the paths and bhumis. His lineage disciples, including Upper Drukpa, Lower Drukpa, and the transmission through the masters of the main seat, also composed many classifications of the four yogas in the form of texts, sayings, and advice. As a result, nowadays these four yogas are very well known in this precious practice lineage, and it is quite amazing that distinctions and degrees of experience and realization of the practice are considered very relevant for this time. Phagmo Drupa presented the better-known twelve subdivisions of the four yogas in the following way:

> Lesser one-pointedness is when the mind sees the identity of bliss and clarity, middling is when its samadhi is mastered, and greater is when it has become continuous. Lesser simplicity is when one's mind is realized as unoriginated, middling is when it is realized as rootless, and greater is when all misconceptions regarding the external and the internal have been resolved. Lesser one taste is when samsara and nirvana have merged into one, middling is when dualistic fixation has been cut, and greater is when all phenomena have subsided into equality. Lesser nonmeditation is when one is free from meditator and object of meditation, middling is when the

> original seat of natural presence is captured, and greater is when a nondual merging with luminosity has occurred.

The meaning of this quotation shall be explained later.

These twelve yogas do not occur in strict consecutive order. For instance, without having completed the experience and realization of greater one-pointedness, lesser or middling simplicity may take place. Without having completed those of greater simplicity, lesser or middling one taste may take place. Without having completed those of greater one taste, lesser or middling nonmeditation may take place. Therefore, the explanations do not spell out the order of occurrence. That being so, the experiences and realizations have been explained mostly according to the way they took place in the personal experience of past practitioners of the practice lineage who, relying only on staying in solitude, hoisted the victory banner of practice. Besides, their explanations have to do with individuals of the gradual type, and they haven't conclusively specified the references to the sudden and leap type of individuals.[48] Regarding practitioners of current times especially, who for the most part are lazy and carried away by distraction, the way experiences and realizations take place may not coincide exactly with the way they are explained in the teachings. Nonetheless, even nowadays there are people of higher intelligence who received the blessings of the guru and in whom the realized essence has arisen exactly as it is. Since the past gurus of the practice lineage considered it important for their practitioners to measure the extent of their spiritual practice, I am explaining these points based on their teachings.

## Explanation of This Classification

This includes explanations on: (1) the yoga of one-pointedness, (2) the yoga of simplicity, (3) the yoga of one taste, and (4) the yoga of nonmeditation.

## The Yoga of One-Pointedness

This includes explanations on its: (1) identity, (2) experience, (3) strayings, (4) classification, (5) sustaining and enhancing techniques, and (6) borderlines.

## The Identity of One-Pointedness

The meaning of the term "one-pointedness" is that one's mind remains in the natural state with one-pointed undistracted mindfulness, or when stillness and movement have merged and awareness is one-pointed. "Well then," you may ask, "doesn't this contradict the explanation that the realization of the natural state happens in simplicity?" There is no contradiction, as there are enormous differences between them, such as the object of meditation being one's mind, external and internal phenomena being distinct, the clinging to experience and the object of conviction in one case, and the absence of these in the other. Some explain shamatha as being one-pointedness, when the mind rests in the state of nonthought with vividly clear cognizance which (in this case of one-pointedness) remains deluded. Some others consider that when a conviction of an understanding of emptiness dawns on the shamatha itself, delusion appears to be purified. The first one is decisively inadmissible because even though shamatha may have merely arisen flawlessly, it completely lacks the conviction of vipashyana. The other one also does not hold true because it is simply an intellectual understanding of emptiness; it lacks the conviction of vipashyana, which sees mind essence. Therefore, in "seeing mind essence," "seeing" requires that awareness rests one-pointedly, stillness and movement merge as equal taste, and there is a wakefulness that recognizes one's essence. So it is said, "At the time of one-pointedness, the essence is seen." Lord Yangonpa said:

> Mind moving to thought is the gate to the natural state.
> To recognize your essence is the key point of practice.

> When your original face is seen, it merges with yourself.
> See if there is a thought apart from yourself.
> A meditation where the wall between stillness and movement has collapsed will occur.

We must understand the way of sustaining one-pointedness as explained.

## The Experience of One-Pointedness

At the time of lesser one-pointedness, resting composed is such that the experiences of clarity, nonthought, and bliss are tangible. It may happen that you sustain the practice while clinging to them. If thoughts and perceptions arise from this experience, in most cases you will not be under their sway; they cannot stand on their own and are freed by themselves. So you think, "This is meditation," and clinging to that conviction arises. At times, it will also happen that you are unable to liberate thoughts. In the ensuing phenomena, you will feel joyful by and large, and this will arise as concrete. In the ensuing cognizance, you will uphold it through mindfulness. With an experience of empty clarity, a conceptual stance will arise that thinks, "It is empty" or "It is a projection of the mind." The lucidity in dreams is barely enhanced, so your dreams will not be much different than before. Some say they have more dreams but will identify fewer. It may be difficult to rest composed so you think, "Meditation is not happening to me." Alternatively, you may feel you are having quite a good meditation. Thus, there will be great waxing and waning in your practice. Devotion to the guru, pure perception toward Dharma siblings, and compassion to beings are born.

In middling one-pointedness, a stable samadhi endowed with the experiences of clarity, nonthought, and bliss takes place. Sometimes even though you are not meditating, you completely enter samadhi. In these experiences, thoughts and perceptions occur less often than before, and whatever arises is released by itself. Ensuing phenomena have the experience of empty clarity, so the mood is carefree and vibrant. At times, this is reified. By identifying all sudden thoughts, they dissipate in stillness. Due to its strength you feel very much like meditating. While dreaming, experiences may or may not come, as appropriate. To some people dreams decrease in number. There is joy in meditation.

At the time of greater one-pointedness, since a samadhi endowed with the experience of empty clarity arises uninterruptedly, thoughts cannot proliferate much, and while in stillness they subside by themselves. An unshakable stillness takes place. Typically, you enter dreams in that state and have a conviction that clings to good and bad. Many experiences of void occur in the mind—empty bliss, empty awareness, thoughts as empty clarity, and phenomena as empty appearances. Experiences in which you feel that all phenomena are like dreams and illusions increase. Some conditioned qualities such as mild clairvoyance are also born. Once you are accustomed to this, it becomes constant and leads to complacency in not meditating. Devotion, pure perception, and other qualities are also born.

## Removing Strayings and Clearing Faults in One-Pointedness

We have already discussed extensively how to clear the faults of the strayings related to this point. Here, and just to hint at its regular meaning, some people do not clearly see stillness and movement with a precise distinction, yet say that from the beginning they neither forget nor are distracted. However, what they are actually doing is guarding the meditation one-sidedly, and that is considered to be apathetic shamatha. If that is practiced as the meditation, even if it were sustained for an eon, no qualities would be born, and it is said that it would become cause for rebirth as an animal. To remove this obstacle, one must reinforce mindful knowing and develop the potential based on the perception of phenomena.

Furthermore, some say that when sudden thoughts and the mindfulness that identifies them meet on the spot, that would be the undesirable and the antidote meeting chest to chest, and it may become the main practice of someone in the path of connection. This happens often to some people, and they feel self-important, claiming that they are sustaining whatever arises. Although one may sustain this, one's spiritual practice will never be developed, so it must be abandoned. Through this experience of one-pointedness all thoughts are subdued, and even if they don't emerge for a while, as soon as the experience wanes, they will revive. It is said that to revert from that change is similar to what happens to a red-hot iron when it cools.[49] Conceited attachment to that experience is born and when this is solidified, experience has slipped to concept. This is an extremely serious straying. Practitioners of low intelligence who have followed a guru for a short time may devote their whole life to a superficial practice stuck to the glue of meditative experience, but they will not recognize mind essence, and even if they do, they will lose it again. Lord Gampopa said:

> A view lacking realization
> May be called free of extremes, but it is conceptually fabricated.
> Those meditators who have not reached certainty
> May have a good samadhi, but it is the cause of samsara.

As said by Lord Drikungpa:

> Left uncorrected,[50] good experiences
> Are causes for rebirth in the higher states of the gods.

If these experiences are sustained without attachment, they will constitute the basis or root of all sublime qualities. It is also important not to give in to conceptual attachment or clinging to the naked nature of mind itself. The Great Brahmin said:

> No matter what your object of attachment is, give it up!

Lord Gampopa said:

> The meditator who has dualistic clinging
> Has experiences, but that's not the real thing.

Once that experience has vanished, some people go completely into an ordinary state and think, "My meditation is lost," after which they exert effort, but nothing happens as before. No matter how much they try, not one atom of it takes place again. It is said that the very moment these experiences disappear is when the nature of mind should be introduced. Therefore, it should be recognized right at awareness, on the spot. Without that introduction, since there would be no one subduing conceptual thoughts, their view and conduct would be in accordance with those of ordinary people. Following their karma, they could possibly be reborn in such states as the lower realms. If the guru is far away and they cannot find a realized experienced yogin in their stead, without further ado they should place their total trust in their own guru and make supplications. If they do so, once they receive the blessings, they will recognize the realization.

## The Classification of One-Pointedness

This includes explanations on: (1) the three types of one-pointedness, (2) the four types of one-pointedness, and (3) the six types of one-pointedness.

## The Three Types of One-Pointedness

Once the samadhi endowed with the experience of the bliss of mind essence—empty clarity—has dawned, beginning around the moment of finding it hard to sustain up to when meditation comes at will, that is lesser one-pointedness. At times, samadhi arises even when one is not meditating, and since it remains stable, one has mastered it; that is middling one-pointedness. Once the experience of that samadhi becomes uninterrupted day and night, both in meditation and postmeditation, and awareness turns completely into the continuity of that empty clarity, that is greater one-pointedness.

## The Four Types of One-Pointedness (Applying the Four Yogas to Each of Them, Thus Adding Up to Sixteen)

First, once coarse and subtle thoughts have subsided, to rest while in empty clarity is the one-pointedness of one-pointedness. Second, to cut off assumptions derived from fixating on the characteristics of the identity of stillness is the simplicity of one-pointedness. Third, to unite bliss, clarity, and nonthought without acceptance or rejection is the one taste of one-pointedness. Fourth, to know that the cognizance that is having the experience has no true existence is the nonmeditation of one-pointedness.

## The Six Types of One-Pointedness

We will follow the classification made by Lord Gyare. First, whether the essence is seen or not: That mind essence has no intrinsic existence whatsoever means it is "empty." Although empty, because its manifestations are unimpeded, it is "lucid." The essence of one-pointedness is seen when you are confident that the cognizance of inseparable lucidity and emptiness is like the center of a clear sky, and a thought-free conviction that it is self-knowing dawns.

On the other hand, the mind may be simply resting vividly awake on the experiences of bliss, clarity, and nonthought, yet a conviction about the wisdom of self-knowing awareness hasn't been reached. If so, it hasn't merged with the experience of vipashyana, and there is an experience of not being certain about phenomena, like a child looking at the moon's reflection in water. This means the essence hasn't been seen.

Second, whether the potential is developed or not: While in the state of composure of the samadhi of bliss, clarity, and nonthought and imbued with the conviction of self-knowing awareness, if you are able to rest at will whenever you want to, then the potential is developed. But if sometimes you meditate and it doesn't happen, or it happens although you have not meditated, then the potential hasn't yet developed.

Third, whether thoughts arise as meditation or not: Thoughts arise as meditation when, by simply recognizing all thoughts that arise, they spontaneously turn into the continuity of the natural state, and during the experience of sleep, the mind enters luminosity. But if thoughts are unable to subside, even through retentive mindfulness, and you need to draw them in with the meditation hook and consequently place them in meditation, then thoughts are not arising as meditation.

Fourth, whether qualities are born or not: Through stillness, mind does not become involved with external objects, so it turns away from the eight worldly preoccupations. When outer and inner germs have been eliminated, and one can show miracles such as some clairvoyance and control over the elements, the qualities of one-pointedness have dawned. But if the mind is not pliable or peaceful, the qualities of meditation haven't been sifted from the refuse, and you have not been able to bring about the ordinary signs of progress, then the qualities haven't yet dawned.

Fifth, whether the conventional level is mastered or not: In the ensuing cognizance of the perceptions of lucid samadhi, when there is a final conclusion about interdependence arising inevitably from coarse or subtle, inner or outer, cause and effect, and so abandonment and acceptance are carried out correspondingly, then the conventional level is mastered. But if you have not found certainty regarding that sort of interdependence and are careless about acceptance and rejection connected with cause and effect, then you have not mastered the conventional level.

Sixth, whether the seed of rupakaya has been planted or not: When conceptual compassion for beings is born within the radiance of such meditation, and you are able to make vast altruistic aspirations, the seed of rupakaya has been planted. But if the samadhi is dimmed by all sorts of experiences, you find compassion difficult to arise, and you strive for the sake of your own peace and well-being, then the seed of rupakaya hasn't been planted.

## The Techniques for Sustaining and Enhancing One-Pointedness

At the time of the third one-pointedness, persevere in staying in retreat in the mountains, sealing the entrance to your room, and observing silence. If you are strongly contaminated,[51] the mind will not be pliable and your intelligence will dim, so shun offerings that create obscurations. Even when the contamination is weak, samadhi will not be clear and its obstacles and faults will abound, so strongly refrain from contamination and take care of cleanliness and behavior. If you are contaminated, get rid of it. Even when the mind is undistracted and loosely one-pointed, no matter what good or bad experiences arise, sustain the recognition of the essence upon them, while free from dualistic fixation, blocking, or acquiring. Those who have mostly dullness and agitation should apply the specific techniques to eliminate each of them and look at the essence many times. If dullness is so heavy that it is a big fault, so you should purify negativities applying any suitable method. Ask your guru for empowerment and take many empowerments of samadhi. Carry out sacred feasts, make offerings, and practice generosity. Consult your guru and experienced Dharma friends and eliminate the fault. When the fault is very intense, you don't feel like consulting your guru and Dharma friends, and many wrong ideas arise. That is an obstacle of the maras, so strive in taking refuge. Summon up the strength of weariness, renunciation, devotion, pure perception, and compassion, and meditate. After some days you may rest and do some suitable physical exercise.

Then, as explained before, guard the samadhi sustaining it one-pointedly through mindfulness of movement or retentive mindfulness (whichever is applicable) like a crane waiting for a fish. In the ensuing cognizance period, don't pursue objects of intellectual analysis, thought-free stillness, savoring the experiences, or the perceiver and perceived. Don't be attached to good experiences or regard bad ones as faults, but sustain the samadhi without succumbing to the fixation of stopping or acquiring whatever arises in your mind. If the experience is dense, it obscures the essence, so over and again get rid of the moisture of experiences. Strengthen awareness, sustaining precisely the fresh cognizance that doesn't fall into making corrections. At times, also read the liberating lives of the past masters of the practice lineage, and learn how through hardships and exertion they stuck to their practice. Also, read vajra songs of realization, and so forth, and feel that also you will cultivate the fortitude to follow a similar way of life.

In case you have sustained the yoga of one-pointedness for many years but you have not progressed to simplicity, it is said that the following three attachments should be abandoned. Regarding letting go of attachment to your ego, and so to cut off the bonds of desire and attachment to this life, keep away from crowds. Get rid of attachment and aversion to friend or foe, and shed the shackles of mundane life. Offer your body to the guru. When clinging dearly to your body, carry out the many worship rituals of a simple practitioner.

Regarding giving up attachment to wealth, offer the guru whatever riches you have that please them. To the assembly of yidams offer ritual torma and sacred feasts. Give vajra siblings all you have that pleases them. Cast away the desire for abundant happiness, food, or high position. Disregard food, clothing, and talk. Practice the conduct explained earlier such as the one similar to that of a [wounded] deer. Give up dwellings that induce attachments, aversions, and distractions, such as your native place. If, no matter how hard you try, you are unable to abandon these, maintain silence for a few years.

Regarding letting go of attachment to samadhi, destroy all pleasing and likable experiences in which you trust. Resolve not to regard anything that arises in the natural state as good or bad. Don't let anything distract you from the raw, original mind essence as it is, devoid of experiences however it may be, and rest in nonmeditation. Lord Gampopa said:

> At the beginning, while learning, train in making cognizance vividly lucid. Then train in nondistraction. Then train in not being distracted from the essence of awareness. Once you are habituated to this, conviction will be born in you.

Lord Gyare said:

> Once you are in one-pointedness, you should destroy experiences and practice nonmeditation.

In particular, at all times and in every situation, gradually enhance your spiritual practice by persevering in making supplications to your realized authentic guru with genuine devotion, placing your complete trust in them. In due course, the pure and impure parts of awareness will be separated, attachment to experience will be cleansed, you will realize the nature of mind as it is, and the realization of simplicity will dawn.

## The Borderlines of One-Pointedness

Among other borderlines the teachings indicated the following. Practice lower than one-pointedness is defiled. The meditation of simplicity is undefiled. Up to one-pointedness knowing is conceptual; thereafter it is nonconceptual wisdom. Up to one-pointedness it is a worldly meditation; thereafter it transcends mundane meditation. Up to one-pointedness it is the ground of engagement through aspiration; thereafter it is engagement through capacity. Up to one-pointedness the absolute is a designation; thereafter it is the actual absolute. Up to one-pointedness it is inferential valid cognition; from simplicity onward it is evident valid cognition.

Lesser one-pointedness is equivalent to the lesser path of accumulation. During middling one-pointedness, since you have attained the samadhi of Dharma flow, this completes both the middling and greater paths of accumulation. Since in greater one-pointedness the wisdom of the path of connection is born, it is equivalent to the actual path of connection. Thus, since you don't traverse through greater one-pointedness beyond the supreme attribute—the highest attainment within worldly systems—the three levels of one-pointedness are on the plane of the mundane.

## The Yoga of Simplicity

This includes explanations on: (1) definition of the identity, (2) experience, (3) strayings, (4) classification, (5) sustaining and enhancing techniques, and (6) borderlines.

## The Definition of the Identity of Simplicity

The term *simplicity* stands for the following: By purifying your obscurations and receiving the blessings of your guru, you will come to know the essence of mahamudra. The mind becomes joyful, and the undesirable and antidote are cognized as nondual. Therefore, you don't need a rigid antidote like before, and your mind becomes open and expansive. From the natural luminosity of mind essence all kinds of things arise, yet they turn into the expanse of thoroughly knowing the nature, after which it is sufficient to let them be. Since there is no need to deliberately fixate on stopping and acquiring, joy is born. At that time, devotion to the guru also increases, and your mind will merge with the Dharma. Regarding this, Gyalwa Yangonpa said:

> Karmic fruition is awakened, blessings are received, and experience culminates. From these three interdependencies, in time the truth of Dharma, the absence of elaborations, is seen. What is seen? Itself is seen. Who sees? It is seen by itself. How is the seeing? The seeing is nondual, without the division of subject and object. In between the ceasing of past cognizance and the birth of future cognizance, the cognizance of nowness itself is recognized, not as an object.

And:

> Furthermore, at that instant of realization the mind is pulled out from the sheath of subject and object. Words, conventions, theories, and experiences have become external husks and peel off.

Furthermore:

> That thoughts arise as dharmakaya is in fact the manner of arising corresponding to lesser simplicity. Apply the great key point to whatever arises.

When it is said that thoughts are dharmakaya at the time of simplicity, it does not mean that you have realized the dharmakaya as such, free of obscurations. What is meant here is that thoughts simply have the dharmakaya nature. In other words, the empty essence of the mind is dharmakaya, and you know that the myriad forms that arise from its natural radiance are all identical. Since the realization of the natural state occurs once meditator and object of meditation are comprehended as indivisible, it is said that thoughts are dharmakaya. Thus, apart from that there is no need to make any choices at all, for even an instant, so you will have an open state of mind. Apart from the flow of simply knowing the nature of your own mind, you don't need to rely on dualistic antidotes, deliberately adopting and rejecting. Since there is no need for meditator and object of meditation, this is why it is called "free from object of meditation."

Moreover, the masters of the past have referred to the confidence of realization in the following terms. The unconditioned absolute nature is evidently seen. Since there is no longer reified samsaric suffering, that is the bhumi of supreme joy. The border between samsara and nirvana is opened. Misconceptions and doubts are eliminated. The three divisions of time are realized as one. One instant of mind knows everything. When looking outside there are no conceptual elaborations. When looking inside there are no conceptual elaborations. Cognizance being unsupported, awareness does not touch anything at all, and it is free from all conceptual elaborations. The essence of awareness will be as if some solid value was inserted in its core, or as if its skin was peeled off, or like the heart entering the essence. At that point the essence is found. If not, it hasn't been recognized. An undefiled joy blooms, like a pauper who has found a treasure. A mind with crystal clear joy and delight unfolds. Then, by meditating persistently, all deluded thoughts are purified and an awareness that has shed effortful practice becomes unelaborated. That is called the yoga of simplicity. Lord Gotsangpa said:

> After purifying the experiences of one-pointedness, realization happens gradually. The various things that appear are realized as simplicity, and once both thinking and capturing through mindfulness have been purified, the realization becomes ordinary, free, and relaxed. This is called "seeing the essence of meditation."

Here "ordinary" has three meanings. The first is the ordinariness of thoughts: It is this instant of thought. The second is the ordinariness of experience: It is to rest without object after the mindfulness which recognizes the thought and the thought itself are both purified. This is the realization of greater one-pointedness and the experience of lesser simplicity, while the essence has still not been seen. The third is the ordinariness of realization: In the essence of an instant of thought, uncontaminated by both samsara and nirvana, there is in itself an ever-present natural luminosity. When it is identified, the thought subsides by itself. In other words, regardless of pure or impure, whatever arises in an instant is not blocked, but instead it is recognized. That recognition has indeed been taught as being the ordinariness of realization. Also, Lord Gyare said:

> It has been taught that the difference between one-pointedness and simplicity is whether thoughts arise as dharmakaya or not. While looking at the origination, abiding, and cessation of a thought, you see the essence of mind but do not see the actual genuine state. By seeing the genuine mind essence, without regarding the origination, abiding, and cessation of the thought even for an instant, its form arises fresh and in its natural condition, so what happens is precisely what is

> meant by "self-liberation of spontaneous arising."[52] Besides, regarding the mind free from origination, abiding, and cessation, the masters of the past said that from the perspective of awareness, instantaneous awareness is not blocked, and from the perspective of emptiness, it is unborn; it does not dwell in nondual awareness and emptiness and it is also not "inseparable," so it transcends concept. When this is recognized you are free from the afflictive obscuration. Since there is no stain of fixating on that, you are free from the cognitive obscuration.

Here, some people believe that the absence of conceptual constructs of subject and object is the meaning of simplicity. Others deem the conviction of recognizing all phenomena as emptiness to be what simplicity means. Neither of these is acceptable. The first is unacceptable because mere thought-free shamatha would then become simplicity; the second is unacceptable because the attachment to the conviction about things being empty and not real would then become simplicity. Therefore, the teachings say that it is at the time of simplicity that the nature of mind is realized. Mind nature is explained to be like space: unconditioned and changeless. The sutras say, "Profound, peaceful, free of constructs, luminous, and unconditioned." Also the *Sublime Continuum* says:

> What is the luminous nature of mind like?
> It is changeless like space.

## The Experience of Simplicity

Even though the essence of all phenomena is free from the conceptual constructs of origination, abiding, and cessation, you cling to the fixation on the emptiness of everything. In the ensuing cognizance, a fixation arises reifying friend and foe, attachment and aversion, and sleep and dreaming also mostly arise as delusion. There are great highs and lows in your spiritual practice. Toward the guru and Dharma siblings, as well as your own practice, sometimes you have faith and conviction is born; at times doubts can arise.

At the time of middling simplicity, no matter what, a small attachment results from the experience of clinging to emptiness. The experience of habitual patterns of thoughts shines vividly. Empty awareness and empty thought movement do not arise as concrete entities. They are not blocked as being insubstantial entities and do not dwell as separate entities. They are realized as being free from origination, abiding, and cessation. At this time, once the root of conceptual thought has been cut, misconceptions based on thought movement are resolved, but reified hope and fear occasionally appear based on phenomena. In the ensuing cognizance and dreaming, various delusions and nondelusions take place. Toward the guru, Dharma siblings, and spiritual practice, highs and lows of faith, doubts, and so forth occasionally happen. At times you think that there is no buddhahood to be attained or no hell to be reborn in.

At the time of greater simplicity, by having cut off the root of all samsaric phenomena, misconceptions regarding all external and internal things are resolved, and hope and fear die out. Without hope and fear regarding all phenomena as empty or not empty, and so forth, the mind becomes open and totally free. Also, all perceptions arise as empty and lacking intrinsic identity. In the ensuing cognizance, the fact that all thoughts have been purified does not completely result in a sole vividly lucid cognizance. Nonetheless, together with the pure, good experience of empty cognizance and empty phenomena, daytime meditation is uninterrupted. Yet, since that continuity is not fully held by mindfulness, at times you must resort to retentive mindfulness. While dreaming, delusion and grasping occasionally happen. Sometimes you think you have realized the natural state, devoid of buddhahood to be attained or hells to be reborn in. Even very profound teachings are understood. Mind essence arises as the guru. Phenomena arise as allies of spiritual practice. At any rate, attachment diminishes, and the mind turns away from the eight worldly preoccupations. Nevertheless, it is said there is a danger that you may think that you now no longer need a guru, become proud, feel self-important, despise others, and so forth.

## The Strayings of Simplicity, Clearing Faults

At this point, with a strong experience of emptiness, the cause and effect of karma is seen as lacking true existence. Knowing them not to be true, there is a danger that you muddle up what is to be adopted and abandoned, in which case it would be as the saying goes, "performing simplicity influenced by nothingness." This straying happens here.

When it is said "cause and effect arises as emptiness," it means that the seed of things as they are was planted, but the seed of things as they appear is ruined. Recognized absolute with unrecognized relative results in "the maras' work of spreading out negation."[53] Regarding this, by knowing the infallibility of the cause and effect of karma, act properly, adopting and rejecting. Knowing the conventional to be dependently originated, exert yourself in practicing with the two truths in equal terms. Furthermore, if you go along with fixation, your practice will become as is said, "cut grass that is not dry yet,"[54] "human footprints turned into dog's footprints,"[55] and "meditation born without a boss." Therefore, emphasizing undistracted nonmeditation, sustain it without clinging to, adopting, or rejecting the mere occurrence of the myriad perceptions of samsara and nirvana, good and bad.

## The Classification of Simplicity

This includes explanations on: (1) the three types of simplicity, (2) the four types of simplicity, and (3) the six types of simplicity.

## The Three Types of Simplicity

You may have realized mind essence as being free from the conceptual constructs of origination and cessation, yet you are not free from experiencing the conviction fixated on emptiness, are afraid of wandering in samsara, and hope to attain nirvana. This is lesser simplicity. When the mind has been cleansed of the experience of fixating on phenomena and emptiness, you realize mind essence as rootless and without basis. Nevertheless, the fixation on hope and fear based on outer objects of perception takes place, so misconceptions haven't been resolved. This is middling simplicity. Once you are free from the conviction and fixation on the emptiness of all external and internal phenomena—of the world and beings, of samsara and nirvana—and there is no longer any hope and fear, doubts and misconceptions are severed. This is greater simplicity.

## The Four Types of Simplicity

The four yogas are each classified into four subdivisions, adding up to sixteen subdivisions, which include the four types of simplicity. First, any thought that arises goes into the state of nonorigination; this is one-pointedness of simplicity. Second, as the objects of perception of the six spheres have no attributes, misconceptions fixating on these are resolved; this is simplicity of simplicity. Third, not to adopt or reject any thought that arises is one taste of simplicity. Fourth, the experience of emptiness purified is nonmeditation of simplicity.

## The Six Types of Simplicity

In the context of the four yogas each classified into six subdivisions, there are twenty-four subdivisions, which include the six types of simplicity.

First, in terms of whether the essence is seen or not: In seeing the simplicity of the essence, the fixation on conviction is freed. When the root of the one who experiences it as simplicity has been cut, if all constructs are totally freed in the state of purity, the essence of simplicity is seen. In this, fixating on emptiness or everything connected to conviction is an experience of simplicity. But if there is a slight experience of the division between perceiver and perceived, although there may be experience and realization in simplicity, the essence hasn't been seen.

Second, in terms of whether the potential has developed or not: By recognizing the essence of all phenomena of samsara and nirvana, there will not even be a tiny bit of hope or fear, or of fixation on emptiness. If reifications about everything are eliminated within simplicity, the potential of simplicity has been developed. However, if thoughts are known to be unborn, but the experiences of hope and fear and fixation on emptiness based on objects of perception haven't been purified, the potential hasn't developed.

Third, in terms of whether thoughts arise as meditation or not: First, all thoughts and thinking are realized as being empty movements in the state of awareness, and all phenomena arise in the equality of bare recognition as empty phenomena. Then, when all ensuing cognizance and ensuing phenomena arise as the realization of resting in composure, thoughts arise as meditation. But if the realization of resting in composure does not occur in thinking and perceptions, and the ensuing cognizance and perceptions are not taken as the path, this results in spiritual practice not being accomplished based on experience. Then, thoughts do not arise as meditation.

Fourth, in terms of whether sublime qualities are born or not: Having met the path that awakens the qualities, such as the path of means, if this connects with the signs of accomplishment and realization, the qualities of simplicity have dawned. Absolute reality may have been realized, but if it hasn't turned into conditions on the path and there is no manifestation of the signs of accomplishment, the qualities haven't dawned.

Fifth, whether the relative level has been mastered or not: By realizing that cause and effect is the radiance of emptiness, its basic nature is nothing whatsoever. Nonetheless, interdependence is such that conditions are flexible and can be managed. All phenomena occur from a collection of factors; they are born from conditions. When they are known to be just an illusory cause and effect, an illusory mental projection, the relative level has been mastered. But not having eliminated the ignorance of being deluded about suchness, if you are veiled by the ignorance of being deluded about cause and effect and do not understand that interdependence, then the relative level hasn't been mastered.

Sixth, whether the seed of rupakaya has been planted or not: Once the expression of the realization of emptiness has arisen as nonreferential compassion, when through the mechanisms of bodhichitta, aspirations, and so forth, you know how to set up the right interdependencies in ensuing phenomena without reifying, then you have planted the seed of rupakaya. But if it is difficult to arouse compassion despite having realized emptiness, and you don't know how to set up the right conditions of interdependence to help others, then the seed of rupakaya hasn't been planted.

## The Techniques for Sustaining and Enhancing Simplicity

Once you have abandoned the three types of attachment during the three stages of simplicity, you should strive in solitude, keep silent, and seal the door to your meditation dwelling. Offerings of torma and supplications to the guru should be kept to a minimum. As has been explained, it is best to keep conceptual spiritual practices to a minimum. So leave them aside for some time and give birth to the meditation without allowing it to be without a master, so to speak. If you are forgetful at first, train only in a retentive mindfulness of emptiness. You must precisely sustain a stable mind essence. Lord Lhatsewa said:

> The essence of all phenomena is the natural coemergent wisdom, or absolute truth, utterly nondwelling indivisible mahamudra, ordinary mind not fabricated by anyone, the awareness that knows itself, raw and naked. This is precisely what is sustained. The great Lord Translator Marpa said, "In the mountain hermitage blazing like fire, with a claw I caught the mind of emptiness."

If you don't slip from recognizing your awareness, you will feel all good and bad situations as allies, you will neither adopt nor reject anything that arises, and although you don't deliberately meditate, you will not be distracted even for a moment. This undistracted nonmeditation is called "the path of the self-existing essence of its own accord." Always sustain it with perseverance. Also from time to time, generate conditioned merit, such as making offerings and practicing generosity. Practice devotion, pure perception, and compassion, and reflect on the interdependence of cause and effect. Request profound discussions with the guru and realized Dharma siblings and friends. Read such texts as the vajra songs of realization of the lineage siddhas and sing them melodiously. Tuning yourself to the realized essence, develop conviction. At that time, you should sharpen awareness and lay it bare, lest dullness prevents you from detecting the meditation stains and distinguishing meditation and postmeditation. Having laid awareness bare, know each of the three types of meditation and postmeditation. Without falling prey to ensuing cognizance, you should practice sustaining the prevalence of emptiness. Lord Gampopa said:

> During the yoga of simplicity, it is important to avoid remaining apathetic. Instead, sharpen awareness.

And Lord Gyare said:

> Once you have reached the time of simplicity,
> Meditate merging all phenomena included in the two groups.

Thus he explains that, having developed a sharp cognizance, you merge it with the variety of phenomena and meditate on simplicity. Lord Yangonpa said:

> Don't lose the freshness of undistracted mindfulness.
> Don't fabricate the nonmeditated natural state.
> Don't wish to verbalize inconceivable awareness.
> Sustain openly without contaminating with analysis.
> In meditation, the mother and child of simplicity will meet.

He instructs us to reinforce retentive mindfulness so we don't slip away from the face of simplicity and become distracted from it. Since it will not do to modify its natural state, don't meditate on anything else as new. Don't analyze awareness, which is beyond thought, words, or expression, but sustain it casually. You should rely on these points.

If it happens that joy and cognizance diminish, you want to leave, your heart is unhappy, and so forth, carry out the appropriate practices of the path of means: blazing and dripping, supreme tummo, or yogic exercises. Once the realization of greater simplicity dawns, if you practice for a year but there is no progress, again let go of the three attachments, take empowerments, confess damaged and broken commitments, and so forth, and supplicate that your realization increases. While meditating on your deity, reflect on the suffering of the hells, and when you are definite about that in your mind, rest composed in the state of simplicity. Similarly, thinking about the happiness and bliss of the gods, rest in simplicity. Contemplating the samsaric condition, rest in simplicity. Considering the natural state of nirvana, rest in simplicity. Sometimes go to the top of a mountain and relax in simplicity. At times go to a crowded place and relax in simplicity. While controlling wind-energies in a session, stare at appearances and relax in simplicity. These will bring about enhancement.

Sometimes go to a place where fierce gods and demons dwell or to a place where there is a great show. When sustaining awareness in these places without lapsing, magical manifestations of spirits and demons occur, whether actually appearing or manifesting in a visionary experience. All kinds of undesirable things, such reactions as excitation and depression, will happen. These are called the "arising of testing." At that point, see them as your parents while in the state of great altruistic love, and in order to repay your karmic debts, offer your whole body to the spirits and demons. Say these words, "You who like meat, eat my flesh! You who like blood, drink my blood! If it takes too long, eat it raw! If you have time, cook it and eat! If you can carry it, take it away!" After casting all away from your mind, rest in the continuity of the Dharma without wavering. This will bring about effortless progress in your spiritual practice, the strength of awareness will increase more and more, and a feeling of certainty that the nature of this crisp and clear ordinary mind abides as the dharmakaya will dawn from within. This is called "the extent of completion." When the practice has become continuous throughout day and night, this is what the omniscient Drukpa has described as a small awakening free from the bardo. Don't follow after the many kinds of perceptions stirred up by circumstances. If you disregard the cause and effect of karma, this would be straying, so practice instantaneous giving and taking. Since positive qualities such as generosity are practices, offer one hundred tormas every single day. Altruistic work is similar to aspirations, so make vast aspirations. If you carry all this out while in the undistracted state, it is called the "wisdom display" or "expression of dharmakaya." Practicing this way, toward all the phenomena of samsara and nirvana, you will eventually neither block nor acquire through being free from conceptual constructs or not, being empty or not, adopting or rejecting, and so forth. Whatever takes place will arise as mahamudra, the yoga of one taste, fresh and not faded.

## The Borderlines of Simplicity

Since the truth of absolute reality is seen in lesser simplicity, through this you are free from the fears of samsara and are close to attaining enlightenment. Seeing that you benefit beings a special joy dawns, so this is the first bhumi, the "Supreme Joy." In middling simplicity, through the power of realizing that all phenomena are rootless and without basis, ethical discipline will no longer be contaminated by violations, so this is the second bhumi, the "Immaculate." In greater simplicity, all phenomena arise as luminosity, as appearances devoid of true nature, so this is the third bhumi, the "Illuminating."

## The Yoga of One Taste

This includes explanations on: (1) identity, (2) experience, (3) strayings, (4) classification, (5) techniques for sustaining and enhancing, and (6) borderlines.

## The Identity of One Taste

As to the meaning of the yoga of one taste, the general teachings in this regard explain that all phenomena included in the world and beings, samsara and nirvana, have one taste in emptiness—the absolute reality. This is referred to as "one taste." The Great Brahmin said:

> The sacred guru himself is the one who provokes the realization that all myriad phenomena are of one meaning and have a single identity in emptiness.

Shawaripa said:

> Just like the Ganges and all other rivers
> Are of one taste in the salty ocean,
> Know that conventional mind and the variety of mental events
> Are of one taste in the dharmadhatu.

However, in our case the meaning of one taste is as follows. Although the dualistic phenomena of different kinds, visible and invisible, are a multiplicity, in their inseparable essence they are of one taste, therefore it is called one taste. Lord Phagmo Drupa said:

> The myriad visible and invisible phenomena are mind, and empty.
> Empty and not empty are inseparable in one taste, and empty.
> Realized and not realized are of one taste. Meditation and postmeditation are undivided.
> Meditation and nonmeditation are of one taste in the state of purity.
> Elaborate and unelaborate are of one taste in dharmadhatu.

Also Lord Zhang agreed with these words.

Some people who define one taste as in the general teachings, in the sense that the essence of all phenomena is of one taste in emptiness, consider that one taste as viewed in our case is inadmissible. That being so, the yoga corresponding to their view should be called the yoga of one taste, but if we said that then lesser and middling simplicity should also be called the yoga of one taste for the same reason. In other words, at the time of simplicity when all phenomena are realized as emptiness, although from the perspective of emptiness this coincides with one taste it doesn't from the point of view of phenomena. Therefore, when you realize genuine one taste in the absence of the realization of actual indivisibility, it is said that without fading or being incomplete, phenomena arise indivisibly with emptiness, so myriad dualistic phenomena are indivisible in one taste. If this is the meaning ascribed to one taste at this point, it would be admissible.

## The Experience of One Taste

At the time of lesser one taste, although everything is realized as having the essence of the genuine state, there is a fixation on that experience and conviction. In the ensuing cognizance, perceptions of the six spheres disturbed by violent objects or situations will unsettle the practice. Also, on occasion, dualistic reified perceptions casually take place, and due to these habitual patterns, delusion and fixation occasionally may occur during dreamtime. At times, an experience of inseparable body, phenomena, and mind is also born. Nonetheless, it is said that devotion, compassion, and respect for cause and effect could diminish.

During middling one taste, there is freedom from the dualistic fixation of realized object and realizer, experienced object and experiencer. The fixation of dualistically holding on to phenomena and mind is uprooted. In the ensuing cognizance and dreaming, delusion is reduced compared to before, and the reifying fixation does not increase. A capacity to benefit or harm external disciples comes about.

In greater one taste, the realization that the unceasing expression of the genuine state of equality appears as the myriad things, free from reification and duality, takes place continuously throughout day and night. With the merging of meditation and postmeditation having culminated, this becomes the river-flow yoga. In thought-free perception, a slight feeling that phenomena are undetermined occurs through sheer clarity. In the ensuing cognizance, there is no grasping at phenomena, which appears as an illusory empty lucidity. There, a subtle, detected dualistic perception occasionally arises. One does not grasp at dreams, which arise unimpeded and barely hazy, and sometimes it happens that there are no dreams. At this point, a subtle supernormal cognition arises. Predictions by the yidam and dakini take place, and it is said that envy has completely subsided.

## The Strayings of One Taste, Clearing Faults

At this point, since thoughts arise as meditation, the unspecified interdependencies[56] arise from within, and this is the way of the natural state and distinguishing features of all phenomena. The knowledge arising from meditation that concludes, "This is how they are," and the like, spreads like a forest fire. If you follow that, knowledge becomes analytical and the freshness of awareness is lost, so it becomes hard to capture the all-sufficient royal seat. Since theoretical understanding and book Dharma jargon can be excellent but actual experience weak, if in the daytime distraction occurs, dreams will be deceptive, and so you will stray. You will feel like composing poetry and songs of realization. Once the perceiver and perceived of the eight worldly preoccupations well up, you will feel you can master any dharmic and worldly matter, and so attachment and self-importance take place. Due to this, while you see this fault in others and point it out in them, you see your own faults as insignificant and keep them in a tight fist. You envy your fellow Dharma practitioners and compete with them. You have vague thoughts such as "From now on, why shouldn't I engage in this or that worldly activity?" If you follow that thought, you will lose the all-sufficient royal seat, and as a result you will spread your mess everywhere. You misunderstand the flattery of nuns and sponsors and cherish it, thinking it benefits you. You wrongly regard the advice of the guru and Dharma friends and siblings, and this makes it easy for obstacles to manifest. Ambition will prevent you from completing what you set out to do. You feel distraught at others' criticism.

Since your experience is unsteady, you will not feel settled and will come to regard a populated place as a better option. This is the straying known as "floating in the wave of mixed experiences," and it pertains to one taste. In other words, it is difficult to take good conditions as the path. It is said that the concept of envy will be like the wind blowing in your ear. That will be the time when siddhis and obstacles will struggle, so there will be either great gain or great danger. When the manifestation of sublime qualities is close to being completed, it will be very difficult for them to find room within the context of your merit. Lord Gyare said such things as:

> Don't put out the fire that is boiling the water. Don't break the flying wings of a vulture. Don't throw your hard-earned wealth in the water. Don't close the lid of the treasure. Don't let your autumn crops be spoiled by frost.

At this time, unshaken by any conditions that may occur, the foremost antidote is to practice devotion, recite fierce renunciation mantras, and train in self-liberation free of grasping. Lord Gotsangpa said:

> Until your desire for having experiences has ended, don't break the method for realization.

Hence, if you are able to remain in cutting off both coarse and subtle occurrences of such a desire, all obstacles will vanish within themselves; all siddhis will fall like rain; gods, demons, and men will be overpowered; the royal seat of dharmakaya, your own purpose, will be captured; and the benefit for others will spontaneously take place without effort. On account of this, such a realized yogin is referred to as a brave person. Since this is said to be the greatest merit, you should definitely practice in this way.

## The Classification of One Taste

This includes three explanations: (1) the three types of one taste, (2) the four types of one taste, and (3) the six types of one taste.

## The Three Types of One Taste

You may have realized that all phenomena subsumed in such twofold groups as samsara and nirvana are of one taste in the indivisible essence of mahamudra, yet you have a slight attachment to the conviction of having experienced that. This is lesser one taste. Once your grasping at the conviction of the experience of multiplicity in one taste has been purified, neither the object grasped is left outside nor the grasping mind is left inside; rather phenomena and mind are vividly actualized as being inseparable. This is middling one taste. Thus, when realizing multiplicity in one taste and that realization of one taste arises as the multiplicity of phenomena, the whole world and beings settle in the state of the genuine nature. This is greater one taste.

## The Four Types of One Taste

In the context of the four yogas each classified into four subdivisions, there are sixteen subdivisions, which include the four types of one taste. First, to rest still without fixation in the state of the single realization of the multiplicity of phenomena is one-pointedness of one taste. Second, to have resolved the misconception of holding phenomena and mind as two entities is simplicity of one taste. Third, free from the rejection and acceptance of blocking or acquiring phenomena and emptiness, body, mind, and phenomena merge together; this is one taste of one taste. Fourth, the purified experience of meditator and object of meditation is nonmeditation of one taste.

## The Six Types of One Taste

In the context of the four yogas each classified into six subdivisions, there are twenty-four subdivisions, which include the six types of one taste. First, in terms of whether the essence is seen or not: When you recognize all phenomena of the six sense groups spontaneously in their natural state without needing to contaminate them with alterations, the essence has been seen, for that is the realization of one taste. But if you are still fixated on something to be liberated or obtained, you remain not completely convinced, and your mind stream is mixed with slight stains of blocking and acquiring, that would be a meditative experience of one taste, so the essence hasn't been seen.

Second, in terms of whether the potential has been developed or not: Even if the sky and earth have turned upside down, you don't use an antidote to alter the equality of all phenomena of the world and beings, of samsara and nirvana. Instead you spontaneously realize multiplicity in one taste through the sufficiency of self-knowing awareness. When, as a result of that realization, you master the multiple phenomena so that emptiness is constantly present in everything, then the potential has been developed. But if the realization of one taste during meditation does not merge with postmeditation, and the objects of the five sensory gateways appear as such, then you perceive them dualistically, although you may have realized them in meditation as nondual. This is referred to as not being released from the seal of dualistic perception. If you remain not free from the slight stains of blocking and acquiring, then the potential hasn't been developed.

Third, in terms of whether thoughts arise as meditation or not: By merging phenomena and mind into one, ego-fixation is uprooted and exhausted, the afflictive consciousness is purified, and based on the nonexistence of inherent identity in the self, the inherent identity of the other is also nonexistent. The merging together of oneself, others, phenomena, and mind frees you from sexual desire, and envy subsides from its core. You are not bound to go after, nor free to come out of, the unimpeded perceptions of the six sense groups; their appearance is sufficient. If all this takes place, thoughts arise as meditation. But if, by recognizing the perceptions of the six sense groups, you need to acquire or liberate through mindfulness, then thoughts do not arise as meditation.

Fourth, in terms of whether sublime qualities are born or not: As a result of body, mind, and phenomena merging into one and arising without duality as multiplicity, you master the elements and can perform miracles. Through supernormal perception and superior wisdom, you have command of external and internal phenomena, so the sublime qualities of being in the pure bhumis arise. In a moment of cognizance, good things of samsara and nirvana are accomplished, imperfections and defects are abandoned, and since you are capable of developing the sublime qualities, you master thoughts. The karma accumulated in your previous births to be experienced after many eons in the Avici hell, which has been dormant, surges forth on its own as a mere disturbing dream, and thus it is purified by itself. Also, virtuous karma that would ripen after many eons is rendered evident right at this time. You master karma. Having realized the three divisions of time to be the same, in a single moment you see them as indivisible, eons are condensed into an instant, and an instant opens into eons. You master time. Since body, mind, and phenomena are integrated, space and the palm of your hand are equal; the billion world systems fit into a few grains; one is transformed into many, and many are made into one; you emanate as any of the six types of beings taking their specific form and teach the Dharma in their corresponding language, and so forth. You master phenomena. With the throat *nadis* having opened, the treasury of Dharma surges forth, the lord of speech is realized, your self-confidence to write texts is unimpeded, and there is no confusion regarding the meaning of Buddha's scriptures. Without hindrances you know everything there is to know, so you master primordial wisdom. If the power to perform these and other miracles has been attained, the qualities of one taste have dawned. But if, even though you have had some realization of one taste, the conditions of the path to awaken the qualities are feeble and hence the signs of accomplishment haven't been brought forth, then the qualities haven't been born.

Fifth, in terms of whether the relative level has been mastered or not: The manifold phenomena are inseparable and of one taste in the essence of one realization, a realization that masters the manifold cause and effect. An instant of dependent origination appears clearly as the wheel of cause and effect, like brocade laid over the center of the sun. In the experience of a moment of cognizance, samsara and nirvana are separated into two. You adopt virtue and abstain from wrongdoing, and train to increase the purification of obscurations. In empty absolute reality, empty phenomena arise. Space-like cause and effect is actualized. Since the connection with habitual patterns has been cut, the cause and effect of karma does not persist in the second instant. Since you are aware that the arising, cause, abidance, basis, and destruction of all phenomena of samsara, nirvana, and the path are circumstantial factors, upon the movement of body, voice, and mind—or at the very least, a rolling stone or stick—you will know what faults and qualities are to be rejected and which to be adopted. External phenomena, down to birds and mice, reveal the Dharma to you. Thus, realizing that phenomena have the natural characteristics of your mind, your knowledge of interdependence and cause and effect reaches perfection, and the relative level has been mastered. One taste is realized to be the distinguishing feature of mind. Misconceptions based on phenomena are cleared away by the mind. The relative cognizance is prajña, so the ignorance that results in delusion regarding cause and effect is dispelled, and the wisdom aspect of knowing all things in existence should be born. But if the one taste of emptiness does not arise in the multiplicity of cause and effect, the relative level hasn't been mastered.

Sixth, in terms of whether the seed of rupakaya has been planted or not: When multiplicity is realized in one taste, one taste takes command over multiplicity. At that time, all-pervading compassion and effortless activity take place. You become the lord of all samsara and nirvana. Clouds of visible and invisible retinues and wealth gather. Together with gods, the world makes offerings and becomes your crown jewel. This is cause and effect beyond control.[57] Lord Phagmo Drupa said:

> When you have earnestly cut the root
> And are suspended in the state of one taste,
> The great flag is hoisted on the glorious mountain,
> And all needs are satisfied without having to do so.
> Isn't this cause and effect beyond control?

At this point, it is time to put on the belt of accomplishing the welfare of others. If at that time, constantly in command of the five excellences,[58] you cease to devote your life to accumulating merit and instead open the treasure chest of altruism, the seed of rupakaya has been planted. On the other hand, although you may have realized multiplicity in one taste and one taste arises as multiplicity, the natural expression of that realization does not surge as compassion. Therefore, if you haven't opened the treasure chest of altruism, you haven't planted the seed of rupakaya.

## The Technique for Sustaining and Enhancing One Taste

At the time of the three stages of one taste, stay mostly in an isolated place. Every now and then also stay among people. Meditation or nonmeditation, being mindful or not, doesn't seem to make any difference. When in solitude, it is vital to sustain the realized essence undistractedly with perfect mindfulness. Gampopa said:

> At the time of the yoga of multiplicity in one taste, it is important not to mix this with theoretical ordinary aspects, but rather experience it within.

Thus, he says that the strength of the realization of one taste is precisely what should be drawn forth. Lord Gyare said:

> On the attainment of the yoga of one taste
> Is where the seed of altruism lies.
> One does not make evaluations,
> Yet the right interdependencies take place without reifying.

He thus explains that by making vast aspirations for benefiting others, all excellent interdependent conditions are set. Lord Yangonpa said:

> The five senses arising on the objects are the unimpeded natural radiance.
> The objects born from nonfixation are the unborn basic nature.
> Though attachment to perceptions is not blocked, the natural flow of meditation stops it.
> Manifested emptiness arises beyond concept; that is the path left to itself.

> Not regarding phenomena as defective is to have cast away fixation.
> The meditation has arrived at the expanse of one taste.

Here he explains that no matter what or how phenomena arise, fixation is to be abandoned. You should understand all these references.

The manner of enhancement is for the most part similar to that of greater simplicity. During lesser and middling one taste, there is a possibility that the aspects of method—such as acceptance and rejection in relation to cause and effect, as well as devotion, pure perception, or compassion—may be overlooked, so you should reinforce them through practice. Set up all the conditions for a positive result and forsake all negative conditions. It is important to act in accordance with adopting and rejecting what is positive and negative. As Lord Gomtsul said:

> Generally, though the meaning of nonduality has been realized,
> What is good should not be despoiled but searched for.
> Though the meaning of nonmeditation has been realized,
> Skillful service to the guru should not be despoiled but searched for.
> Though in conduct there is no adoption or rejection,
> Seek to avoid creating conditions for others to act negatively.
> Though there is no hope or fear in fruition,
> Seek to avoid leaving afflictions in free rein.

You may have realized greater one taste, but the capacity to benefit or harm hasn't arisen, and signs such as supernormal perception and predictions by dakinis haven't occurred. This is because you have damaged the samaya or become contaminated by the veil of others' violation of samaya, hence you should offer ardent confession. Make a thousand *tsatsas* and offer a flower to each while you supplicate, "Please completely eliminate my contamination." In addition, perform mantra rituals designed to clear away these contaminations, and carry out appropriate virtuous actions. If events such as signs of realization appear, avoid self-importance or reacting with likes and dislikes concerning them. If this happens, it means that a mara has set in. Whether you bring benefit or do harm, all these are your own mind, including the maras, and so forth. Think that the mind is like space, without center or fringe. Then, as soon as one taste is born again, don't be afraid of thoughts and don't have a liking for qualities; faults will be unable to beguile you. If once again you have strong envy, many afflictive emotions, coarse thoughts, likes and dislikes, or you are easily irritated, Mara has entered your mind. After recognizing this, be cautious about your spiritual practice. In general, it has been said that you should recognize all that conflicts with meditation as actual maras.

Eliminating the faults in this way and sustaining the practice will purify the stains of experience. The realization of the path will merge with the natural state of the essence, after which there will be no division between meditation and postmeditation, being mindful or distracted. The realization of nonmeditation will have arisen at that point.

## The Borderlines of One Taste

The natural expression of the wisdom of lesser one taste purifies or burns the undesirable into groundlessness, so this is the fourth bhumi, the "Brilliant." In middling one taste there are two subdivisions. During meditative composure there is multiplicity in one taste. During postmeditation, when mingling each phenomenon with mind in multiplicity, since sentient beings are not conceptualized, it is difficult to guard yourself from deliberately training to benefit them and from being partial toward your own mind's peace and well-being. Therefore, this is the fifth bhumi, "Difficult to Accomplish." Then, in the ensuing cognizance one taste arises in multiplicity; this is the time when emptiness is ever present. All phenomena of samsara and nirvana are realized as mind essence. Since one has actualized that this fact is instant awareness, this is the sixth bhumi, the "Actualized." Also, in greater one taste there are two levels. The first is that the path, having parted far from the ordinary, so this is the seventh bhumi, the "Far Reaching." The second is that, since concepts of subject and object are of one taste, the realization cannot be shaken; this is the eighth bhumi, the "Unshakable."

## The Yoga of Nonmeditation

This includes explanations on: (1) identity, (2) experience, (3) strayings, (4) classifications, (5) technique for sustaining, and (6) borderlines.

## The Identity of Nonmeditation

A simple general explanation of the meaning of nonmeditation is that there is no thing as an object of meditation that is taken as a reference point, or else, it refers to resting in nonmeditation through the fact of the absence of true nature. As said in the *Kalachakra* and the *Guhyasamaja Tantra*:

> Since there is nothing concrete, there is no meditation,
> And there is nothing to be meditated upon.
> Since there is neither something nor nothing,
> Meditation has no frame of reference.

Since meditator and what is meditated upon are nondual, the resting is in nonmeditation. As said by the Great Brahmin:

> *Kyema!* It is not said that what has no true nature is something to be meditated upon.
> If the concepts of meditator and object of meditation are two,
> Due to the mind fixating on duality, the awakening mind is abandoned . . .

Based on this reason, some people oppose these two ways of defining it as inadmissible because in the first case, the yogas of simplicity and above would become the yoga of nonmeditation, and in the second case, the yoga of one taste would also become the yoga of nonmeditation. Well then, why is this? At the time of one taste, there is a subtle concept of meditator and object of meditation. Once this has been purified, all that remains is the realization that there is no longer a division between meditation and postmeditation, mindfulness and nonmindfulness. Since meditative effort and activity have been transcended, that is what is called nonmeditation. Shawaripa said:

> To the realized, there is no meditator and object of meditation.
> The sky finds no reference point in the sky.
> Similarly, through being empty, emptiness is not to be meditated upon.
> Nondual cognizance is like water and milk.
> The myriad things have the one taste of unceasing great bliss.

As Lord Zhang said:

> When the yoga of nonmeditation arises,
> The essence of awareness is freed from support.
> The yogin has nothing to meditate upon.
> There is no meditator; it has become pervasive.

## The Experience of Nonmeditation

In lesser nonmeditation, dualistic perception is mostly purified. There is no need to deliberately meditate and hold through mindfulness, and all phenomena arise as meditation. Generally, it happens that while you don't waver from meditation, in the ensuing cognizance there is what is called "unrecognized absence of concepts." It has been taught that a residue of ignorance or unknowing, a part of the ground consciousness, lingers in a concept-free neutral mind. This is taken to be a stain of negative habits. In the ensuing cognizance, karma cannot be accumulated, yet fleeting impure concepts fixated on wisdom arise as illusory. During dreams, a slight, unrecognized reification arises.

In middling nonmeditation, even that subtle illusory dualistic perception is purified. The entire day and night become the continuous realization of nonmeditation. In the ensuing phenomena, there is an extremely subtle aspect of unrecognized absence of thought, which is said to arise as natural lucidity and completely agree with the flow of the basic nature. This itself is an extremely subtle stain of negative tendencies, and it is also partially present at nighttime.

In greater nonmeditation, that extremely subtle aspect of unrecognized absence of thoughts is also purified into wisdom, after which natural luminosity and realized luminosity merge. Therefore, this becomes the infinite expanse of primordial wisdom, conventionally known as "awakening into the dharmakaya," the accomplishment of one's own purpose. Its radiance embraces all without bias. From the interdependent connection with the pure perception of those to be trained, the image of rupakaya appears for their benefit. As long as there is samsara, the altruistic work is carried out spontaneously.

## The Strayings of Nonmeditation

We are including this explanation only to follow the same pattern regarding this chapter about strayings discussed in the previous three yogas because in nonmeditation there are no strayings. As Gotsangpa said:

> In the daytime, ensuing phenomena are but an obvious illusion or a lucid emptiness. It is said that for the duration of just one finger snap, a slight gap may arise, but without applying mindfulness—as commonly defined—it will purify itself on its own within the essence. At any rate, it will simply be as if the sun of nonmeditation were obscured by a cloud.

Since there is neither meditator nor meditation object, the practice becomes solely resting in composure. Nonetheless, as internally dualistic cognizance is not exhausted, wisdom is self-dimmed; path wisdom is not completely purified into fruition wisdom. Externally, since knowable things have not become exhausted, if you are not free from a slight dualistic perception of whatever there is, this is said to become a straying. So by also identifying these subtle dualistic fixations and purifying them, the whole of samsara and nirvana becomes the single great dharmakaya. The actualization of greater nonmeditation merges with luminosity and that is the actualization of the indivisibility of no more learning.

## The Classification of Nonmeditation

This includes explanations on: (1) the three types of nonmeditation, (2) the four types of nonmeditation, and (3) the six types of nonmeditation.

## The Three Types of Nonmeditation

There is neither a need to hold through mindfulness nor a need to deliberately rest in composure. All phenomena arise as meditation, and there is no division between meditator and object of meditation. As long as a slight clinging to the experience of illusion arises, that is lesser nonmeditation. Once you are free from such a fixation, the whole day and night becomes the continuous realization of nonmeditation, so you have captured the original state of natural presence. In the ensuing phenomena, there is a subtle aspect of consciousness that arises as natural luminosity. This is middling nonmeditation. When that subtle aspect of consciousness becomes wisdom, the two luminosities merge, and this becomes the sole infinite expanse. This is greater nonmeditation.

## The Four Types of Nonmeditation

In the context of the four yogas each classified into four subdivisions, there are sixteen subdivisions, which include the four types of nonmeditation. First, to rest without wavering from the continuity of suchness is one-pointedness of nonmeditation. Second, to have resolved misconceptions regarding all existing knowable phenomena is simplicity of nonmeditation. Third, benefiting others without acceptance or rejection is one taste of nonmeditation. Fourth, the purification of the self-obscuration of wisdom is nonmeditation of nonmeditation.

## The Six Types of Nonmeditation

In the context of the four yogas each classified into six subdivisions, there are twenty-four subdivisions, which include the six types of nonmeditation.

First, in terms of whether the essence is seen or not: When, within the realization of nonmeditation, the experience of having anything to be held by mindfulness or to be familiarized with is all the time utterly purified, then the essence of nonmeditation has been seen. But if in that realization there is still something to be familiarized with or a clarity to become slightly enhanced, then the essence has not been seen.

Second, in terms of whether the potential has been developed or not: When in the realized wisdom there is absolutely no stain of dualistic fixation and no part of mind essence that hasn't been recognized, knowing and knowable have disappeared into one, and it has become inseparable with dharmadhatu wisdom. Then the potential of nonmeditation has been developed. But if external knowable things haven't ceased so that you are not free from a subtle duality toward external phenomena, and there is a slight unrecognized absence of concepts, then the potential hasn't been developed.

Third, in terms of whether thoughts arise as meditation or not: When you are free from the five aggregates, body, mind, and phenomena are liberated from the three chains[59] into the absence of phenomena. Once this happens, if the ground consciousness has become purified into its original state, then thoughts arise as meditation. But even though the six sense groups and the afflictive consciousness may have been purified, if a subtle dormant tendency to fixate on the perception of body and mind and a slight stain of experience remain, then thoughts are not arising as meditation.

Fourth, in terms of whether sublime qualities have been born or not: When the body has turned into the rainbow wisdom rupakaya and the mind into luminous dharmakaya, if buddha fields appear as infinite purity, the qualities of nonmeditation have been born. But if, regarding skillful means, the mode of interdependence hasn't been acquired and the strength of the realized prajña is feeble, there still lingers a slight impure perception of and fixation to the body and mind and to the world and beings. Then the qualities of nonmeditation haven't been born.

Fifth, in terms of whether the relative level has been mastered or not: When you have perfected and actualized things as they are and everything in existence—as well as the powers, types of fearlessness, the unique dharmas, and the remaining buddha qualities—then the relative level has become purified and reached perfection; it has been mastered. Although you may have realized things as they are, due to the stain of the three chains, the extremely subtle knowledge of everything in existence has not been actualized. If so, the relative hasn't been purified, and you haven't mastered it.

Sixth, in terms of whether the seed of rupakaya has been planted or not: Yourself and others, the world and its inhabitants, the animate and the inanimate, and all things have become the single dharmakaya, essence of the three vajras. Thus, awakened to perfect buddhahood, you pervade without duality the mind streams of beings and the compassionate energy of the buddhas. If through this, the stream of supreme nirmanakayas is uninterrupted until samsara has emptied, then the purpose of the rupakaya's activity has been actualized. But if it hasn't, and you must depend on the time of the three buddha fields,[60] then the potency of the seed of rupakaya has not ripened.

## The Technique for Sustaining Nonmeditation

Even though nonmeditation has the divisions thus explained, when it comes to the final perfection of nonmeditation arising in this life, one's mind clearly knows it is buddha all of a sudden. One then has deep certainty that there is nothing undesirable to be eliminated, no antidote to rely on, nothing to be purified, no mind that purifies, and that one is beyond dying or not dying. However, while meditation and postmeditation haven't integrated, that sudden conviction alone is not considered to be an indication that nonmeditation has taken place. Regarding the way of sustaining that experience Lord Gampopa said:

> At the time of the yoga of nonmeditation it is important not to stick to the glue of experience. You must not be attached to experiences.

Thus he says that at this point you should be cautious about sticking to an experience. So no matter whether the experience is good or bad, it is vital not to block or acquire, or become attached. You have to train by means of a constant recognition of all aspects of dormant mental tendencies; therefore, the root of meditation is undistracted perfect mindfulness or nonconceptual mindfulness. For this reason, no matter what happens in this life, plant the victory banner of practice. It is considered that through undistracted nonmeditation, ordinary cognizance is brought to its perfection. Lord Gyare said:

> The lowest nonmeditation is similar to one taste.
> The way of carrying out the practice is the same.
> The highest nonmeditation is buddhahood.
> It is totally free of action and effort.

Thus, the way of purifying, training, and sustaining in lesser and middling nonmeditation is the same as in one taste. Lord Yangonpa said:

> The object of meditation and the meditating mind—
> Look with awareness whether they are two.
> In nondual awareness divested from support,
> Sustain evenly the cognizance free of thinking.
> A continuous cycle of meditation throughout day and night will occur.

This very awareness where meditator and object of meditation are inseparable, divested of support and reference point, is a cognizance free from thinking and mental constructs. He explains that this is to be evenly sustained of its own accord. The meaning of nonthinking and free from mental constructions has been explained earlier.

In general, the experience of meditation that is continuously present, similar to the one in nonmeditation, happens also during one-pointedness. The bare inseparability between meditator and object of meditation in nonmeditation also occurs in simplicity. In the yoga of nonmeditation, whatever appears arises as meditation, so there is no separation between meditation and postmeditation; that alone also happens during one taste. Therefore, all these are but mere particularities of meditation experience. They are not the realized nonmeditation as it is, so you should know the distinctions. The final realization of nonmeditation coincides with the attainment of perfect enlightenment, yet for those who haven't perfected nonmeditation in this life, the nonmeditation dawned in this life is considered to be a mere denomination. As Lord Gyare said:

> Nonmeditation is the seat of dharmakaya.
> In most cases nonmeditation becomes a denomination.

## The Borderlines of Nonmeditation

By possessing the qualities of lesser nonmeditation, you are in the ninth bhumi, the "Sublime Intelligence." In middling nonmeditation, altruistic work happens effortlessly and the rain of Dharma spreads ceaselessly; this is the tenth bhumi, the "Cloud of Dharma." Greater nonmeditation is such that all phenomena have become infinite purity, so this is the eleventh bhumi, the "Universal Illumination." In general, in these four divisions of each of the four yogas, which add up to sixteen, or more, don't deem a lower level to be higher than what it is. Roughly evaluate your practice and do not overrate it. Lengom asked Lord Gomtsul about the difference between the four yogas, and he replied:

> One-pointedness is knowing the essence of mind.
> Simplicity is knowing the nature of mind.
> One taste is knowing the nature of phenomena.
> So-called nonmeditation, oh, I have no clue!

Thus, he didn't make any acknowledgment about nonmeditation. Among the disciples of Lord Phagmo Drupa, there were said to be three and a half who had realized one taste. Also, Lord Gotsangpa, Orgyenpa, and others admitted nothing more than just one taste. Most of the masters of the past have said that their realization was not higher than greater and middling simplicity. Leaving aside the question of whether past saints reached the borderline of awakening to buddhahood—one's own purpose—they spoke of their level of realization in accordance with what was to be revealed to specific disciples.

Nowadays, those who acknowledge having the realization of nonmeditation based on simply one taste don't know the system of the four yogas precisely. However, they feel that something like that is to be proclaimed, and so they speak about it. That is nothing more than blatant pride and foolish talk. What is the use of chattering about higher levels when one hasn't experienced the lower ones? Someone who has realized the genuine perfect mindfulness of the past masters is as rare as a star in the daytime. The lower is given higher names. For instance, even though one hasn't realized more than lesser simplicity, one claims to have middling simplicity, and having no higher than a middling level, one proclaims having the greater level, and so forth. This is unbefitting. If, knowing how it really is, you speak in that way, you would be a hypocrite influenced by the eight worldly preoccupations and the ten wrongdoings, falsely proclaiming yourself a guru. Dharma and your mind stream not merging . . . What a pity! How frightening! What is the use of speaking like that?

No matter what realization of the essence you may have, it is all right to talk about it as being that itself. There is no need to embellish it with fancy words. If you apply a term to it, your guru will say, "You are giving your practice names as to this or that, high, low, or middling." Even though there are no nice words to be said about the meditation, if you have a firm certainty and conviction about your realization of the essence, that is sufficient. Lord Lhatsewa said:

> Generally, if the genuine realization of simplicity arises, that is sufficient. It is pointless to scrutinize one taste and the rest.

> There are many who have high assertions about their unsubstantiated experience, so be careful.

That being the case, regarding the essence of the practice, the right thing to do is to not verbally exaggerate (externally) and to properly sustain mind essence (internally). It would not be suitable for you to be swollen with pride; it is said that meditators are bound by meditation, and this is their undoing. What is called Dharma must go hand in hand with it being an antidote to the afflictions, so although you may have a good mind practice, you should recognize and purify the stains of the veil of pride and babbling about "high levels."

We have clarified the divisions of the four yogas here. In terms of enumerations, it is considered that they can't be covered by explanations, and there is no end to them. However, regarding the key point, the most important purpose and certainty is that, once you have recognized the natural state—the mind's original condition as it is—you should not contaminate the natural flow with conceptual fabrications. It is important to understand that the key way of sustaining ordinary cognizance is to allow it to be of its own accord. This is all that matters. Lord Tilopa said:

> What is nonconceptual is not realized by conceptual Dharma.
> Nonaction is not found through the Dharma of action.
> If you wish to realize the meaning of nonconceptual and nonaction,
> Inquire into awareness and rest in mind essence.

Siddha Lingchen Repa said:

> Lord, you told me to meditate on the innate essence,
> And meditate is what I did;
> It so happened that meditation object and meditator simply vanished,
> And no postmeditation was there to hold.

Lord Gyalwang said:

> Some say that emptiness is empty;
> Since there is neither someone emptying nor anything emptied,
> There is nothing done nor fabricated.
> The innate is somehow empty by nature.

And also, the wisdom dakini Niguma expressed these words:

> If you don't see whatever arises as meditation,
> How will it do to rely on an antidote?
> It doesn't work to reject objects and situations.
> If you know them to be illusory, they are free within themselves.

Hence, loosen up and resolve on the continuous flow of nonconceptuality, the self-knowing aware mind that is free from dualistically clinging to an object of meditation. Regarding its unceasing expression—the manifestation of thoughts and phenomena of all kinds—by thoroughly knowing their nature, in unfixated postmeditation release them in self-liberation. In the ensuing cognizance, when starting to cling to dualistic perceptions, don't be carried away by that, even for a moment. Cultivate liberation within their own nature of the diversity of good and bad conditions, as well as that of actions of neutral value.

Using the basis of mind as the path is not all there is to it. Beginning with the development of bodhichitta, supplications, aspirations, determination, and so forth, seal all your karma and activity toward the path of enlightenment. Train the natural expression of your realization in such practices as devotion, generation stage, pure perception, compassion, bodhichitta, and aspirations. Besides these, attach importance to developing the potential of the realization in the expanse of great indivisibility within which guru and your mind, generation and completion, infinite purity, emptiness and compassion, aspirations within the purity of the three spheres, and so forth are inseparable from the basic nature of awareness. In the practice of interdependence, it is important to perfectly set up the gateway of dependent origination without muddling the two truths.

I have thus considered it necessary to explain the divisions of the four yogas from the perspective of experience because it is very hard to do so based on the fundamental texts. In particular, it is extremely difficult to do this for the latter yogas, which do not take place in the field of the intellect. Nonetheless, taking as a basis the advice of those of both greater and lesser capacities, Lord Gampopa, as well as the teachings of Lord Gyare, Gampopa Tashi Namgyal, and other siddhas of the past, and indirectly ornamenting it with my trifling experience and realization, I have explained these systems in detail.

# 11. Utilizing Events on the Path

F. The Stage of Training on Utilization
  1. The Time and Conduct for Using as the Path
  2. The Common Key Point of Using as the Path
  3. The Six Types of Using as the Path Explained One by One
    a. Using Thoughts as the Path and Taking Bad Omens as Auspicious
    b. Using Afflictions as the Path and Transmuting Poison into Ambrosia
    c. Using Gods and Demons as the Path and Magnetizing Obstacles as Siddhis
    d. Using Suffering as the Path and Instructions on Bodhichitta
    e. Taking Sickness as the Path and Equalizing the Elements
    f. Using Death as the Path and Pointing Out Mother and Child Dharmata

## The Stage of Training on Utilization at the Stage of Conduct

This includes explanations on: (1) the time and conduct for using [all events] as the path, (2) the common key point of using as the path, and (3) the six types of using as the path explained one by one.

## The Time and Conduct for Using as the Path

At the time of using as the path, generally you should see the essence of coemergent mind and, in particular, totally see the essence of coemergent thoughts and coemergent phenomena. Then, through the presence of the practice, ensuing cognizance and ensuing phenomena should arise mostly as postmeditation. Once that happens, you should use them as the path. This is because otherwise—without recognizing the essence of the three coemergences—you are unable to use as the path the knowing of a situation as it is.

We now turn to the time when you need to apply the method of using as the path. Even though in meditation the realization of seeing the essence has arisen, you are carried away by the perceptions and cognitions of this life, so the clinging of desire and aversion solidifies. You remain an ordinary person and your mind, upset by intense situations, is anxious, making it hard to take these naturally as the path. While you are at leisure and happy, you cease to recognize your dormant thoughts. In brief, it will be difficult to automatically take situations as the path through the practice. When apprehensive thoughts like hopes and fears make the mind unsuitable, you should apply the conduct of using any situation as the path. When meditation arises continuously in an isolated place, you should also apply this conduct to situations that may occur in order to stabilize and enhance your practice. So whenever moments of anxiety arise in the mind, use them as the path. Elsewhere, when the mindfulness of meditation and postmeditation has become undistracted, if you discard sustaining the natural state of its own accord and thereafter apply such techniques as antidotes or inverted meditations for the purpose of using situations as the path, then you have slipped into the corresponding deviation, as explained before.

Regarding the time to enter into action, in the *Two Segments* it is said:

> When attaining warmth,
> If you feel like going into action
> And you have the desire to accomplish,
> This is exactly the action to carry out.

Here it says that once you find signs of progress (warmth), you should engage in the conduct. Besides, here in the practice lineage, conduct is considered to be related necessarily to timing. Some people who haven't recognized the essence of mind simply have shamatha experiences. Some others don't even have that. They go to such places as charnel grounds and crossroads for the sake of pretense, fame, or gain. Thus, at first they endure hardships, and later they seem to be impervious. But their spiritual practice does not progress properly because, through these ways, they are aware neither of the thought essence to be taken as the path nor of the natural state of the mind that is to be used as the path.

As to the purpose of conduct, it is not only for the sake of taking sensual objects as the path, but also for equalizing all steady and moving minds in the essence of dharmata. As said in the *Two Segments*:

> The conduct through the perishable body explained earlier
> Has not been taught to be for the sake of enjoyments.
> No matter whether the mind is steady or moving,
> It is meant to test your mind.

Regarding the actual conduct, in the father tantras there are three types of conduct: elaborate, unelaborate, and extremely unelaborate. In the mother tantras there are three types of conduct: secret, yogic, and victorious on all fronts. In the practice system of the Old Tradition (Nyingma) we find four types of conduct: the Samantabhadra conduct, the hidden secret conduct, the yogic awareness conduct, and the totally victorious conduct. Other types of conduct also have been taught, such as the beginner's conduct, the conduct of mastering wisdom, the conduct of strongly mastering wisdom, and the four types of liberating conduct. In other words, if a tantric practitioner is connected with the profound pith instructions of generation and completion, that conduct is also evidently aligned with the mahamudra conduct. This is because we find that the Nyingma practice system, the *dohas* of the Great Brahmin, and the mahamudra texts by Lord Shawaripa, Virupa, and Tilopa teach that those types of conduct should be practiced as is fit. Nonetheless, as to what is accepted in this practice lineage, in the *Kalachakra* it is said:

> For ordained persons, the conduct of desire is prohibited in most cases. For the practitioner, the conduct of desire is just meant to enhance the meditation, so there is no conflict with that of an ordained person. Therefore, it is acceptable for this conduct to be simply carried out secretly in harmony with the Samantabhadra, the unelaborate, the extremely unelaborate, and the totally victorious types of conduct.

Regarding the place where conduct is carried out, in such places as a monastery or village where the state of mind is carefree, the outer and inner interdependent conditions to perform the conduct are incomplete because in these places internally brutal thoughts and afflictions will not surge strongly in the mind. Since this intense upsurge that is to be used as the mahamudra path would be missing, by and large you would remain at ease in the state of laziness and indolence. Although you may have practiced meditation for many years during your entire life, you don't cope with situations. While happy and at leisure, you neglect to sustain your spiritual practice, and if an afflictive situation happens, you slip into being an ordinary person. Therefore, in terms of enhancing the practice, staying in such places as a monastery or village for three years is considered to be less effective than staying only one month in wild, terrifying places, where you integrate practice with situations, carrying out secret conduct. Because of this, it has been explained that one should cut off ordinary talk and stay on fearsome, dreadful mountain peaks; rough hermitages where magical manifestations of nonhumans appear; charnel grounds with frightening corpses, skeletons, and so forth; in front of a tree owned by such beings as nagas or *tsen*; empty towns where *pretas*, demons, and the like gather; and crossroads where simple practitioners have previously practiced making offerings and practicing generosity.

As to confidence in carrying out the conduct, according to the Kadampas of the past there are five requisites: to wander in mountain hermitages without hypocrisy, to overcome situations through antidotes, to master the instructions, to restore health through faith, and to be able to remove subtle harm through capacity. Lord Gampopa considered that the four requirements for attaining confidence are: the instructions, the capacity, the experience, and the view. As Mahasiddha Zhang said:

> Mastering the treasure of instructions, not being defeated by the hosts of external and internal maras, keeping pure ethics without hypocrisy, and so forth; after conquering these by yourself, wander in mountain hermitages.

As to the actual conduct, there are five similes. Conduct like a wounded deer: A wounded deer doesn't associate with fellow deer but instead remains alone without having any consideration for anything else. Similarly, one has no interest in the aims of this life, such as being attached to friends or eliminating foes, or entertaining and flattering patrons. Rather, one abandons friends and carries out the conduct in solitude.

Lion-like conduct: Just as a lion feels no anxiety amid hordes of deer or savage beasts, there is no fear in one's mind either toward external obstacles created by humans or nonhumans, or internal obstacles of events stirred by thoughts.

Conduct like wind in the sky: Just as the wind in the sky is insubstantial and sticks to nothing but transparently moves in total freedom, there is no desire and yearning for or attachment to body, wealth, happiness, well-being, fame, and so forth, but the mind is left to be transparent and freely open.

Space-like conduct: Just as there is no support in space, the mind takes support neither from aims to do this or that, nor from reference points with or without characteristics.

Crazy-like conduct: Just as the mind of a crazy person has no reference points whatsoever, there is no attachment to such reactions as blocking or acquiring, adopting or rejecting, or whatever it may be, in terms of good or bad.

It is considered that through these five types of conduct, no matter what outer or inner situation occurs, it will be taken as the path and become an enhancement toward the natural state.

## The Common Key Point of Using as the Path: An Explanation on What Is to Be Used as the Path

At this point, what is to be used as the path are the obscuring, unbridled thoughts of subject and object resulting from ignorance because these are precisely what makes one sink into samsara. Moreover, in the *Enlightenment of Vairochana Tantra* it is said:

> Thoughts are the great ignorance;
> They are what plunges us into the ocean of samsara.

When you use those very thoughts as the path through the instructions, instead of slipping into them as they appear, they arise as wisdom essence and purify samsara. In the *Two Segments* it is said:

> Thoughts themselves purify thoughts,
> And existence itself purifies existence.

The Great Brahmin said:

> Thoughts are great wisdom;
> They are what dries the ocean of samsara.

Naropa and Maitripa said:

> Self-liberated thoughts are great wisdom.

Well then, you may think, "Before it was said that it is indeed sufficient to recognize thoughts as dharmakaya. So what is the purpose of later on using thoughts as the path?" For people who became enlightened instantly, it is possible that they were completely liberated on the spot. However, most practitioners need to focus on the key point after that recognition by using thoughts as the path. When sustaining the mindfulness of practice, most subtle thoughts are purified into wisdom, but in most cases, you are unable to purify coarse thoughts or thoughts occurring in the ensuing cognizance. Thoughts abound continuously and, in the midst of them, meditation is only entered fleetingly in bits and pieces. After slipping into thoughts at their will, many think thoughts are dharmakaya or wisdom and lapse into that conceptual label. Not only that, even though during simplicity in meditation, subtle thoughts arise as dharmakaya through undistracted mindfulness, very strong conceptions of attachment and aversion to some extent fail to arise as dharmakaya. Also at the time of one taste, disturbing thoughts provoked by severe circumstances do not turn into spiritual practice. All kinds of occurrences have been mentioned. Therefore, using as the path is important even for those with higher realization. Nowadays even people who have meditated for many years and are having a glimpse of the face of meditation don't progress significantly, and various forms of depression arise. All this is due to not having applied the key point of using as the path. Therefore, all beginners and advanced meditators should strongly cultivate this key point and master it. This crucial point depends on the skill for stabilizing the flow of mindfulness that each person has according to their degree. Lord Drikungpa said:

> Children, when you totally concentrate, there is nothing other than that.
> Why so? Because if you master mindfulness, you master meditation.

He also advised the river-flow yogins to cherish undistracted mindfulness.

All other forms of using as the path are a variation of using thoughts as the path, so the strength of all the rest resides precisely in using thoughts as the path. In other words, just as the hollowness of all bamboos is known by knowing the hollowness of one bamboo, the diversity of thoughts should be known in the same way. Lord Gampopa considered that since the dharmakaya way of using thoughts as the path was foremost, from it the diversity of other forms to be used as the path follows suit. Generally, Lord Gampopa and other masters classified six types of using as the path, of which some were taught as the main subject and others in a fragmented form. In particular, the lord protector of beings Tsangpa Gyare extracted from Lord Rechungpa's treasury of pith instructions the one named equal taste, which is extremely renowned in this glorious extended Drukpa lineage of actual truth.

There are three important key points in all the systems of using as the path, like the ones we have considered. First, "identify thoughts." No matter what good or bad situations manifest or arise, don't slip right into them but start by identifying them. From the beginning, always be careful about precisely this, like being cautious of an enemy, and strengthen the antidote. Then, "get rid of ego-clinging." Toward whatever arises, don't be contaminated by attachment or aversion, blocking or acquiring. Abandoning the bonds of ego-clinging, never grasp or view in terms of quality or defect, but rather rest in the continuous state untouched by concept. Finally, "clear the treacherous path of hope and fear." By proceeding in this way, don't have any hopes or fears at all, such as hope that something may come or fear that it may not, or neither hope of using as the path nor fear of not doing so. If a subtle hope or fear arises, let it be without modifying and let go completely into nonclinging. You should know these three key points in all instances of using as the path.

## The Six Types of Using as the Path Explained One by One

This includes instructions on: (1) using thoughts as the path and taking bad omens as auspicious, (2) using afflictions as the path and transmuting poison into ambrosia, (3) using gods and demons as the path and magnetizing obstacles as siddhis, (4) using suffering as the path and bodhichitta, (5) taking sickness as the path and equalizing the elements, and (6) using death as the path and pointing out mother and child dharmata.

## Using Thoughts as the Path and Taking Bad Omens as Auspicious

As said in the *Two Segments*:

> Just as water inside the ear
> Should be extracted by more water,
> Similarly, a thought about a thing
> Should be cleansed by a thought.

A thought is cleansed by a thought, and the way to do that is, rather than taking a thought as something to be rejected, to use the thought as the path, as an essence thought. Lord Gampopa said:

> Internally in the mind, don't reject a thought, but regard it as kind, as indispensable, as needed, as delightful. This being so, thoughts are essence thoughts, thoughts are friends, thoughts are the path, thoughts are fuel for prajña.

As to actually using thoughts as the path, you should start by identifying the thought. Once a thought—subtle or coarse, virtuous or unvirtuous—arises in the mind, if it makes the mind apprehensive and provokes a vivid like or dislike, don't be casual about it but identify it through sharp mindfulness.

Then, get rid of ego-clinging. It is not a matter of not conceptualizing it, drawing in the mind, and applying the antidote of meditating on concept-free wisdom. It also does not entail investigating such aspects as the origin, abode, and exit of the thought, leading to a conclusion that it lacks true nature. Neither is it a question of being casual about the thought so you follow it, and then you sustain the practice through mindfulness. Instead, once you simply identify the thought, just as it is, fresh and complete, place the core of your practice right upon it. Don't cling at all to flaw or quality, block, follow, or conceptually modify the thought in any way whatsoever. Sustain loosely with vivid clarity, openly, awake, and without fixating. By doing so, there is no need to reject or adopt, block or acquire, contaminate with alterations, or manipulate any arising thought. Instead, that very thought will vividly arise as meditation, and that is what is meant by taking thoughts as the path. Maitripa said:

> The adventitious thought in nonorigination
> Itself has the essence of space.
> These two have never been apart from the beginning.
> I declare that these two are of one taste.

Lord Gampopa said:

> An uncontaminated thought is the nature of dharmata.
> Know how to free it into its original state without alteration.

Lord Gotsangpa said:

> Again, when a thought is born,
> Sharply catch it through awareness
> And rest at ease right there.
> There is no doubt it will be freed into its original state.

And:

> Thought movement is insubstantial like the breeze.
> Not clinging to it, movement is all right.
> That is what is meant by thoughts arising as meditation.
> By knowing its essence, you are free from blocking and
> acquiring.

Those who are not accomplished yogins will, at first, feel irritated in their hearts by a turmoil of thought movements, and their spiritual practice will also be somehow disturbed. However, since thoughts and karma pranas are working together, this is an experience of disturbed karma pranas. In fact all this is part of the practice, so the thought at some point will spontaneously be taken as the path easily within the practice. Once familiarized, simply identifying the thought will turn it into practice.

Finally, "clear the treacherous path of hope and fear." In terms of using as the path according to this system, don't be at all anxious or ponder over the hope of taking as the path, fear of not doing so, and so on. Let go without evaluating, clinging, or leaving any trace. Know how to use other matters as the path in ways similar to these.

## Using Afflictions as the Path and Instructions on Transmuting Poison into Ambrosia

As said in the *Two Segments*:

> Just as those boiled by boiling
> And further heated up by fire,
> Those burned by the fire of desire
> Will be further burned by the fire of desire.

In the *Samputa Tantra* it is said:

> Desire purifies desire.
> Hatred cleanses hatred.
> Dullness cleanses dullness.
> Pride cleanses pride.
> Envy cleanses envy.
> Vajra holders cleanse everything.

As said, through using afflictions themselves and equalizing their taste with dharmata, while their forms are of afflictions, their essence arises as the five wisdoms. One by one, once desire is purified into discerning wisdom, aggression into dharmadhatu wisdom, ignorance into mirrorlike wisdom, pride into wisdom of equality, and envy into all-accomplishing wisdom, one actualizes the level of the five buddhas. As the *Samputa Tantra* states:

> Wisdom and afflictions go equally.
> These are the five families,
> Five wisdoms and five buddhas.

Therefore, by following the instructions of using as the path, you may enjoy the six sensual objects without being contaminated by their flaws. It is similar to transmuting poison into nectar. In the *Two Segments* it is said:

> The never-ending karmas of beings
> That bind them in whichever way,
> If they have the method, through those karmas themselves
> They will be freed from the bondage of samsara.

As the Great Brahmin said:

> By relying on the objects, they don't contaminate.
> Water does not touch the petals of the utpala flower.
> Likewise, for yogins who have taken refuge in the root,
> And who possess the poison mantras, how can poison
> penetrate them?

And:

> Just like salty ocean water
> Becomes as sweet as vapor in clouds,
> On benefiting others through a stable mind,
> The poison of the objects also turns into nectar.

As to actually using afflictions as the path, in the case of desire: you may feel desire and attachment toward the world or its inhabitants, and therefore want to possess them. Recognize the mind that acutely yearns to do so. Regarding aggression toward such objects as enemies and obstructing spirits, or similar situations, you react with displeasure. Recognize that disturbed, resentful mind. Regarding ignorance, you may delight in sleeping, and your present mind may be cloudy, dull, lethargic, and so forth. Recognize precisely that unclear mind. As to pride, based on others I bolster myself; thinking that I am better than them makes me proud, and so forth. Once arrogance is born, your mind clings to feeling better than others. Recognize that very mind. Regarding envy, your mind feels unhappy because of others' wealth, and so on. Recognize the mind that is disturbed by a deep feeling of loss.

When these are identified, rest right on them without any manipulation. Extend the continuity of nondistraction, give up ego-clinging, and avoid the uneasiness of hope and fear. If you have hope, rest on hope, and if there is fear, rest on fear, and so forth. You should know to rest on such events, as explained before.

At times, either actual desire or anger arises toward an objective, afflictive condition (such as an object of desire or hatred), or you do something that increases its strength so that the affliction is boosted. Somehow your breathing is uneasy, your expression changes, and your body fidgets and shakes, so that fierce desire or anger either takes place or is deliberately stoked up. Identify that thought itself, and apply the rest of the instructions. It has been explained that however strong the emotion may be, this path is very effective in powerfully purifying the afflictions as such. As Maitripa said:

> The afflictions are the great wisdom.
> Like wind to forest fires, they are a yogin's aid.

The way in which they are taken as the path or not has been explained before and by persevering in using them as the path, the essence of the afflictions will emerge nakedly. The wisdoms will not be found anywhere apart from the five poisons, which will be freed in their original condition.

## Using Gods and Demons as the Path and Instructions on Magnetizing Obstacles as Siddhis

As has been said, "Concepts are obstacles. All obstacles arise from conceptual thoughts." Naropa said:

> Sickness and obstacles from harmful spirits,
> If subsumed, they are condensed in concepts.
> If sick, it is the concept itself that is sick.
> If harmed, it is the concept itself that is harmed.
> If dying, it is the concept itself that dies.
> If born, it is the concept itself that is born.
> Happiness, suffering, and so forth
> All are conceptual thoughts.
> In the mind there is nothing whatsoever.
> If the basis and root of thought are cut,
> Sickness and harmful spirits will not arise.

And the Great Lord [Milarepa] said:

> Perceiving demons, thinking demons, clinging to demons,
> They may arise, but they do so from the yogin himself.
> They may dissolve, but they dissolve into the yogin himself.
> Generally all demons are a magical display of the mind.
> If the yogin doesn't see it as his own empty projection
> But clings to it as a concrete demon, he is deluded.

And the female demon Drag Sinmo said to Milarepa:

> If through the original cause of delusion in your mind,
> The thought of enemy hadn't arisen,
> How could Drag Sinmo emerge as an enemy?
> Besides, the demon of habitual patterns arises from the mind alone.

> If you don't know the absolute nature of mind,
> Your ordering me to leave will not make me go away.

Hence, as mentioned in these and other quotations, all demon-clinging is a magical display of one's own conceptual thought. The apparent forms of gods and demons are but the experience of mentally solidified thought. For instance, this is similar to a rope that, once one has clung to it as a snake, appears to be a snake. As to the causes and conditions that give rise to events such as these, in one's body, which is a result of karmic ripening, the wind-energy has entered the channels where the three poisonous afflictions reside, and this is followed by the corresponding grasping thoughts and deluded perceptions. It has been taught that they arise from fixated thoughts and perceptions corresponding to each of the afflictions. Thus, from ignorant dullness arise nagas and earth-owning spirits, from aggression arise *tsen* and harmful male spirits, from desire arise harmful female spirits such as *sinmo*. Later on, once these become part of the path and arise as spiritual practice, and fixated concepts clear away, then cheerfulness will follow suit, harm caused by harmful spirits will subside, and all of them will be subdued. This will occur like the plates of a weighing scale—as one goes up, the other goes down.

Regarding the manner of using this as the path, Lord Gampopa said:

> It has been taught that one manner is to examine the four harmful spirits, whereby one becomes convinced that they have no true nature. However, that manner is slightly at odds with the method of equal taste. In the manner of focusing on the vital point in regard to gods and demons, the way is to rest without modifying on the continuous nonduality of one's mind and the concept of demon being one's own projection. What is said elsewhere about taking gods and demons as the path coincides precisely with this way.

As to actually using them as the path, whether gods and demons magically manifest or not, your mind is anxious that it may happen, and a vivid sense of grief arises. Alternatively you may feel afraid and panic. When any of these situations occurs, put on the armor of knowing that these gods and demons arise from habitual patterns and are in your own mind. With that, sharply recognize your frightened mind. Apply the main core of the practice onto this itself and, barely undistracted, prolong its continuity. If hope and fear arise, sustain the practice right on them, as was explained before.

No matter how intense the magical display may be, it is to be underrated. It may appear as fearsome, such as sky and earth clashing, gods and demons fighting, hitting and slashing each other with weapons, being burnt in fire, and being plunged into water. Thinking that the apparitions taking place are something other than mental, the experience of fear greatly increases. Be it the one who is afraid, the concept holding on to demons, the adversity, the sickness, the pain, the drowsiness, or so forth, the main point is to simply recognize that itself and, resting on it without modifying, to deepen the practice. If you equalize the taste in that way, all hopes stop, all fears are welcome, happiness is cast away, suffering is accepted, gain is given up, loss is acquired, fame is obliterated, obscurity is let go, criticism is accepted, and praise is an obstacle. If, on any good or bad circumstance you are able to remain firm like a mountain, for sickness you will not need to call a doctor, and for harmful spirits you will not need healing ceremonies. This point alone will place you in the company of realized yogins and experienced meditators.

## Using Suffering as the Path and Instructions on Bodhichitta

Since the seeds of happiness and suffering are but an image of something gone by in the past, you need to know first how to correct the cause, then how to eliminate the conditions, and finally how to conquer the fruition. Strong karma ripens in this life as something that is evidenced and experienced. There is also karma that is experienced in the future, in a later life, and there is karma that is experienced after a number of lives. This is all there is to it: karma produced by us does not ripen in others. Therefore, as said in a supplication:

> I follow the infallible cause and effect of virtuous and negative actions.
> Since karma will not ripen in anyone else
> Except in the body and mind of the perpetrator,
> Bless me so that I may accomplish adoption and rejection even at the risk of my life.

Regarding correction of the cause, you should earnestly exert yourself in confessing—by means of the four powers—the negative actions that were done in the past. As to eliminating the conditions, any cause and effect of your virtuous and negative actions belongs to the past. Later, when encountering a situation akin to the cause, this coincidence will easily transform the condition into virtuous or negative. So from the point of view of guru yoga, supplicate your guru. It is most important to persevere in mastering the ability to train in your own suffering and that of others. As to conquering the fruition, you must supplicate, make aspirations, and endeavor to apply methods to avoid it happening in the future.

In other words, while suffering is occurring, recognize it and don't allow yourself to be contaminated by the wish to be free from that suffering for your sake alone, as in the story of the friend's daughter. Take upon yourself the type of suffering afflicting others that is similar to yours, and train your mind through a firm resolve to exchange yourself for others. Wishing that all beginningless obscurations and negativities rising on the ground consciousness may be purified, be joyful. If unhappiness surges in your mind, identify it and apply the main practice without distraction, extending its continuity. Without hope and fear, if these events happen, follow the way of resting there as before. Finally, without losing the continuity of the experience of practice, and motivated by love and compassion toward all beings, cultivate bodhichitta and plant excellent altruistic aspirations. If there weren't seeds of negative actions and obscurations, suffering would have no way to arise; so when it does arise, be happy as it means that negativity and obscurations are wearing down. If these are being eliminated, there is no reason for suffering to arise. Lord Phagmo Drupa said:

If you understand this point wholeheartedly,
All suffering will be great bliss.

When you don't yield to the attitude of rejecting suffering but instead use it as the path, you will harvest bountiful happiness. On the contrary, if you get involved with Dharma practice for comfort and cling to that, you will get tired and feel that you are having to face difficulties. As taught:

In the hut where hunger and cold converge,
Have the courage to forbear these hardships.

These words stress the importance of the purpose.

Once absolute bodhichitta has been captured, everything becomes easier. At that time, the radiance of loving compassion toward the never-ending suffering of beings is unceasing. Its essence or nature cannot be found to truly exist; it is emptiness. The heart of mahayana is to be aware of that essence, so consider emptiness and compassion as indivisible, or the bodhichitta of emptiness as having the core of compassion. In a doha it is said:

When the mind perfectly meditates
On inseparable emptiness and compassion,
That is the teaching of Buddha, Dharma, and Sangha.

Also in the *Samputa*:

The true nature devoid of conceptual elaborations
Is renowned for possessing wisdom.
Like the wish-fulfilling gem,
Compassion benefits beings without exception.

By using suffering as the path in that way, through knowing its nature, in the state of great bliss the attitude of rejecting suffering is also liberated into its original condition. Then it automatically or spontaneously becomes the amusement of illusion.

## Taking Sickness as the Path and Instructions on Equalizing the Elements

Generally speaking, the basic cause of sickness is ignorance, which induces karma and afflictive emotions to generate sickness. The secondary conditions for all sicknesses start with the movement of karmic energies which, when it strikes, disturbs the four elements and creates a health imbalance. As a consequence, a feeling of suffering occurs in body and mind which leads from sickness to pain and so on.

Sickness can be classified into sickness arising from wind-energy, bile, phlegm, or a conjunction of all three, adding up to 404 types. There are numerous explanations on treatments to cure illnesses, but here we are concerned with curing the main cause, ignorance, and the profound treatment consists of sustaining awareness-wisdom. As to clearing away the conditions, since these consist of disturbed karmic energies, through the key point of unifying mind and energy, they will be purified into their original state. Therefore, sustaining the genuine state, the unfabricated mind, is profound. In regard to defeating the fruition, since this is the feeling of suffering, in order to let it go as tasteless and insubstantial, meditating on emptiness, the natural state, is profound. For these reasons, to cause chronic or new sicknesses to subside, it is considered more profound to use them as the path than to rely on other remedies.

As to actually using sickness as the path, when there is pain, don't slip into blocking it or curing it. No matter what disturbance in the elements or pain arises, think that it is a cause for purifying negativity, recognize the vivid feeling of physical and mental sickness and pain itself, and entrust the core of the meditation to that very recognition. Sustain that lucidly without altering or contaminating it with the attitude of blocking or accomplishing. At times, investigate ego-fixation in the one who is sick, hurting, experiencing, and so forth, and rest without modifying in the continuity of the indefinable essence.

Moreover, it is important to bear that painful illness gladly. When Lord Gotsangpa was afflicted by a very serious ailment for a long time, if the pain became very intense, he would join his palms, smile, and say, "The Three Jewels are being very compassionate." When the pain started to recede, with an expression of sadness and displeasure he would say, "Aren't the guru and all sublime beings sorry for me? I am recovering from my illness. The obscurations and negativities of this lazy person are not being cleansed!" Later on he would say, "What is impossible for others is possible for me. When others are happy, they laugh, and when they suffer, they cry. When I am happy, I cry, and when I suffer, I laugh." Based on his spiritual practice of using sickness as the path, all his convictions were reaffirmed. In fact, he considered sickness to be a broom that sweeps away obscurations and a guide that turns obstacles into siddhis.

Finally, don't indulge in any way in hopes that the illness will be cured, in fears that it will not be, or in any other reaction. Rather, rest decisively in great equanimity. When you are not able to equalize the taste based on the view as we have explained, and instead you are taken over by the young thief of hope and fear, then emphasize the excellent key point of inverted meditation. If you are unable to apply inverted meditation to this now, you will be unable to in the future, so it is an important key point for dealing with death.

In all other cases, check whether such practices as inverted meditation are compatible with the Buddhist path or not, and practice according to your own capability. It is said that you should seek the right conditions with what is good for you. So, in regard to taking physical illness as spiritual practice—the specialty of a yogin—since the body is the support for attaining enlightenment, it will not do to approach this situation from a silly understanding of Dharma that takes no account of whether or not you may die. So, at the conventional level, apply a treatment to become cured and rely on the right conditions, while at the ultimate level, practice free of hope and fear based on awareness. If you make no progress with the treatment, delight in sickness and be happy with death. As it is said in praise of the top-level practitioner:

> Delighting in sickness, happy with death,
> Not calling the doctor when sick,

> Not making rites to ward off demons,
> This is a child of the Drukpas endowed with good karma.

Since the root of sickness and negative influences depends on devotion to the guru, you should understand these words:

> Even if you don't resort to numerous treatments,
> Wearing the armor of emptiness is very important.
> In everything, guru yoga is auspicious.

In regard to using as the path the obstacle of hopes and fears, don't hope to get better here by making rituals. In order to abandon attachment to things, make offerings to the guru and the Three Jewels and give up wealth. This is the supreme method for adversities to arise as allies. Besides, if someone carries the responsibility of being *tokden* stands as the sublime guru who has accepted you, kindly confer empowerment and other rites to create an interdependent connection, you should use that as the path on the basis of your wish. Further, for a *tokden* to bow before a guru because they hope to be cured of a disease and ask for an empowerment because they fear dying would be an authentic hoisting of the victory banner of disgrace. Also, it would be improper to carry out worldly healing rites.

If one forces unsuitable food on a sick person who feels revulsion to food, this will disturb their mind and prevent healing. Just like by wishing to go to a foreign land one makes a connection and dies there, it is said that the sick person will be born in a place where food and drink are not available, or other similar situations. So be careful about this. Above all, when it comes to a practitioner who is not so advanced, if you insist on healing treatments and protection rites that are unsuitable, their mind will be disturbed, and there is a danger that you will spoil many interdependent connections. Therefore, be cautious about going against their mental dispositions. Some believe that once a person has realization, they will not be stricken by pain. That is really not the case. As long as we are together with this guesthouse of a body composed of the elements, there is no way to prevent the pain of sickness caused by the disturbance of the elements. But for the realized person there is no grief about the pain.

Furthermore, by this method in which you are bringing sickness into the fold of experience, whether pain comes from sitting cross-legged for a long time or from other types of illness afflicting the body, we believe that if you apply the method and use sickness as the path the pain will be relieved. Thus, by sustaining the practice on the sickness for a long time without mistaking its key point, eventually you will not regard pain and ego-clinging as enemies or want to reject them. They will arise as meditation and dissolve into the inconceivable and ineffable expanse. By knowing them to be primordially pure, they will be realized as emptiness. By equalizing the elements, heat and cold, it is believed that your recovery from the sickness and your progress in your practice will coincide.

## Using Death as the Path and Instructions Pointing Out Mother and Child Dharmata

To begin with, since you understand that your lifetime is uncertain, you need to be habituated to use as practice all thoughts and experiences that may happen whenever a situation threatens your life. For instance, the birth of a thought illustrates birth and its cessation is similar to death. Likewise, going to sleep is like death and waking up like birth. Ultimately, it is a matter of a difference in the subtlety of concepts, as nothing is beyond a concept. Therefore, if sick, it is the concept of sickness, and if dying, it is also the concept of dying, so for individuals who have not entered the path it is as said, "Conceptual thought is the great ignorance that plunges us into samsara." Whereas for a yogin, it is said, "The thought called death is what leads them to the dakini realm." Thus, it is as Machig Labdron said:

> My death is nothing more than being free from beneath a great mountain.[61]

In the pith instructions by Machig on using the moment of death as the path, it is said that we should let go of attachment to country, servants, food, wealth, and so forth. If we are unable to give these up, since thoughts have great power at the moment of death, this will be cause for a bad rebirth. In the past, a bhikshu was attached to his own begging bowl and was reborn as a snake. Attachment to people, food, or gold also led to rebirth as a snake. Some were attached to food and were reborn in their stove as a scorpion that experienced immeasurable suffering. Since there are many examples such as these, listen to this unerring guide: don't let your mind be attached or cling to anything whatsoever. If you are wealthy, make pleasing offerings to the guru; offer delightful ritual tormas to the yidam, dakini, and protectors; make pleasurable feast offerings to the vajra siblings and give everything away; and so forth. Cast negative objects and situations far away and set up all good interdependent connections properly.

When the time comes, adopt the postures of a lying lion, or if sitting upright, adopt the key points of the body posture. Beforehand, give away your body in the form of a ransom rite to the Dharma and all beings, and make altruistic aspirations that you will benefit beings on a large scale for as long as you stay alive. As to the main part, visualize on the crown of your head the buddha in whom you believe and their buddha field inseparable from your root guru, and with fervent devotion ask to be compassionately accepted. Make your supplication with the feeling, "Guide me on the path!" Furthermore, knowing that all is of one taste in the essence of mind, your own awareness, engage in using all as the path.

Due to the strong solidity of this life and knowing that you will be separated from it, what is to be used as the path are the thoughts in your mind at the moment of death, including the accompanying experiences. The latter are a sense of anxiety, of losing confidence, and of weeping, as well as the subsequent visionary experiences that occur during the dissolution of the elements, the experiences of appearance and increase, and the variety of experiences that arise one by one.

As to the manner of using as path, if you engage in hope and fear in terms of the following, then they are all obstacles to using as the path: feeling anxiety due to dislike and aversion toward all these experiences; your mind settling into the ego-clinging of judging whether it is this or that; your resting in the final meditation[62] or not; and your having entered the path or not. So begin by simply recognizing these thoughts and experiences, then apply the core of the practice onto them, and barely rest on not being distracted from the nature of mind. Don't contaminate it with attitudes such as that of blocking or acquiring, but by applying the other explanations given earlier, sustain it without clinging. At the conclusion, rest composed in the nonduality of the guru and your own mind, and look to see whether that flows. There is nothing more profound than resting composed in the nondual nature of the guru and your mind, the continuity of the great all-embracing dharmakaya, free of action. Orgyen Rinpoche said:

> The highest level of yogin performs the dharmakaya transference.[63] To remain in the continuity of natural dzogchen, where neither the place to be transferred to nor the one doing the transference has true existence, is the ultimate transference.

If awareness is transferred in this way, the purpose will be accomplished. At that point, if you are concerned about how well it is going, there is a danger that this may hinder the path. In general, on reaching this point it becomes obvious whether you are brave or not. Don't be uptight, instead be joyful; it is important not to be tense, but cheerful.

Regarding this point, the instructions on mind training in the mahayana also include transference at the time of death. Although there is a great deal of boasting about these instructions, it is explained that there is nothing more profound than sustaining whatever arises without fixation. After completing the dissolution stage in that manner, natural luminosity will spontaneously arise, which, when merging with the mother and child luminosity practiced during the path, will be like water poured into water. Becoming like space merging with space, it is explained that one awakens into dharmakaya. This meaning is mentioned in the following citations. In a tantra it is said:

> The thought that is called death
> Is what leads one to the dakini realm.

And:

> In one instant there is a special separation.
> In one instant there is buddhahood.

Lord Gampopa said:

> Thought moves from one to the other:
> Where is dying there?
> In perfect dharmakaya,
> Where is dying there?
> In fading rainbow drawings,
> Where is dying there?
> In birthless and deathless mind,
> Where is dying there?

As has been taught, it may be that you are not very accustomed to using death as the path, and hence you are unable to awaken to buddhahood within the state of indivisible awareness and space. Yet during the bardo or at the time of conception in rebirth, because death was previously used as the path in any appropriate way, you will be in control. Otherwise, at the very least through the strength of the interdependent connection, the karmic result will be completed in the next life. This moment of death definitely happens to all sentient beings, and there is no telling when it will come to you, so look for this trustworthy escape. The parents, relatives, wealth, and possessions of this life—whatever it may be—for sure, there is no way they will accompany you from here. The smart cultivate primordial awareness. The intelligent give up what is perishable. This is important.

# 12. Identifying and Traversing the Paths and Bhumis

G. Identifying the Paths and Bhumis and the Manner of Traversing Them
  1. Identifying the Paths and Bhumis
  2. The Manner of Traversing the Paths and Bhumis

## Identifying the Paths and Bhumis and the Manner of Traversing Them

This includes explanations on: (1) identifying the paths and bhumis, and (2) the manner of traversing the paths and bhumis.

## Identifying the Paths and Bhumis

These are subsumed in the following quotation:

> The paths of accumulation, connection,
> Seeing, meditation,
> And culmination,
> These are thus subsumed into five.

In the text *Torch of the Path to Enlightenment*, these five paths are rightly taught as follows. The path of accumulation is what is traversed by people of the lower and middling capacities, who start by laying the foundation of the path through practicing their corresponding teachings, then cultivate the bodhichitta of aspiration and application, and then endeavor to generate the two accumulations of merit and wisdom. The words "once one gradually attains the signs of accomplishment in the practice" refer to the path of connection. Through "having attained the Joyful One and rest," the author referred to the paths of seeing, meditation, and culmination.

Regarding the path of accumulation, someone belonging to that spiritual family starts by developing the bodhichitta toward supreme enlightenment, and after receiving the instructions from the master, they strive in every way to practice what is virtuous until the warmth of wisdom is born. This may occur in one of four ways according to whether it has happened through realization, aspiration, higher wish, or accomplishment. It is called the path of accumulation for two reasons. The first is that merit is generated so the practitioner becomes a suitable vessel for experiencing all that has to do with realization, such as the signs of accomplishment in the practice. The second is that this path is the basis for the merit that is compatible with the attainment of liberation. At this stage, one practices twelve points of the Dharma leading to enlightenment: the four applications of mindfulness, the four aspects of right renunciation, and the four stages of miraculous ability. The four applications of mindfulness are: mindfulness applied to the body, sensations, mind, and phenomena. These correspond to the stage of the lower path of accumulation. The four aspects of right renunciation are: to abandon anything negative and unvirtuous that has occurred; not to give rise to what has not yet occurred; to give rise to what is virtuous as a remedy; and to increase the virtue that has arisen. These correspond to the stage of the middling path of accumulation. The four stages of miraculous ability are those that correspond to the samadhis of determination, perseverance, mind, and inquiry. These belong to the stage of the greater path of accumulation.

The path of connection starts after the culmination of the higher path of accumulation. In it are born a realization of the four noble truths as well as the four aspects of definite discernment conducive to that: meditative warmth, climax, acceptance, and the highest worldly spiritual attainment. It is called the path of connection because one connects with the realization of the four truths. Furthermore, at the stage of warmth and its climax, five faculties are present: faith, perseverance, mindfulness, samadhi, and knowledge. At the stage of acceptance and highest worldly spiritual attainment, these five aspects are present as five strengths: faith, perseverance, mindfulness, samadhi, and knowledge.

The path of seeing starts after the highest worldly spiritual attainment. It entails calm abiding on the four noble truths as an object and the corresponding insight. Each of the four truths has four aspects. In the case of suffering, there is: acceptance of the Dharma leading to the knowledge of suffering; actual knowledge of suffering; acceptance of the knowledge of the discernment of suffering; and the subsequent knowledge of the discernment of suffering. The same applies to the other three truths, so altogether they include sixteen instances of acceptance and knowledge. It is called the path of seeing because the noble truths that had not previously been seen are now seen. This stage includes the seven factors of enlightenment, namely: perfect mindfulness, perfect discernment of phenomena, perfect perseverance, perfect joy, perfect thorough training, perfect samadhi, and perfect equanimity.

The path of meditation starts after the path of seeing has been born. It can be a worldly path or a path transcending worldly existence. The worldly path consists of the first to fourth worldly concentrations and the fourfold spheres of perception: infinite space, infinite consciousness, nothing whatsoever, and neither perception nor nonperception. These meditations have three purposes: to subdue the afflictions through rejecting them in meditation, to accomplish such exceptional qualities as the four boundless states of mind, and to establish the support for the path that transcends worldly existence.

The path transcending worldly existence consists of calm abiding that has as its object the two types of wisdom and the accompanying insight of vipashyana. As mentioned earlier, in the path of seeing, there are two acceptances and two types of knowledge for each of the four truths. Of these sixteen aspects, eight acceptances are completed in the path of seeing. In the path of meditation, one becomes familiarized with the eight forms of knowledge through the practices of shamatha and vipashyana, related to the four concentrations and three formless samadhis. Furthermore, part of the knowledge of phenomena is to become familiarized with the realization of absolute reality. Part of the continuity of knowledge is to become familiarized with the realization of primordial wisdom. The sphere of neither perception nor nonperception is worldly because it fails to completely remove the cause of perception. It is called the path of meditation because the meditation generates familiarity with the suchness that has been realized in the path of seeing. At this stage, the noble eightfold path is followed, namely: right view, right understanding, right speech, right completion of action, right livelihood, right effort, right mindfulness, and right samadhi.

Regarding the path of culmination, after the vajra-like samadhi, one realizes that thereafter the causes for rebirth have ended, and they will never happen again. The vajra-like samadhi happens at the time of the path of abandonment that comes at the end of the path of meditation, and is included in the path of connection and the unobstructed path. This samadhi is called diamond-like (vajra) because it is indestructible, hard, stable, uniform, and pervasive. It is "indestructible" because it cannot be damaged by worldly activity; "hard" because it is not destroyed by any obscuration; "stable" because it is unmoved by thought; "uniform" because it has an equal taste throughout; and "pervasive" because it does not objectify the suchness common to everything knowable. "The realization that thereafter the causes for rebirth have ended" means that because the causes or origin of suffering have come to an end, the primordial wisdom focuses on the four truths. "The realization that they will never happen again" means that the primordial wisdom focuses on the four truths because of the resultant elimination of suffering. Moreover, the wisdom focusing on the cause being exhausted, and the effect being that it will not arise again, is the cognizance of exhaustion and nonarising. All these are called the path of culmination because one has reached the perfection of learning. Since one has proceeded to the citadel of nirvana, it is called the path of culmination. At this stage, there are ten topics that need no learning, starting with right view and ending with right samadhi, right liberation, and right wisdom. The ten dharmas that need no learning are further subsumed into five immaculate groups. Learning-free right speech, right completion of action, and right livelihood belong to the group of ethics; right mindfulness and right samadhi belong to the group of samadhi; and right view, right understanding, and right effort belong to the group of knowledge. Right liberation belongs to the group of liberation. Right cognizance belongs to the group of seeing the liberating wisdom.

Are the bhumis included in these five paths? The thirteen bhumis are summarized as in the following quotation:

> The beginners, those of devoted conduct,
> The ten bodhisattva bhumis,
> And the level of buddhahood—
> Thus ten and three subsume all the bhumis.

In the *Torch of the Path to Enlightenment* these are indicated as:

> The Joyful One and the others will be attained.

The Joyful One refers to the first bhumi, and the others refer to the two lower and the ten higher ones. The beginner's level is the stage of the path of accumulation because our immature being is brought to maturation. The level of devoted conduct is the path of connection because inspiration for the meaning of emptiness is simply brought forth. At this time, whatever is incompatible with the paramitas—such as avarice, afflictions that are abandoned through insight, and the cognitive obscuration, which are all designations—are all subdued and will not rise again. The ten bodhisattva bhumis range from the first, "Joyful One," to the tenth, "Cloud of Dharma." As mentioned in the *Sutra of the Ten Sublime Bhumis*:

> O sons of the conquerors, these are the ten bhumis of the bodhisattvas, the bhumi called the Joyful One and the rest.

In this context, the first bhumi, Joyful One, is the phase corresponding to the dawning of the path of seeing, in which the meaning of emptiness is directly realized. From the second to the tenth bhumi correspond to the phase of the path of meditation, in which familiarity with the suchness realized in the first bhumi takes place.

These ten bhumis of the bodhisattva should be understood in two manners: general and specific. The general manner consists of three aspects: the identity of the bhumis, their definition, and the reason for classifying them as ten. The identity includes the training of one's being to realize the absence of intrinsic identity in phenomena assisted by the corresponding samadhi. They are defined as bhumis (grounds) because each constitutes the basis of its corresponding qualities, and because they are the basis for the one that follows. Another meaning is that those on the bhumis remain enjoying primordial wisdom, like the cow pen where a cow stays [chewing the cud]. They are bhumis because that wisdom is traversed like a running horse. They are bhumis because that wisdom constitutes the ground on which all the sublime qualities are born, like an arable field. They are classified as ten because of the considerations required for each. The specific manner involves nine points for each of the bhumis, namely: specific name, specific definition, specific training, specific practice, specific purification, specific realization, specific abandonment, specific birthplace, and specific power.

The specific name of the first bhumi is Joyful One.

Its specific definition is that it is joyful because one comes close to enlightenment and accomplishes the welfare of beings on the attainment of this bhumi. As said in the *Ornament of Sutras*:

> On getting closer to enlightenment
> And seeing that the welfare of beings is accomplished,
> Immense joy is born;
> This is why this bhumi is called the Joyful One.

Specific training involves training in the ten points, such as having no deceitful thoughts toward anyone. By training in the ten points, one attains this bhumi. As said in the *Ornament of Clear Realization*:

> Through the ten trainings
> The first bhumi is attained.

Specific practice means that a bodhisattva who is on this bhumi, although practicing all ten perfections, predominantly practices the perfection of generosity in particular, wishing to bring satisfaction to all beings. As said in the *Sutra of the Ten Sublime Bhumis*:

> Out of the ten perfections, what is practiced most in the first bhumi is generosity. This does not mean that the other nine are not practiced.

Specific purification is explained in the *Sutra of the Ten Sublime Bhumis*:

> In the Joyful One, on account of the great vision and strong aspirations, many hundreds, thousands, and millions of buddhas manifest. Upon seeing them, the bodhisattvas make offerings and venerate them with the highest altruistic attitude, and in a similar manner, pay respects to their community of followers. That root of virtue is dedicated to the attainment of unsurpassable enlightenment. They also hear the Dharma from those buddhas, receive it, memorize it, and diligently put it into practice. Through the four means of attraction, they ripen beings.

For many eons, they venerate and follow the Buddha, Dharma, and Sangha; they bring beings to complete maturity; and they dedicate the merit toward unsurpassable enlightenment. Through these three causes the root of merit is vastly increased and purified. As is said:

> The more fine gold is heated by jewelers, the clearer, purer, and more pliable to one's wish it becomes. Likewise, the roots of virtue of the bodhisattvas in the first bhumi become totally cleansed, completely purified, and pliable to their wishes.

Specific realization means that, although in general all ten bhumis are alike in the realization that happens during resting in composure, there are differences in the subsequent stage depending on how certainty is induced. Thus, when explained individually, in the first bhumi the dharmadhatu is realized as extending everywhere, whereby the equality of self and others is attained. Hence the *Discernment of the Middle Way and the Extremes* alludes to "extending everywhere."

Specific abandonment, in terms of the afflictive obscurations, means the complete abandonment in this bhumi of the eighty-two afflictions that are capable of being eliminated by seeing the truth. In terms of the three types of cognitive obscurations, the layers are stripped like the bark of a tree. Furthermore, there is freedom from the five fears. As said in the *Sutra of the Ten Sublime Bhumis*:

> The five fears that are eliminated in the bhumi Joyful One are: the fear of not making a living, the fear of not getting praise, the fear of death, the fear of the miserable realms, and the fear of being amid followers.

Specific birthplace means that in most cases a bodhisattva in this bhumi will take birth in the world of Jambudvipa as a universal monarch who will remove the stain of avarice from beings. In the *Jewel Garland* it is said:

> Through their maturity,
> They will become a universal monarch in Jambudvipa.

Although this is the indicated birthplace, when considering the nature of the bodhisattvas, they will manifest in different forms for the sake of benefiting those to be trained by them, as can be seen in the *Jataka*.

Specific power is as said:

> The bodhisattva in the bhumi Joyful One is willingly diligent. If he is an ordained person, in an instant he accomplishes a hundred samadhis and settles in meditative absorptions, sees a hundred buddhas, comprehends their blessings, illuminates

> a hundred world spheres, goes to a hundred buddha fields, shakes a hundred world systems, ripens a hundred beings, remains for a hundred eons, knows the limits of one hundred previous and future eons, opens a hundred doors of the Dharma, and manifests in a hundred physical forms, each surrounded by a hundred bodhisattvas.

The specific name of the second bhumi is Immaculate.

Its specific definition is that, since it is free from the stain of unethical discipline, it is called Immaculate. Thus, it is said:

> Because it is free from the stain of unethical discipline,
> It is called the Immaculate bhumi.

Specific training means following the eight trainings, such as discipline and gratitude. Thus:

> There is ethics, gratitude, patience,
> Immense joy, and great loving compassion.

Specific practice means that a bodhisattva in this bhumi, although practicing all ten perfections, practices predominantly the perfection of ethics.

Specific purity means that, through the three causes explained earlier, the root of merit is extensively purified. As said:

> Fine gold is further purified by experienced jewelers after dipping it in acid and heating it. Likewise, the roots of virtue of the bodhisattvas on the second bhumi become greater, purer, more refined, and more pliable than before.

Specific realization means that the dharmadhatu is realized as being supreme. The bodhisattva thinks, "I will exert myself to accomplish this aspect in the purification of everything." Therefore it is considered to be "supreme."

Specific abandonment means that, in terms of afflictive obscurations, from the second to the tenth bhumi there are sixteen afflictive obscurations capable of being abandoned through meditation. Although their seeds are not eliminated and still remain, their manifestations are subdued. Regarding the cognitive obscurations, the common ones are eliminated.

Specific birth means that, in most cases, a bodhisattva in this second bhumi will be born as a universal monarch ruling over the four continents, and will establish beings in the ten positive actions after having turned them away from the ten wrongdoings. As said:

> By their maturity,
> Through the glorious ten jewels,
> They become a universal monarch for the benefit of beings.

Specific power means that, in an instant, one accomplishes a thousand samadhis and absorptions. The rest is the same as in the previous bhumi except that a hundred should be replaced by a thousand wherever it appears.

The specific name of the third bhumi is Illuminator.

Its specific definition is that because the lights of Dharma and samadhi are so bright, this bhumi illuminates the great light of Dharma in others. Thus, it is called the Illuminator. As said:

> Since it brightens the great light of Dharma,
> It is called the Illuminator.

Specific training entails training in five points, such as being insatiable in listening to the Dharma. As said:

> Never tiring of listening to the Dharma,
> Teaching it without material interests.

Specific practice means that a bodhisattva in this bhumi, apart from generally practicing the ten bhumis, particularly emphasizes the paramita of patience.

Specific purity means, as in the previous cases, that through the three causes, the root of merit is extensively purified. As said:

> Just as when fine gold is purified by a jeweler it does not lose weight while all the stains are eliminated, similarly the root of merit of a bodhisattva who is in the third bhumi does not decrease but becomes extremely pure, cleansed, and pliable.

Specific realization means that a bodhisattva who is in this bhumi realizes the supreme meaning of the Dharma that describes the dharmadhatu. To receive even one word of that Dharma, the bodhisattva would jump into a billion fires. As said:

> This is the supreme meaning in accordance with the cause.

Specific birth means that a bodhisattva who is in this bhumi in most cases will become Indra, the lord of gods, and will be skillful in releasing beings from their attachment to desire. As said:

> Powerful lord of gods,
> He skillfully reverts the attachment of desire.

Specific power means that, in an instant, he accomplishes a hundred thousand samadhis. The rest is as in the previous bhumi except that a thousand should be replaced by a hundred thousand.

The specific name of the fourth bhumi is Radiant.

Its specific definition is that it is called Radiant because in this bhumi the radiance of the wisdom of all the factors conducive to enlightenment burns away the two obscurations. As said:

> This bhumi possesses
> The light that burns away
> The factors unfavorable for enlightenment;
> It is Radiant because it burns away the two [obscurations].

Specific training consists of ten activities, such as living in seclusion. As said:

> Living in forests, contented, with few desires,
> Training with purity, adhering to vows . . .

Specific practice means that a bodhisattva who is in this bhumi, apart from generally practicing the ten paramitas, emphasizes the paramita of perseverance.

Specific purity means that, through the three causes mentioned earlier, the root of merit is extensively purified. As said:

> Just as gold ornaments made by an experienced jeweler are not outshone by ornaments not made of gold, the root of merit of a bodhisattva who is in the fourth bhumi is not outshone by the root of merit of the bodhisattvas in the lower bhumis.

Specific realization means that a bodhisattva who is in this bhumi realizes the meaning of complete nonfixation and is free from attachment to Dharma. As said:

> The meaning of complete nonfixation . . .

Specific birth means that a bodhisattva who is in this bhumi will usually be born as the king of gods in the Supreme Strife-Free realm and will be skilled in destroying the belief in the existence of a self. As said:

> They become a king in the Supreme Strife-Free god realm
> And are skilled in destroying
> The belief in the existence of a self.

Specific power means that, in an instant, he accomplishes ten million samadhis. The rest is as in the previous bhumi except that a hundred thousand should be replaced by ten million.

The specific name of the fifth bhumi is Difficult to Train.

Its specific definition is that it entails two difficulties: striving to ripen beings and avoiding emotional disturbance when they respond adversely. As said:

> To accomplish the welfare of beings
> And guard one's own mind
> Is difficult for intelligent people.
> Therefore it is called Difficult to Train.

Specific training means that this bhumi is attained by abandoning ten actions, such as associating with laypeople for the sake of gain or the like. As said:

> To yearn for acquaintances and home.
> To live in busy places.

Specific practice means that a bodhisattva in this bhumi, although generally practicing the ten paramitas, emphasizes the paramita of concentration.

Specific purity means that, through the three causes mentioned earlier, the root of merit is extensively purified. As said:

> Fine gold polished and studded with all kinds of precious jewels by an experienced jeweler is unrivaled and cannot be matched by other types of gold. Similarly, since the root of merit of a bodhisattva who is in the fifth bhumi is very pure because it is examined by skillful means and knowledge, it is unmatched by those of the bodhisattvas who are in the lower bhumis.

Specific realization means that a bodhisattva who is in this bhumi realizes the meaning of the absence of separate natures and knows the ten equanimities. As said:

> Natures are not diverse . . .

Specific birth means that in most cases a bodhisattva in this bhumi will be reborn as a king in the Tushita god realm and will be an expert in refuting the views of non-Buddhists. As said:

> Through their maturity,
> They become a king among Tushita gods
> Who refutes the afflicted views
> Of all non-Buddhists.

Specific power means that, in an instant, he accomplishes ten billion meditative stabilities. The rest is as in the previous bhumi except that ten million should be replaced by ten billion.

The specific name of the sixth bhumi is Actualized.

Its specific definition is that it is called Actualized because samsara and nirvana become evident. This is because on the basis of the paramita of transcendent knowledge, a bodhisattva dwells in neither samsara nor nirvana.

> Based on the perfection of transcendent knowledge,
> Samsara and nirvana
> Are both actualized.
> Therefore it is called the Actualized.

Specific training is perfecting the six factors, such as generosity, and abandoning the six factors, such as desiring the level of shravakas. Through these trainings this bhumi is attained. Thus:

> By perfecting generosity, ethics, patience, perseverance,
> Concentration and transcendent knowledge . . .

Specific practice is that a bodhisattva in this bhumi, although generally practicing the ten paramitas, emphasizes the paramita of transcendent knowledge.

Specific purity means that, through the three causes mentioned earlier, the root of merit is greatly enhanced and purified. As said:

> Gold studded with lapis lazuli by a clever jeweler is unmatched by other types of gold. Similarly, since the root of merit of a bodhisattva who is in the sixth bhumi is very pure and luminous because it is examined by skillful means and knowledge, it is unmatched by those of the bodhisattvas who are in the lower bhumis.

Specific realization means that those in this bhumi have realized the meaning of affliction and purity in such a way that, in interdependence, affliction and purity are known to be nothing whatsoever. As said:

> Affliction is a concept, not truly existing . . .

Specific birth means that a bodhisattva in this bhumi will usually be reborn a king among the Sunirmita gods and be skillful in counteracting the pride of sentient beings. As said:

> Through their maturity
> They become a god among the Sunirmita,
> Shravakas cannot match them,
> And they counteract overweening pride.

Specific power means that, in an instant, he accomplishes ten trillion meditative stabilities. The rest is as in the previous bhumi except that ten billion should be replaced by ten trillion.

The specific name of the seventh bhumi is Far Reaching.

Its specific definition means that one reaches far because this bhumi is connected to the single path to be traversed, so one's training reaches culmination. As said:

> Because it is connected to the single path to be traversed,
> It is known as the Far Reaching bhumi.

Specific training consists of attaining this bhumi by abandoning the twenty fixations, such as ego-clinging, and relying on knowing the three doors to liberation and the rest of the twenty opposing factors. As said:

> Fixating on self and sentient beings . . .

And:

> Knowing the three doors to liberation . . .

Specific practice is that a bodhisattva in this bhumi, although generally practicing the ten paramitas, emphasizes the paramita of method.

Specific purity means that, through the three causes mentioned earlier, the root of merit is extensively purified. As said:

> If a master jeweler studs gold with all kinds of precious jewels and makes it extremely beautiful, it cannot be surpassed by any other ornament in the world. Similarly, since the root of merit of a bodhisattva who is in the seventh bhumi is extremely pure, it cannot be surpassed by those of the shravakas or bodhisattvas who are in the lower bhumis.

Specific realization means that a bodhisattva who is in this bhumi realizes the meaning of nondifferentiation in that there is no difference in the distinguishing characteristics of the Dharma found in the sutras and in other teachings. As said:

> No differentiations . . .

Specific birth means that a bodhisattva who is in this bhumi in most cases will be reborn a king among the Vashavartin gods and be skilled in understanding the type of knowledge of the shravakas and pratyeka buddhas.[64] As said:

> Through their maturity
> They become a king of the Vashavartin gods

> And a supreme teacher
> Who truly realizes the four noble truths.

Specific power means that, in an instant, he accomplishes ten quadrillion meditative stabilities. The rest is as in the previous bhumi except that ten trillion should be replaced by ten quadrillion.

The specific name of the eighth bhumi is Unshakable.

Its specific definition is that it is unshaken by effort toward discerning the presence or absence of characteristics.[65] As said:

> Because it is unshaken by the twofold conceptualization,
> It is called the Unshakable.

Specific training consists in attaining this bhumi through eight practices, such as knowing the activity of all beings as it is. As said:

> They know the minds of beings
> And love them through supernormal cognition.

Specific practice is that a bodhisattva in this bhumi, although generally practicing the ten paramitas, emphasizes the paramita of altruistic aspiration.

Specific purity means that, through the three causes mentioned earlier, the root of merit is extensively purified. As said:

> Just as the finished gold ornament made by an artistic jeweler worn on the neck of the king of the world cannot be surpassed by any other ornament worn by common people, the root of merit of a bodhisattva who is in the eighth bhumi is extremely pure, so it is not surpassed by those of the shravakas or bodhisattvas who are in all bhumis from the seventh down.

Specific realization means that since a bodhisattva who is in this bhumi is free from conceptual discrimination of all phenomena and has fully comprehended them to be like space, he is not terrified or frightened by the meaning of emptiness and nonorigination. He is said to have attained forbearance regarding the nonorigination of phenomena. Through this acceptance he realizes that phenomena neither increase nor decrease. He does not see anything that can be more or less defiled or purified. As said:

> Neither decreasing nor increasing . . .

And:

> The place of the four masteries.

These are mastery over absence of conceptual thought, pure buddha fields, primordial wisdom, and activity. A bodhisattva who is in the eighth bhumi realizes that it is precisely here that he masters the absence of conceptual thought and the pure buddha fields. Furthermore, he is said to possess the ten powers over: length of life, mind, necessities, karma, birth, aspiration, motivation, miracle, wisdom, and proclamation of the Dharma.

Specific birth means that in most cases he becomes Brahma who rules over the first level of the billion world systems, and he has great skill in establishing the teachings of the arhats, pratyeka buddhas, and so forth. As said:

> Through their maturity
> They become Brahma, the king of the billion [world systems],
> And are unparalleled
> In establishing the teachings of arhats and pratyeka buddhas.

Specific power means that, in an instant, he accomplishes as many samadhis as there are atoms in one hundred thousand of one billion world systems. The rest is as in the previous bhumi except that ten quadrillion should be replaced by this number.

The specific name of the ninth bhumi is Good Intelligence.

Its specific definition means that its name derives from an excellent discerning intelligence. As said:

> In this bhumi, intelligence is of excellent discernment,
> So it is called Good Intelligence.

Specific training involves the twelve practices, such as unlimited aspirations. As said:

> Aspirations are limitless,
> And they know the language of gods and other beings.

Specific practice is that a bodhisattva in this bhumi, although generally practicing the ten paramitas, emphasizes the paramita of power.

Specific purity means that, through the three causes mentioned earlier, the root of merit is greatly enhanced and purified. As said:

> Just as the finished fine gold ornament made by an experienced jeweler worn on the head or neck of a universal emperor cannot be surpassed by any other ornament worn by the kings of these worlds and beings of the four continents, the root of merit of a bodhisattva who is in the ninth bhumi is adorned with the intense brilliance of wisdom so it is not surpassed by those of the shravakas or bodhisattvas in all preceding bhumis.

Specific realization consists in realizing, out of the four masteries, the mastery of remaining in primordial wisdom, due to having attained the four types of right discerning knowledge, which are mentioned in the *Sutra of the Ten Sublime Bhumis*:

> The right discerning cognizance of Dharma, meanings, languages, and eloquence. These are always present.

Specific birth means that in most cases he becomes Brahma who rules over the intermediate level of the billion world system, and can answer all questions. As said:

> Through their maturity
> They become Brahma, the lord of the second level of the billion world system.
> On answering the questions of beings,
> They cannot be beaten by arhats, and so forth.

Specific power means that, in an instant, he accomplishes as many samadhis as there are atoms in a hundred million countless buddha fields. The rest is as in the previous bhumi replacing the number accordingly.

The specific name of the tenth bhumi is Cloud of Dharma.

Its specific definition is so called because the bodhisattva who is in this bhumi showers the rain of Dharma like a cloud, abating the most minute afflictions of beings. Another reason why it is called "cloud" is that he possesses the doors to samadhis and dharanis that pervade everything like the sky. As said:

> Because it covers the sky of Dharma
> With the two types of clouds, it is called Cloud of Dharma.

Specific training is not discussed in the *Ornament of Clear Realization* but in the *Sutra of the Ten Sublime Bhumis*:

> O sons of the conquerors, in this way the bodhisattva up to the ninth bhumi has differentiated and discriminated countless objects of knowledge through a discerning mind.

It then defines the tenth bhumi as the one of the ten trainings that empowers the bodhisattva for the wisdom of omniscience. When a reference is made to the bhumi in which the bodhisattva is initiated into omniscient wisdom, that is the tenth bhumi. Why is the tenth bhumi called the "bhumi of empowerment into omniscient wisdom"? This is because the bodhisattva in this bhumi is empowered by the light rays of the buddhas in the ten directions. This is more extensively discussed in the *Sutra of the Ten Sublime Bhumis*, and it coincides with what was taught by Maitreya and also found in the *Maitreyatikka*. In the vajrayana it is said that, at the end of the tenth bhumi, the bodhisattva is empowered by the buddhas in the ten directions, whereby he becomes enlightened. This coincides with what was said before, and although the reply to the question differs, there is no discrepancy in the meaning. In the *Jewel Garland*, it is said:

> Because the bodhisattva
> Is empowered by the light rays of the buddhas.

Specific practice is that a bodhisattva in this bhumi, although generally practicing the ten paramitas, emphasizes the paramita of primordial wisdom.

Specific purity means that, through the three causes mentioned earlier, the root of merit is extensively purified. As said:

> The great ornaments of a god, studded by precious jewels, are not created by craftsmen or artists. When the king of the gods wears them on his powerful head or neck they cannot be surpassed by the ornaments of gods and men. Similarly, the causes of primordial wisdom of a bodhisattva on the tenth bhumi cannot be defeated by ordinary beings, shravakas, or bodhisattvas up to the ninth bhumi.

Specific realization consists, out of the four masteries, of remaining in the mastery over activity. This is because he manifests at will myriad emanations through which he benefits beings.

Specific birth means that a bodhisattva in this bhumi becomes Maheshvara, the king of gods, and is skilled in revealing the teaching of the paramitas to ordinary beings, shravakas, and bodhisattvas. As said:

> Through their maturity,
> They become the lord of the pure abode gods,
> And master infinite wisdom.
> They are the supreme Maheshvara.

Specific power means that, in an instant, he accomplishes as many samadhis as there are atoms in ten million times one-hundred-thousand-billion countless, inexpressible buddha fields. The rest is as in the previous bhumi replacing the number accordingly. Moreover, from every pore of his body he is instantly able to manifest countless buddhas and innumerable retinues of bodhisattvas. He can display many beings such as gods and men. He can teach the Dharma in accordance with those to be trained, while taking the form of Indra, Brahma, world guardians, kings, shravakas, and tathagatas. Thus, in *Entering the Middle Way*,

> From the pores of his body he can display perfect buddhas
> Surrounded by countless bodhisattvas,
> As well as gods, men, and asuras,
> In every single instant.

This completes the explanation on the ten bodhisattva bhumis.

The bhumi of a buddha is at the stage of the path of culmination. Through the birth of the vajra-like samadhi, the afflictive obscurations that are eliminated through meditation and the cognitive obscurations, which are like the heart of them all, are suddenly eliminated. In this way, one will tread these bhumis through three incalculable eons. As said in the *Sutra of the Ten Sublime Bhumis*:

> These are reached by perfectly accomplishing them throughout three incalculable great eons. Through the first great incalculable eon, after perfectly going beyond the stage of devoted conduct, one attains the Joyful One; this is achieved through constant dedication and not without it. Through the second great incalculable eon one goes beyond the Joyful One up to the seventh bhumi, Far Reaching, and attains the eighth,

> Unshakable, with absolute certainty because such a bodhisattva endowed with an excellent intention has a definite dedication. Through the third great incalculable eon, after properly transcending the eighth and ninth bhumis, the bodhisattva attains the tenth bhumi, Cloud of Dharma. Among them, the bodhisattvas who exert great effort skip many intermediate eons, and others may skip a whole great eon, but you should know that none will skip an incalculable eon.

## The Manner of Traversing the Paths and Bhumis

In our case, vajrayana is superior to the sutra path, which involves enduring hardships for a long time. In general it is a shortcut, in particular its profound key point is the true meaning, and its distinguishing feature is that—as has been taught—the paths and bhumis are rapidly traversed with one unsurpassable realization. The essence of mahamudra, absolute reality, is an all-sufficient path, and it is inadequate to make distinctions in terms of the essential absolute reality. Therefore, as regards the true meaning, it is considered not fit to evaluate the stages of the paths and bhumis. In the *Commentary on Entering the Middle Way* it is said:

> Since it is a matter of the nature of cognizance, distinctions cannot be made in terms of their essence. Just as the learned cannot describe and see the traces of a bird in the sky, the sons of the conquerors also are unable to describe all the bhumis, let alone hear about them. Similarly, if the bhumis of the bodhisattvas cannot be spoken of, how may they be heard?

In the *Clear Meaning Commentary* [to the *Ornament of Clear Realization*] it is said:

> As explained, since at the time of the path of seeing, the subjective experience is indivisible from its object [emptiness],

> the paths of seeing and meditation have become indivisible. Therefore, it is said that the path of meditation as such cannot be accurately described. From the perspective of the essence, there are no distinctions and this accords with the explanation. Nonetheless, you may wonder how progress along the paths and bhumis is made while sustaining meditation. For those of duller faculties, there are the paths and bhumis of the sutras and, in the case of the four yogas of meditation, there is the way of evaluating the measure of the paths and of the bhumis.

The great siddha Zhang said:

> In all-sufficient mahamudra
> The unintelligent ponder paths and bhumis, and they become confused.
> However, so as to please the unintelligent,
> Here the paths and bhumis of the path of characteristics
> Will also be pondered at the outset.

What is the pondering like? Among many citations, we find in the *Abhidharma*:

> Because what cannot be seen is seen, it is the path of seeing.
> Due to becoming familiarized with the seeing, it is the path of meditation.

Also in the teachings of Maitreya it is said:

> Not seeing is the path of seeing.

Hence, the Dharma of realization of the Kagyu gurus is aligned with the sutra and tantra words of the Victorious One, a connection being made with the five paths and ten bhumis. Zhang Rinpoche said:

> The dawn of brilliant realization
> Is the path of seeing and the bhumi Joyful One.
> Developing familiarity with the realization of equal taste
> Is equivalent to the path of meditation.
> Once there is no meditation that is the path of perfection.

As is explicitly indicated here, the dawn of the realization of nonduality or indivisibility is the path of seeing and the first bhumi. Developing familiarity with that realization is equivalent to the path of meditation and takes place from the second to the tenth bhumis. Since nonmeditation has been taught as being the path of culmination and the level of buddhahood, there is no explanation that would actually link it with simplicity. However, when wondering whether simplicity is considered to be the path of seeing and the first bhumi, if it were so, it would imply that one-pointedness falls into the path of connection. Lord Gyare said:

> Although there is no need for bhumis and so forth during the path,
> If taught, this is how it would be acknowledged.
> Offering of a mandala is the path of accumulation.
> Dawn of experience is the path of connection.
> Simplicity is the path of seeing.
> Development of realization is the path of meditation.
> One taste is the eighth bhumi.
> Nonmeditation is the eleventh bhumi, the path of culmination.

The equivalences are viewed as follows. Starting from the foundational practices, generating merit and purifying obscurations is the path of accumulation; one-pointedness is the path of connection; simplicity is the path of seeing; from the dawn of the realization of indivisibility onward, including the levels of one taste, is the path of meditation; lesser and middling nonmeditation are the ninth and tenth bhumis; while greater nonmeditation is the eleventh bhumi and the path of culmination. Lord Gotsangpa said:

> Generation of merit and so forth are the path of accumulation and the beginner's level. One-pointedness is the path of connection and the level of devoted conduct. Simplicity is the path of seeing and the first bhumi. One taste goes from the second to the seventh bhumis. Lesser and middling nonmeditation are the three remaining bhumis; these are the path of meditation. Greater nonmeditation is the path of culmination and the level of buddhahood.

Some classify the experiences and realizations of the four yogas into groups of twelve according to the three levels of each of the yogas. If classified into twenty-four, twelve yogas of experience belong to the four levels of the path of connection, and twelve yogas of realization are classified in the following way: the three levels of one-pointedness belong to the first, second, and third bhumis; the three of simplicity to the fourth, fifth, and sixth bhumis; the three of one taste to the seventh, eighth, and ninth bhumis; and the three of nonmeditation to the tenth, eleventh, and twelfth bhumis. This is another way in which the connections are presented.

In particular, the three levels—lesser, middling, and greater—at the stage of one-pointedness belong to the path of connection. The four kinds of definite discernment are as follows: Seeing the essence of mind is called meditative warmth; the birth of conviction about that is climax; that circumstances cannot harm it is acceptance; and the continuity of the experience of one-pointedness is viewed as the highest mundane spiritual attainment in the path of accumulation. At this stage the special qualities of the five faculties also take place. How is that? The birth of immeasurable conviction is the faculty of faith; to see the truth without distraction is the faculty of mindfulness; uninterrupted by laziness is the faculty of diligence; uninterrupted meditation is the faculty of samadhi; and realization of the true meaning is the faculty of transcendent knowledge. The development of the potential or the strengthening of each of these five is also referred to as the five strengths.

Having actualized the three levels of one-pointedness, one completes the path of connection and arrives at simplicity. Since the truth that was not seen before is now seen, one attains the path of seeing. At this stage, the paramita path teaches that the practice is on the seven factors of enlightenment, but in fact these arise here automatically. Thus, to rest in the continuity of the natural state of absolute reality as it is is the factor of enlightened samadhi. Not to be mixed with the afflictions is enlightened discernment of the truth. By simply remembering the samadhi, the lingering stains of the path of seeing yet to be eliminated naturally vanish within themselves; therefore this is enlightened memory. To be free from laziness and distraction is enlightened perseverance. To enjoy undefiled blissful joy is enlightened joy. To purify all that must be abandoned without exception is enlightened pliancy. To realize the equality of samsara and nirvana is enlightened equanimity. The seven factors are therefore complete. Furthermore, it has been taught that the various qualities of the path of seeing and the infinite doors of samadhi are attained.

When the genuine realization—the sublime quality of the path of seeing—dawns, since it constitutes the source or foundation of all qualities, it is called "attaining the bhumi." The *Avatamsaka Sutra* says:

> As soon as the bhumi is attained, one is free from the five fears: harm, death, falling to the lower realms, family worries, and anxiety.

As the qualities of the ten bhumis increase more and more, the following bhumis are called the path of meditation. All the periods of resting in composure in this path are solely of undefiled samadhi, and in the ensuing phenomena stage one becomes habituated to the noble eightfold path, which is considered defiled. These eight are right view, right understanding, right speech, right completion of action, right livelihood, right effort, right mindfulness, and right samadhi. In brief, since only right objects are accomplished by these, they only have the multiple distinguishing features of being a path that is superior to the lower vehicles.

Each bhumi has a specific quality at the beginning. The first bhumi has the quality of supreme joy, so it is called Joyful. In this context, at the beginning of simplicity through samadhi there is an increased joy so it belongs to the first bhumi, Joyful. The second bhumi is Immaculate because it is free from the stains eliminated through meditation. The third bhumi is Illuminating because it benefits beings from the strength of the realization. The fourth bhumi is Brilliant because in middling simplicity the predominant wakefulness makes the qualities increase further and further. The fifth bhumi is Hard to Accomplish because the realization of indivisible emptiness and compassion cleanses the stains of habitual tendencies which are difficult to purify. The sixth bhumi is Actualized because during the actualization of greater simplicity, samsara and nirvana are realized as unoriginated.

We have described the above bhumis as well as the paths of shravakas and pratyeka buddhas and the common vehicle. From these onward such dualistic perceptions as samsara and nirvana, or meditation and postmeditation, for the most part are liberated into indivisibility. The beginning of the dawn of the realization of one taste coincides with the seventh bhumi, Far Reaching. In middling one taste, since what is realized never wavers from perfect mindfulness, it is the eighth bhumi, Unshakable. In greater one taste, apart from a mere subtle, illusory, dualistic perception, most other defilements have been purified, so it is the ninth bhumi, Sublime Intelligence. This subtle dualistic perception also vanishes within its original state, so the qualities of the paths and bhumis are consummated; yet residual stains or habitual fixations remain in the ground consciousness, which is extremely subtle cognitive obscuration. This is the stage of lesser and middling nonmeditation. In terms of the general approach, this would be the tenth bhumi, Cloud of Dharma.

From here onward, the bodhisattvas possess the same qualities as the lords of the tenth bhumi, so the subtle habits of the cognitive obscuration, which result in the stain of not recognizing nonconceptuality, also dissolve into the essence of vajra-like wisdom, the naturally occurring self-knowing awareness. This brings about a perpetual freedom from obscuring factors. The strength of the wisdom of things as they are and all that exists, as well as the power of the capacity of knowledge and compassion, is totally complete. At this time, generally this is the actual level of perfect buddhahood, the supreme path of culmination of the common vehicle. In mahamudra, this would be described as greater nonmeditation.

In terms of general vajrayana, at this time while one is free from the veils of habitual patterns of karma and afflictions, there is indeed no path as such to tread or train on. The eleventh bhumi, Universal Light, and the twelfth bhumi, Lotus of Nonattachment, are named after the distinguishing feature or special differentiation of the growth of qualities. These are the two special bhumis instantly actualized, after which dharmakaya is fulfilled for one's own benefit and its display manifests as the rupakaya for the purpose of others. This continuously brings immense benefit to beings pervading space until samsara is emptied. This is the thirteenth bhumi, Vajra Holder, buddhahood itself. Therefore, traversing these bhumis along a progression from one to the other is called the path of learning, and when there is no further progression—when reaching culmination—that is called the path of no learning. The thirteenth bhumi, Vajra Holder, is the completion of the inner vajrayana fruition.

Which are the specific qualities on accomplishing each of these bhumis? When a bodhisattva attains the first bhumi, they are able to emanate in a hundred nirmanakaya buddha fields and traverse them at the same time, meet with a hundred buddhas, and receive teachings of the Dharma. They can simultaneously make a hundred different acts of generosity without any concern, such as giving away their body, life, wealth, kingdom, children, and spouse. They can simultaneously send forth a hundred different light radiations, such as emanating red light and reabsorbing it as white, radiating yellow and gathering it as blue, emanating many light rays and reabsorbing them as few. They are able to simultaneously reveal a hundred Dharma gates to a hundred different disciples according to their individual faculties and constitutions. They can simultaneously enter the one hundred different samadhis taught in the cycle of the *Mother of Buddhas* (*Prajñaparamita*), such as the samadhis of bravery, the army gathering, and the lion's posture. They are able to simultaneously perform 108 miracles such as flying in the sky, entering the earth, being unobstructed by mountains and rocks, not sinking in water, water gushing from their lower body while their upper body is burning (or alternating between them), or springing forth many emanations from a single one and condensing many into one. Thus, seven hundred qualities are mastered.

In the same manner, the second bhumi masters seven thousand, the third seventy thousand, the fourth seven hundred thousand, the fifth seven million, the sixth seventy million, the seventh seven hundred million, the eighth seven billion, the ninth seventy billion, the tenth seven hundred billion, and the twelfth seven hundred trillion. The thirteenth is the bhumi of the Vajra Holder, when the essence of the three kayas is actualized. Since the enumeration of the immense qualities therein is infinite, anyone trying to measure it will find that it defies the domain of conceptual mind.

In this way, here within the path of mahamudra, the pinnacle of all vehicles, all the bhumis and paths of the common vehicles have been discerned and completely included. Therefore, upon the correct actualization of the four yogas, the various qualities of the paths and bhumis, whether attained gradually or instantaneously, are by their nature completely included in them. However, at a superficial level, to some people these qualities are not evidently revealed, which is also a special feature of the vajrayana secret shortcut. Yet according to this system, Lord Gyare said:

> Shravakas with or without ornament,
> Bodhisattvas with or without fame,
> Vajrayana's secret or public conduct,
> Whether their qualities are stable or talked about,
> The qualities of the paths and bhumis are implied.
> These measure the strength of the meditator's training,
> Which results in whether they have or haven't miracles
> And accomplishes the benefit of beings or not.

In a nutshell, the meaning of his many words is that all the qualities of paths and bhumis that have been taught in the path of characteristics are intentionally figurative. In addition, there are many different paths, as well as a variety regarding the signs of paths and bhumis. There can be adorned or unadorned shravakas,[66] as well as renowned or unknown bodhisattvas. Similarly, miracles may or may not arise in this life to meditators on account of their previous level of power of training, and for qualities such as miracles to be accomplished, effort must be made in the worldly and the vajrayana paths.

# 13. How the Fruition Is Finally Completed

H. How the Fruition Is Finally Completed

## How the Fruition Is Finally Completed

Having explained the fruition mahamudra as being the inseparability of the three kayas—the indivisible two kayas—we arrive at the conclusion. The fortunate yogin who sees the original face of ground mahamudra, the natural state of reality, focuses on the practice of the view and meditation of path mahamudra, by which he reaches full familiarity. By having thus perfected the qualities of the paths and bhumis, through the strength of actualizing absolute dharmakaya, the fruition mahamudra, the two kayas arise, and the yogin is truly and completely enlightened within the continuity of the three kayas. Thus, in the *Torch of the Path to Enlightenment*, it is said:

> It won't be long to buddhahood enlightenment.

Regarding buddhahood there is this index:

> Seven points pertain to the kayas of perfect buddhas:
> Nature, name, classification,
> Description, exact number, defining characteristics, and particularity.

First, the nature of a perfect buddha is perfect elimination and perfect wisdom. Perfect elimination means that once the afflictive and cognitive obscurations, and the paths and bhumis, have been dealt with, they are all eliminated without exception at the end of the vajra-like samadhi. Furthermore, the obscurations of absorption and so forth are completely included in these two obscurations, so by eliminating these two all other obscurations are also eliminated. Perfect wisdom is as said in the *Perfection of Wisdom in One Hundred Thousand Verses*:

> The perfect buddha has reached the wisdom of all phenomena free from obscurations.

Also in the twenty-first chapter of this text it is said:

> He possesses the unsurpassable buddha wisdom, turns the wheel of Dharma, and brings beings to full maturity.

In other sutras there are also many explanations about primordial wisdom. In terms of the shastras, in the *Ornament of Sutras* it is said:

> Just as when a single solar ray appears
> All the qualities of light arise,
> Know that the wisdom of the Buddha
> Includes the wisdom of all buddhas.

And:

> Unwavering mirrorlike wisdom,
> Depending on it are the three wisdoms:
> Equanimity, discerning,
> And all accomplishing.

Other shastras also explain the buddhas' wisdom. Based on these texts it is accepted that buddhas have wisdom. In which way do they possess it? In brief, they possess it as the wisdom that knows things as they are and the wisdom that knows everything in existence. The wisdom that knows things as they are is the knowledge of the absolute level. As mentioned earlier, the fulfillment of the vajra-like samadhi is that there is complete familiarity with suchness, from which objectification is transcended. The various forms of conceptualization subside, so the dharmadhatu free of constructs and wisdom free of constructs have the same taste. Therefore, they are inseparable like water poured into water or butter into butter. The great prajña free from [dualistic] perception or not seeing any form whatsoever—said to be like seeing space—is the support of all precious qualities. As said:

> Like water poured into water
> Or butter introduced into butter,
> What is known, the absence of constructs,
> Inseparably merges with the wisdom
> That is said to be the dharmakaya,
> The nature of all the buddhas.

And:

> "See the sky" is an expression used by beings.
> "How to see the sky": find out what it means.
> The Tathagata taught that all phenomena should be seen in that way.
> He cannot find another simile for the "seeing."

The wisdom that knows everything in existence is that which entirely knows the conventional meaning of the relative level. Based on the vajra-like samadhi, all seeds of obscurations are vanquished and this becomes the great transcending wisdom which, through its power, knows and sees the multitude of objects of knowledge included in the three times, like placing a fresh olive on the palm of one's hand. The sutras also accept that buddhas know the relative level. As said:

The different aspects of the cause
For the single eye in a peacock's feather
Are known only to the Omniscient One.
It is the power of omniscience that knows that.

In the *Sublime Continuum* it is said:

With great compassion he knows the universe.
He sees all the worlds . . .

The way the universe is known and seen is not as something concrete but as illusory. Thus, in the *Perfectly Abridged Dharma Sutra* it is said:

For instance, some magicians
Endeavor not to be tricked by their illusion.
So through their higher knowledge
They do not become attached to their magical creation.
Likewise, the enlightened beings
Know the three worlds of existence to be a magical display.

In the *Meeting of Father and Son Sutra* it is said:

One will not be tricked
By the magical apparition created by a magician
When it is seen properly as an illusion.
Look at all beings in that way.
Praise he who sees all and prostrate to him.

In this way, perfect elimination and perfect wisdom are the essential nature of buddhas. In the *Sublime Continuum* it is said:

Buddhahood is indivisible,
But it can be classified according to its aspects of purity:
The attributes of elimination and wisdom,
Like the sun and the sky.

And in the *Ornament of Sutras* it is said:

> The seeds of afflictive and cognitive obscurations in beings remain as such for a long time. The immense elimination completely vanquishes them forever. Once transformed, those who possess the supreme qualities are buddhas.

Regarding the name, why is it called buddha (*sang gye*)? Having awakened (*sang*) from the sleep of ignorance and its network, the mind blooms (*gye*) as the two types of omniscience, therefore it is called *sangye*. As said:

> Because he awakened from the sleep of ignorance
> And expands the mind twofold, he is called *sangye* (buddha).

As explained before, to have awakened from the sleep of ignorance means having perfected the elimination and expanding the mind to the objects of knowledge means having perfected wisdom.

In terms of the classification, buddhahood is classified as dharmakaya, sambhogakaya, and nirmanakaya. In the *Sublime Golden Light Sutra* it is said:

> All tathagatas possess the three kayas: dharmakaya, sambhogakaya, and nirmanakaya.

Well then, you may wonder, "How is it that two, four, and five kayas are mentioned in some scriptural references?" Despite these varied references, all are subsumed in the three kayas. In the *Ornament of Sutras* it is said:

> Know that the three kayas subsume
> The kayas of buddhas.

The description of the three kayas is as follows. The dharmakaya is actual buddhahood. As said in the *Prajñaparamita in Eight Thousand Verses*:

> The Tathagata is not to be regarded as the rupakaya. The Tathagata is the dharmakaya.

In the *King of Samadhi Sutra* it is said:

> The king of the conquerors is not to be regarded as the rupakaya.

The two rupakayas are forms that exist from the blessing of the dharmakaya, the perception of those to be trained, and previous aspirations; know that they appear from the conjunction of these three.

The reason why the number of kayas is exactly three lies in the purpose: one's benefit is the dharmakaya, and the benefit of others is the two aspects of the rupakaya. The dharmakaya is considered to be for one's own benefit because, once it is attained, it is the foundation of all sublime qualities, so the strengths, types of fearlessness, and so forth, are all gathered in it as if they had been summoned. Since the dharmakaya has the two aspects of the rupakaya for the benefit of others, these appear as the sambhogakaya before pure disciples and as the nirmanakaya before impure disciples. Therefore, buddhas definitely have three kayas.

The characteristics of each kaya are as follows. Dharmakaya is a mere designation for the exhaustion of all errors by having realized the dharmadhatu—the truth of emptiness—or for the reversion from the nature of deluded perception. In actual fact, dharmakaya, its defining characteristics, and any attribute that may constitute its ground have no existence whatsoever. Uncontrived self-knowing awareness, the primordial wisdom free from transition or change, increase or decrease, is timelessly pervading the mind streams of all beings in the three worlds. This is precisely what is actualized through the profound crucial method of practice. Apart from this, there is no "buddha dharmakaya" that was not there before and arose as something new.

In terms of its distinguishing attributes, the dharmakaya has eight defining features: equal, profound, eternal, singular, perfect, pure, luminous, and connected with perfect enjoyment. It is equal because the dharmakaya of all buddhas is not different. Profound because, being free from all conceptual constructs, it is hard to realize. Eternal because, being unconditioned, it neither is born nor ceases in the beginning, middle, or end. Singular because, since absolute space and wisdom are not different, they are inseparable. Perfect because, since it is beyond exaggeration and deprecation, it is unmistaken. Pure because it is free from the stains of the three obscurations: afflictive, cognitive, and absorptive. Luminous for it is free from conceptual thought; due to that it is nonconceptual, and in that state it is inconceivable. The radiance of dharmakaya is empty lucidity, the display of wisdom. This and ground dharmakaya are nondual, but abide indivisibly, so it becomes the support of the enjoyment embodying vast sublime qualities. In the *Sublime Continuum* it is said:

> By realizing the dharmadhatu as it is,
> Not having beginning, middle, or end,
> Inseparable, nondual, timeless, immaculate, and concept-free,
> The yogin who rests in composure sees it.

In the *Ornament of Sutras* it is said:

> The svabhavikakaya is sameness,
> Subtle and connected to perfect enjoyment.

The sambhogakaya—the dimension of enjoyment—also has eight defining characteristics: disciples, place, kaya, marks, teaching, deeds, natural presence, and lack of true nature. Who are the disciples participating together? Only the bodhisattvas on the tenth bhumi. Where is the enjoyment taking place? In a pure buddha field. Which is the body through which there is enjoyment? Glorious Vairochana, and the rest. Which are the marks possessed? The thirty-two major and the eighty minor marks of excellence. Which is the teaching for realizing perfect enjoyment? Only the mahayana. What is the activity? It is performing such deeds as predicting bodhisattvas. Spontaneous presence is that all enlightened activity is carried out effortlessly; it happens spontaneously like that of the king of jewels. Lack of true nature is that it manifests in myriad ways, such as forms, but like the colors of a crystal, these emanations lack true nature. In the *Ornament of Sutras* it is said:

> In all sambhogakaya realms,
> Disciples, gatherings, fields, marks,
> Body, teaching, perfect enjoyment,
> And deeds, these are the distinctions.

In the *Ornament of Clear Realization* it is said:

> The major marks being thirty-two,
> The minor marks being eighty,
> So that there is precise mahayana enjoyment,
> The Muni arises in the form of sambhogakaya.

The nirmanakaya also has eight distinguishing characteristics: support, cause, field, time, nature, inducement, ripening, and liberation. Support is the dharmakaya, which is analogous to Unshakable. The cause from which the nirmanakaya arises is great compassion that wishes to benefit the diversity of beings. Field is pure and impure realms. Time is the continuity of the nirmanakaya for as long as the world exists. Nature is the threefold type of emanation: creative emanation (engaging with incomparable skill in various arts, such as playing the lute); incarnate emanation (taking various lower forms such as a rabbit); and supreme emanation (descending from Tushita heaven and entering the womb up to passing into the great peace of nirvana). In the *Ornament of Sutras* it is said:

> By always manifesting as a created, an incarnate, a bodhisattva,
> Or demonstrating *parinirvana*,

This nirmanakaya of the buddha
Is the great means for complete liberation.

Also in the *Sublime Continuum* it is said:

Through the variety of magical manifestations,
The nirmanakaya incarnates taking an evident birth,
Moving from Tushita,
Entering the womb and being born.
It is skilled in the arts,
Takes pleasure in the court of ladies,
Renounces all and endures hardships,
Proceeds to the bodhi tree,
Vanquishes the host of maras, reaches perfection,
Turns the Dharma wheel of enlightenment,
Passes into parinirvana,
And in the impure buddha fields,
Remains for as long as they exist.

The Buddha said that he intentionally entered three types of nirvana to lead ordinary beings to enter any of them in accordance with their kind. The nirmanakaya ripens all the accumulations in those who have entered the path.[67] These are the eight defining characteristics of the nirmanakaya. In the *Ornament of Clear Realization* it is said:

The unceasing nirmanakaya of the Muni
Brings manifold benefits to beings,
Performing deeds impartially,
For as long as samsara exists.

The three particularities are sameness, everlastingness, and manifestation.

Sameness means that the dharmakaya of all buddhas is the same because it is inseparable from the basis, the dharmadhatu.[68] The nirmanakayas of all the buddhas are the same because they have common enlightened activities. In the *Ornament of Sutras* it is said:

> These are the same on account of basis, realization, and activity.

Everlastingness in the case of the dharmakaya means that it is eternal by nature because its essence is ultimately unoriginated and unceasing. The sambhogakaya has the everlasting continuity of the uninterrupted enjoyment of the Dharma. The nirmanakaya is everlasting in its activity because even if it disappeared, it would reveal itself again and again, and even if the suitable conditions ceased, it would not recede but reappear when the time is right. In the *Ornament of the Sutras* it is said:

> By nature and continuity
> Their flow is eternal.

Manifestation means that, since in the dharmadhatu the cognitive obscuration is purified, the dharmakaya arises; since the afflictive obscuration is purified, the sambhogakaya arises; and since the karmic obscuration is purified, the nirmanakaya arises.

The three kayas have seven ancillary qualities of indivisibility. The first quality is that the great bodhisattvas abiding in Akanishta are constantly enjoying the vast and profound Dharma of the vajrayana. The second quality is the union of the wisdom body, endowed with perfect major and minor marks of excellence, with the consort who is its natural radiance. The third ancillary quality is great bliss, because the unstained great bliss is uninterrupted. These three are the particularities of the sambhogakaya. Nonreferential compassion pervades like space, so the fourth quality is a compassion that imbues everything. The fifth quality is unceasing, nonconceptual vast activity that arises spontaneously extending to the limits of samsara. The sixth quality is that of noncessation in that the nirmanakaya does not dwell in the peaceful extreme of nirvana. These are the particularities of the nirmanakaya.

The seventh quality, leading to the particularity of the dharmakaya, is the indivisibility of emptiness and compassion lacking true nature and free from all elaborations. These are the ancillary qualities possessed by the three kayas.

Furthermore, the three kayas also possess the eight qualities of mastery. The first is the mastery of body, as the many aspects of the body tame beings according to their faculties. The second is mastery of speech in that speech ceaselessly turns the wheel of dharma in accordance with beings. The third is the mastery of mind in that mind possesses a nonconceptual compassion. The fourth is the mastery of miracles in that miracles are unimpeded. The fifth is the omnipresent mastery in that samsara and nirvana are equal throughout the three divisions of time, and in perfect enlightenment, they are experienced as having one taste. Even though goddesses in number equal to the atoms in thirty-two Mount Meru make offerings of sensual objects, the kayas are unsullied by desire. This is the mastery of desire, the sixth. The seventh is the mastery of giving rise to whatever is wished for in that, like the wish-fulfilling jewel, the kayas fulfill the hopes and wishes of beings. The eighth is the mastery of abode in that the kayas remain in Akanishta dharmadhatu as the Dharma king of the three spheres of existence. These eight masteries correspond to the enumeration of qualities of the sambhogakaya.

As to nirmanakaya, the inconceivable dharmakaya and sambhogakaya emanations arise in accordance with the beings to be trained, who are like reflections in water bowls. For that, they manifest an infinite pervading array of such emanations as birth, art, and great enlightenment, in accordance with their characteristics. This is what is known as the inexhaustible wheels ornamented by the secrecy of the body, speech, and mind of all the buddhas. So there are never-ending ornamented wheels of body, of speech, and of mind.

The inexhaustible ornamented wheel of body has two aspects: inconceivable secrecy of body, and all kinds of bodies. As to the inconceivable secrecy of body, nobody can grasp the size of a buddha's body. As said in the *Jewel Mound Sutra*:

> Desiring to see the Tathagata's crown protuberance, the bodhisattva Holder of Strength rose to the top of Mount Meru, the thirty-three heavens, the Brahma worlds, and also further up to one billion worlds. In the world called Lotus Endowed, where the king Tathagata Essence of the Lotus Glory ruled, he went up one level after the other and looked, but he could not see the crown protuberance.

Regarding all kinds of bodies, starting from the supreme nirmanakaya, an array of possible forms, extending to the phenomenal worlds that can be known, are revealed in accordance with the characteristics of those to be trained and bring benefit to them.

Regarding speech there are two aspects: inconceivable secrecy of speech, and all kinds of speech. The inconceivable secrecy of speech is such that whether one is right in front of the Buddha or several miles away, his speech is neither too loud nor too soft. Maudgalyayana went to Sukhavati in the west and then also as far as the world called Luminous, a billion worlds away, where the tathagata All-Arising Light Rays resides surrounded by his retinue. When he listened to Buddha's speech, it had not reduced its volume at all. As to all kinds of speech, from the pure language of the gods to that of nagas, yakshas, rakshas, and so forth, he is able to teach the Dharma in the language of each type of being.

In terms of mind also there are two aspects: inconceivable secrecy of mind, and all kinds of mind. The inconceivable secrecy of mind is such that Buddha's mind knows things others cannot know at all. Maudgalyayana, who possessed miraculous powers, was unable to know where his mother was reborn, while the Tathagata could. Also, other arhats could not know whether the householder Glorious Birth had the seed of liberation, so they could not ordain him as a monk. The Tathagata knew that seven lives before, he was born as a dog that, while being driven by a pig, went around a stupa, and thus had the virtuous seed that enabled him to be ordained. All kinds of mind means that he possesses the wisdom that knows things as they are and all things in existence. He knows things as they are, because he knows and actualizes the unfabricated natural state of things. He knows all things in existence because he is free from the stain that prevents knowing or seeing all things that can be known. And since he comprehends each and every interdependent relationship between cause and effect; he knows everything distinctly.

The cause for these accomplishments is that now, at the stage of the path, since one practices focusing on the ultimate level of truth—emptiness and mahamudra—one accomplishes the dharmakaya. In its subsidiary aspect—method—by cultivating bodhichitta, making aspirations, and practicing other pure factors, one accomplishes the nirmanakaya. And from the cause and effect of meditation of the profound generation stage, one accomplishes the sambhogakaya. These practices are not performed separately or alternately, but rather uniting knowledge and method indivisibly within the total purity of the three spheres. By exerting in this way, the result is the accomplishment of the permanent goal of the three kayas having inseparable essence.

Therefore, the many classifications as three, four, or five kayas mentioned earlier have only one essence from which the different names derive in terms of their qualities or functions. In brief, at the time of the present ground, radiance, and expression of mind essence, there is no other description than the three kayas. In this context, in the causal vehicle and the lower tantric systems, there are considerations on other points, biased treatises with hidden intentions, and a variety of other philosophical positions. There are bases of contention regarding such points as whether or not in the dharmakaya there are heads and hands, its buddha field is visible, there is condensed wisdom in Buddha's being, and whether the two rupakayas have feelings in their self-projection. Indeed these are the bases of debate, with many arguments that support or reject these points, including discerning analyses. All these are surely true when applied to each of those instances, yet when considering these heart essences of the vehicles, we don't seek to be dependent on the lower philosophical views. The criterion is to say that while these are all in agreement, they still differ from each other. Why is this criterion applied? It is because in relation to all phenomena included in samsara and nirvana and the phenomenal world, we don't cling or fixate on negation or affirmation, true or false, existent or nonexistent, being or nonbeing, birth or cessation, comings or goings, permanence or annihilation, and so forth. If anything is said to be nonexistent, we fall into the extreme of nihilism; if we fixate on existence, that is the extreme of permanence; and if we think they are neither existent nor nonexistent, we don't transcend the conceptual nature.

In the perception of others, if anything exists let it be so, because the unceasing perceptions never end and the interdependence of cause and effect is unfailing. In those who take things as nonexistent, let it be so because things never waver from the nature of emptiness since nothing has existence in the basic nature. Similarly, it is allowed that things are neither existent nor nonexistent because nothing ever falls into any extreme and they are free from partiality. Therefore, in regard to all things that appear as the world and its inhabitants: To the deluded perception of beings due to impure habitual patterns, there are five solid and concrete elements; to yogins on the path, they appear as their unobstructed mind; to buddhas and bodhisattvas, they appear as the field of self-luminous wisdom. At the ultimate level, everything is nothing other than the spontaneous mind essence. Likewise, internally, all thoughts of cognitive acts and mental states appear to impure deluded beings as having the nature of habitual patterns of karma and afflictions; to yogins on the path, as specific experiences and realizations of view and meditation; to tathagatas, the trikaya buddhas, as the display of wisdom and compassion.

Hence, although in the natural state of the cause or of the ground there is not even an atom of difference, due to the temporary conceptual obscuration, it can be densely veiled, lightly veiled, or free from veils, and that is where differences reside. Therefore, the essence of view, meditation, and conduct is never beyond the indivisible two kayas or the inseparable three kayas. The core reason why it does not and will not go beyond is the great key point of simply relaxing into the continuity of one's uncontrived mind, the mahamudra. By denying and superimposing through a conditioned conceptual mind that which is unconditioned, by being attached to the limitation of words, and by being sectarian through a biased philosophical school, those who debate are similar to children who argue about the height of the sky.

Therefore, rest in the carefree, unfabricated, great equality of the all-pervading expanse. There is no doubt that, transcending the notion of walker and walked-upon, by treading the space of the four yogas, the ten bhumis, the five paths, and the fruition—the spontaneously present three kayas—you will find liberation in that state.

Having listened to the stages of introduction, main part, and conclusion, based on every text, strongly exert yourself in putting them into practice without hesitating even for a moment. In this way, you will become the lord of the whole of samsara and nirvana, and thus realize your own purpose. By purifying obscurations and with the sublime qualities increasing more and more, you will completely attain great perfect enlightenment. Then, working for the benefit of others, you should place all the spheres of sentient beings as limitless as the sky on the precious, free level of enlightenment.

In this way, this guidebook about the true meaning, mahamudra—the supreme or innermost heart essence of Dharma teachings—reaches completion. There have been a lot of explanations, and so as not to elaborate further, now follows the meaning in a nutshell.

We have, only this time, barely obtained this human existence endowed with the freedoms and opportunities. Yet this will not remain for long and the time of death is uncertain, and during death what will benefit us is the sacred Dharma. Apart from the guru and the precious sacred Dharma, nobody else is able to protect us from the fear and suffering at that time. If, in the next life and all future lives, we are caught up in the nature of samsaric sufferings such as those of the lower realms, that would be an extreme form of misery and grief. We have been unable even for a moment to get rid of the suffering of samsara that affects us now during this fleeting human lifetime. So today, let us not be foolish and mistaken, for in the future we will completely lack the means to be free from it. The perpetually valuable sacred Dharma, which brings everlasting benefit to our lives to come, is exactly what we need to accomplish now, no matter what.

If we don't have the Dharma while in this body, we have nothing; whereas if we do have it, we have it all. Today, while you have the choice between having the Dharma or not, or of being happy or miserable, you must make the right choice and, at all times and in all your lives, turn toward the pure and invaluable Dharma. When doing so, in general, abandon negative actions and accomplish good ones, being careful about adoption and avoidance related to cause and effect. In particular, through renunciation and weariness toward this dreamlike meaningless life, observe your vows and samaya purely, not just by spouting the words or superficially. More specifically, if the root of mind is not severed, nothing else will be of benefit. Since precisely your own mind is the root or foundation of all of samsara and nirvana, by taming it through the path of undistracted mindfulness, you will actualize the essence of your awareness, primordially pure dharmakaya. Once you do that, through training in developing devotion, pure perception, compassion, altruistic aspirations, and so forth, set in pervasive and impartial interdependence, you will perfect the fruition of the two or three kayas. Displaying this inconceivable secret, you will benefit beings as limitless as the sky.

To completely attain all the purposes of self and others, some things need to be accomplished. Leaving the definitive oral instructions simply at the level of theory will not enable you to traverse the paths and bhumis. You need to be resolved to practice completely and conclusively on the basis of mind. In this way, for the mental stains to be purified, you need to constantly practice the profound Dharma instructions. Don't be attached to the words of the instructions; what you need is to arouse the actual experience in your being. When you are concerned with what is external, all distractions are the workings of Mara. So you should not allow your mind to go there, but rest composed in the basic nature.

Whether the delusion of the path is eliminated or not depends on the blessings of the guru, so you should exert yourself in making genuine devotional supplications to them. Since the root or foundation of the whole of samsara and nirvana is precisely your own mind, if it is not severed, no matter what else you do, samsara will not be decisively abandoned, so you must cut the root of mind. Unless your mind is never separated from mindful knowing, the path will not be traversed; when residual toxic habits arise, you need to be firmly rooted in undistracted mindfulness. If you don't know the vital point of the practice, you will not move forward on the path, so understand the key point and apply yourself to it!

The heart of all sutras and tantras being the true meaning, you need to plant the pointed-out, true meaning in your mind. Since mahamudra, the genuine primordial wisdom, is your very own mind, by clearing all doubts and misconceptions from within, you should actualize dharmakaya, the primordial purity. The antidotes to whatever arises are mindfulness and other similar qualities, and these need to merge within the nonduality of the undesirable and antidote. Since meditation on the flow of the natural state is not something deliberate, you need to sustain a nonconceptual realization. Whatever appears is the display of dharmakaya, so you must not evaluate anything that arises. Once you know that the natural brilliance of mind essence, the basic nature, is unceasing, you need to rest open and carefree. Don't evaluate appearances as high or low; instead anything that appears needs to arise as meditation. The expression of absolute reality is neither good nor bad, so you should take all that you perceive as the path. The radiance of the unborn arises as myriad things, so you must don whatever appears as ornaments. For innate wisdom to arise uninterruptedly, mindfulness must be present and undivided. All phenomena of sights and sounds are natural forms of the mind, and how you develop the strength of the practice should be in accordance with this. Ultimately, samsara and nirvana are not two, so the knot of dualistic fixation must be untied.

The root of attachment and aggression rests on the mind, so you need to bring the stain of subject and object to an end. In the fruition, there is nothing to eliminate or acquire; this is how it is to be known. Since whatever you need is completely within yourself, confidence must arise in your mind. By having developed all the way to the fruition the potential of compassion, bodhichitta, aspirations, and so forth, you will impartially make the right auspicious connections of the rupakaya, resulting in the two or three kayas being swiftly completed. Through the display of this inconceivable secret, you should fully work for the benefit of beings as limitless as the sky, and totally accomplish all the purposes of yourself and others. Convinced that all these are what needs to be achieved, it is important that you put them into practice.

This is all I will say about the core meaning.

# Appendix: Outline of the Text

# Notes

1. Explanation for "precise significance" is missing.
2. Tib. *rang rig ye shes.*
3. Tib. *gzung 'dzin* (lit. apprehender and apprehended). Throughout the text these will be rendered as subject and object, respectively.
4. The lack of identity of the person and of phenomena.
5. *Shri* means "glorious" in Sanskrit.
6. Tib. *tha mal gyi shes pa.*
7. More clearly, "suchness" is not the "object" of knowledge of self-knowing awareness. For instance, when looking at the sky, we may say "I see the sky," but the empty sky is not an object of the eyes; there is nothing there to see.
8. *Dharmata* (Tib. *chos nyid*) has been left as is or translated as "absolute reality."
9. Implying that when there are two things the rope can connect them, which is not the case here.
10. For the sake of simplicity, meditative composure sometimes will be referred to here as "meditation."
11. The hay looks dry, but inside it is still moist. This means that someone seems to be an advanced practitioner outwardly, but inwardly is not.
12. After leaving human footprints these turn into dog footprints because of any number of conditions, such as wind, rain and so forth. This means that the fruition of good practice is spoiled by ensuing cognizance entailing grasping.
13. In the analogy, we would be considering it to be only snow, not noticing that there is slush beneath it.
14. *Togden* (Tib. *rtogs ldan*) literally means "possessing realization." It applies to advanced yogins who spend most of their lives in retreat.
15. "Meeting and destroying" means that the moment a thought is detected it disappears. "Chasing after" is when one starts to look around where the thought is. "Insubstantial illusion" is when the thought is fuzzy.
16. The text, perhaps mistakenly, mentions four experiences, but the whole passage refers to only the usual three experiences of bliss, clarity, and nonthought.
17. Threefold focus: actor, object of the action, and action, all three conceptualized as concrete entities.

18. Primordial purity and purity of temporary stains.
19. According to 84000 and Lhasey Lotsawa, it seems the correct wording of this citation is: "When one realizes mind, this is wisdom. So one should cultivate the clear understanding of not seeking the Buddha elsewhere."
20. Drukchen, head of the Drukpa Kagyu lineage.
21. "Misconceptions resolved from within" (*sgro 'dogs nang nas chod pa*), "dualistic mind" (*gnyis 'dzin gyi blo*), "stripping the deceiving dualistic fixation" (*gnyis 'dzin gyi skor mgo bud pa*); "self-knowing awareness wisdom" (*so so rang rig pa'i ye shes*), "nonmeditation" (*bsgom med*), "effortless" (*rtsol med*), "fresh" (*so ma*), "unfabricated" (*ma bcos pa*), "self-occurring" (*rang byung*), "awareness" (*rig pa*), "primordial purity" (*ka dag*), "natural purity"(*gnas dag*), "transmuted" (*gnas gyur*), "natural" (*rang bzhin*), "manifestation" (*rnam 'gyur*), "the inseparable two truths" (*bden gnyis dbyer med*), "inseparable samsara and nirvana" (*'khor 'das dbyer med*).
22. The meaning of these correlations between the eight consciousnesses with the five wisdoms should be understood as the latter being the former in their original state, like in the simile of ice being water in its original state.
23. This is in line with the instruction pointing out that, instead of viewing it as that the essence of a thought is dharmakaya, it should be viewed as that the thought itself is dharmakaya.
24. Tib. *nag po kha 'byams* is a figure of speech meaning that everything is hopeless and only bad things happen.
25. The text seems to misquote this as belonging to Gampopa's *Jewel Garland of the Supreme Path*, but it is found in the *Extraordinary Ambrosia of Lord Gampopa's Speech*.
26. Moonlight also illuminating the interior of a house, for instance.
27. Literally it means likes and dislikes: *dga' dang mi dga'*. In this case, it means the hope to perpetuate the experience and the fear of losing it.
28. Udraka (also Udraka Ramaputra; Tib. Lhag spyod) was a teacher of Gautama during his period of asceticism.
29. Tsoknyi Rinpoche explains that Gampopa seems to emphasize the sutra view that stresses emptiness, whereas Milarepa points out the vajrayana aspect of the luminous quality of the essence, as in his well-known instruction: "Bliss, clarity, and nonthought are the yogin's deviation. Bliss, clarity, and nonthought are the pinnacle of the yogin's meditation." This depends on whether there is grasping to the experiences (in the first case), or they are the self-experiences of the realized essence (in the second case).
30. In other words, the yogin who, attached to bliss, clarity, or nonthought, is not habituated to renouncing rebirth in the deva realms of desire, form, or formlessness is like sucking the nectar from a sky-flower.
31. The pure three spheres of non-reified actor, action, or object being acted upon.
32. Tib. *shes bzhin*. Usually translated as "vigilance," "alertness," or "introspection." It is the quality of mind that accompanies mindfulness (*dran

*pa*), overseeing the whole picture and detecting obstacles of drowsiness and agitation, and so forth. "Knowing" is a more literal translation that has mostly been used in the text when connected closely to *dran pa*, as in *dran shes*, "mindful knowing."

33. There is no explanation provided in the text for the second section listed, "Specific Enhancement."
34. Tib. *rbad*, meaning to ward off the attacks of harmful beings.
35. One is like a dummy, has nothing oneself, and cannot harm others.
36. If one hits a swine's nose, it would impair its capacity of discerning food. Blocking fervent, emotionally loaded devotion, would also impair its capacity to refine itself.
37. Tib. *la zla*. Literally "to overcome a mountain pass," meaning one has reached a final conclusion beyond any doubt whatsoever.
38. As it happens through blessings, it cannot be described accurately.
39. Tib. *tha mal*. Literally means "ordinary"; however, in the context of mahamudra it points out the natural, raw, naked mind of our being.
40. The sense of "I now realized the essence" compared to while being distracted is dualistic.
41. To say that it is attained through mindfulness and to be rid of delusion is being fooled by conceptual mind. These two citations by Gampopa refer to a very high level of realization.
42. The top and base of a sand mountain go together: if there is up, there has to be down.
43. The ten Dharma activities are: write the sacred scriptures, make offerings, give generously, hear the Dharma, retain it, read it, explain it, recite it, reflect on its meaning, and meditate on its meaning.
44. A common object can become precious when gilded.
45. The text literally has *zhing*, which means fields, but it does not make much sense. The translator has taken the liberty of replacing it with "hills."
46. The text literally states, "like a Khampa," a person from Eastern Tibet.
47. There seems to be no reference to Bharampa in Milarepa's biography.
48. Quoting Gampopa: "In the case of the sudden type, through the force of great previous training, just by the application of an instruction, one attains realization of stability at that very moment. The essence remains present uninterruptedly, devotion to the lama is great, compassion toward beings is intense, and ego-clinging is gone. No enhancement is required. What is born in that mind stream is sustained by itself; nothing else is needed." The leap type individual progresses gradually up to a point and thereafter takes a sudden leap to the attainment of stability.
49. A red-hot iron reverts to its original state when cold.
50. Tib. *ma bcos pa*. Generally this means that during experiences one should let them be without clinging. Here "uncorrected" means one does grasp at them.
51. It is believed that a negative immaterial influence (Tib. *grib pa*) can

be transmitted through objects or food. This has been translated as contamination.

52. Tib. *rang shar rang grol* literally means "self-occurring," "self-liberated." By "spontaneous arising" what is meant is that the thought is not deliberately produced by the meditator but just arises abruptly. It does not mean self-produced because it does so due to causes and conditions in the alaya.
53. No karma, no good, no bad, and so forth.
54. See note 11.
55. See note 12.
56. Tib. *nges med rten 'brel.* Everything is seen as interdependent without focusing on or specifying any one thing. Arising from within means omniscience starts to emerge.
57. Interdependence is so powerful that it is beyond control. For example, Milarepa did not want respect, yet the interdependence was so strong that people respected him beyond his control.
58. Excellent: teacher, teaching, disciples, place, and time.
59. Three chains: body, speech, and mind.
60. Dharmakaya is beyond time, so if one has a notion of time in that context, it means it was not actually realized.
61. Free from the heavy burden of the three types of suffering.
62. Tib. *thugs dam.* This refers to the state when consciousness remains in the body in meditation after clinical death has occurred.
63. Tib. *pho ba* (pronounced *powa*). A practice to deliberately eject consciousness at death to transfer it to freedom or a buddha field.
64. This paragraph is missing in the text and has been quoted here from Gampopa's *Jewel Ornament of Liberation.*
65. Discernment of the presence of characteristics is, for example, whether there is clarity, bliss, nonthought, and so forth, while the absence of characteristics would be, for instance, "this is dharmakaya, emptiness, awareness, and so forth."
66. Some arhats can perform miracles (adorned) while others cannot (unadorned).
67. The "characteristic of liberation" is missing in the text. From the *Jewel Ornament of Liberation*: "It liberates from the fetters of existence those who have been ripened through their virtuous deeds."
68. The "particularity of the sambhogakaya" is missing in the text. From the *Jewel Ornament of Liberation*: "The sambhogakayas of all buddhas are the same because they are inseparable in their realization."

# Works Cited by the Author

Abhidharma: *Chos mngon pa*
Abhidharmakosha: *Abhidharmakośa*, *Mngon pa mdzod*
Abridgement of Naropa's View: *Na ro pa'i lta ba mdor bsdus*
Abridgement of Words: *Tshig bsdus*
Assemblage of Secrets: *Guhyasamaja*, *Gsang ba 'dus pa*
Avatamsaka Sutra: *Avataṃsaka-sūtra*, *Phal po che'i mdo*
Brilliant Expanse: *Klong gsal*
Buddha Skull Tantra: *Rgyud sangs rgyas thod pa*
Clear Meaning Commentary: *'Grel pa don gsal*
Cloud of Precious Jewels Sutra: *Ratnamegha-sūtra*, *Dkon mchog sprin gyi mdo*
Commentary on Bodhichitta: *Bodhicittavivaraṇa*, *Byang chub sems 'grel*
Commentary on Entering the Middle Way: *Madhyamakāvatāravibhaṅga*, *Dbu ma la 'jug pa'i 'grel pa*
Condensed Tantra, *Saṃcaya-tantra*, *Bsdud rgyud*
Descent into Langka Sutra: *Laṅkāvatāra-sūtra*, *Lang kar gshegs pa'i mdo*
Discernment of the Middle Way and the Extremes: *Madhyāntavibhāga*, *Dbus mtha'*
Discourse Requested by Arya Akashkosha: *Aryagaganagañjaparipṛcchā-sūtra*, *'Phags pa nam mkha' mdzod kyis zhus pa'i mdo*
Discourse Requested by the Close Circle: *Upālipariprccha*, *Nye bar 'khor gyis zhus pa*
Enlightenment of Vairochana Tantra: *Vairocanābhisambodhi*, *Rnam snang mngon byang*
Entering the Middle Way: *Madhyamakāvatāra*, *Dbu ma la 'jug pa*
Five Stages: *Rim lnga*
Four Hundred Verses: Ċatuḥśataka, *Bzhi brgya pa*
Fundamental Wisdom of the Middle Way: *Mūlamadhyamakakārikā*, *Dbu ma rtsa ba shes rab*
Jewel Garland of the Supreme Path: *Lam mchog rin po che'i phreng ba*
Great Ali Kali River Tantra: *Ali kali chu lung chen po'i rgyud*
Great Commentary on Kalachakra: *Dus 'khor 'grel chen*
Heart Sutra, *Prajñāpāramitā hṛdaya-sūtra*, *Shes rab snying po*
Higher Abhidharma: *Mngon pa gong ma*
Illuminating Lamp Tantra: *Sgron ma'i rgyud*
Immortal Vajra Song: *'Chi med rdo rje'i glu*

Inconceivable Secret Sutra: *Gsang ba bsam gyis mi khyab pa'i mdo*
Inconceivable Secret Tantra: *Gsang ba bsam gyis mi khyab pa'i rgyud*
Jataka: *Jātaka*, *Skyes pa'i rabs*
Jewel Garland: *Ratnāvalī*, *Rin chen 'phreng ba*
Jewel Mound Sutra: *Ratnakūṭa-sūtra*, *Dkon mchog brtsegs pa*
Kalachakra: *Kālacakra*, *Dus 'khor*
Kalachakra Root Tantra: *Kālacakramulatantra*, *Dus 'khor rtsa rgyud*
Key Notes on Dzogpa Chenpo: *Rdzogs pa chen po'i gnad kyi zin tig*
King of Samadhi Sutra: *Samādhirāja-sūtra*, *Ting nge 'dzin rgyal po'i mdo*
Leaning Below: *Āmnāyamañjarī*, *Man snye*
Mahamudra Bindu: *Phyag rgya chen po'i thig le*
Meditation Accomplishment Scripture: *Bsgom don grub pa'i lung*
Meeting of Father and Son Sutra: *Yab sras mjal ba'i mdo*
Mound of Gemstones: *Rin chen spungs pa*
Ocean of Dakinis: *Mkha' 'gro rgya mtsho*
Open Teachings of Auspiciousness and Prosperity: *Tshogs chos bkra shis phun tshogs*
Ornament of Clear Realization: *Abhisamāyalaṅkāra*, *Mngon rtogs rgyan*
Ornament of Sutras: *Māhayāna Sūtrālaṅkāra*, *Mdo sde rgyan*
Pemachen (Elucidation of the Difficult Points of Kalachakra): *Dus 'khor gyi dka' 'grel pad ma can*
Perfectly Abridged Dharma Sutra: *Dharmasamgīti-sūtra*, *Chos yang dag par sdud pa*
Prajñaparamita: *Shes rab kyi pha rol tu phyin pa*
Prajñaparamita in Eight Thousand Verses: *Arya Aṣṭasāhasrikā Prajñāpāramitā Sūtra*, *'Phags pa brgyad stong pa shes rab kyi pha rol tu phyin pa'i mdo*
Prajñaparamita in One Hundred Thousand Verses: *Śatasāhasrikā Prajñāpāramitā Sūtra*, *shes rab kyi pha rol tu phyin pa' bum*
Precious Lamp Sutra Dharani: *Ratnatalala-dhāraṇī*, *Dkon mchog ta la'i gzungs*
Public Teaching on the Cycle of Thinking: *Tshogs chos mno 'khor ma*
Realization of the Secret: *Gsang ba grub pa*
Realization of Wisdom: *Ye shes grub pa*
Realms and Transformations of Sound: *Sgra thal 'gyur*
Reciting the Names of Manjushri: *Mañjuśrīnāma Saṃgīti*, *'Djam dpal mtshan brjod*
Revealing the Hidden Characteristic of Mind: *Sems kyi mtshan nyid gab pa mngon du phyung*
Samputa Tantra: *Saṃpuṭa-tantra*, *Sam bu ti*
Secret Amrita King Tantra: *Gsang ba bdud rtsi rgyal po'i rgyud*
Secret Sutra of the Tathagata: *Tathāgatācintyaguhanirdeśa*, *De bzhin gshegs pa'i gsang ba'i mdo*
Secret Wisdom Tantra: *Guhyajñana-tantra*, *Ye shes gsang ba'i rgyud*
Self-Existing Bliss Tantra: *Rgyud rang byung bde ba*
Seventh Unification: *Sbyor ba bdun*
Shravaka Levels: *Śrāvakabhūmi*, *Nyan sa*
Stages of Meditation: *Bhāvanākrama*, *Sgom rim*
Storehouse Tantra: *Bang mdzod*

Sublime Continuum: *Uttaratantra, Rgyud bla ma*
Sublime Golden Light Sutra: *Suvarṇaprabhāsa-sūtra, Mdo sde gser 'od*
Sutra of the Ten Sublime Bhumis: *Aryadaśabhūmika-sūtra, 'Phags pa sa bcu pa'i mdo*
Sutra of the Wisdom at the Moment of Death: *Āryātyayajñāna-sūtra, 'Da' ka ye shes mdo*
Sutra Requested by Mati Sambhava: *Blo gros 'byung gnas kyis zhus pa'i mdo*
Sutra Revealing the Inseparable Dharmadhatu Nature: *Dharmadhātu prakṛtya-saṃbhedanirdeśa-sūtra, Chos kyi dbyings kyi rang bzhin dbyer med pa bstan pa'i mdo*
Sutra That Unravels the Intent: *Saṃdhinirmocana-sūtra, Dgongs pa nges par 'grel pa'i mdo*
Torch of the Path to Enlightenment: *Bodhipathapradīpa, Byang chub lam gyi sgron me*
Torch of the Vehicles: *Theg sgron*
Two Segments: *Hevajra-mūlatantra-rāja, Rgyud rtags gnyis*
Utterly Nondwelling Mahamudra Tantra: *Chag rgya chen po rab tu mi gnas pae'i rgyud*
Utterly Nondwelling Suchness Sutra: *De kho na nyid rab tu mi gnas pa'i mdo*
Vajra Dome Tantra: *Vajrapañjara-tantra, Rdo rje gur*
Vajra Peak Tantra: *Vajraśekhara-tantra; Rgyud rdo rje rtse mo*
Way of the Bodhisattva: *Bodhicaryāvatāra, Byang chub sems dpa'i spyod pa la 'jug pa*
Wisdom Equal to Space: *Ye shes mkha' mnyam*
Words Distinguishing the Two Truths Composed in a Chapter: *Bden pa gnyis rnam par 'byed pa'i tshig le'ur byas pa*

# Index